C000113187

ON THE ROCK-WALL OF ILLIMANI

THE
BOLIVIAN ANDES

A RECORD OF CLIMBING & EXPLORATION
IN THE CORDILLERA REAL IN THE
YEARS 1898 AND 1900

BY

SIR MARTIN CONWAY

ILLUSTRATED

NEW YORK AND LONDON
HARPER & BROTHERS PUBLISHERS
1901

TO

GEN. JOSÉ MANUEL PANDO

PRESIDENT

OF THE

REPUBLIC OF BOLIVIA

CONTENTS

ILLUSTRATIONS

ILLUSTRATIONS

ILLUSTRATIONS

THE BOLIVIAN ANDES

CHAPTER I

LONDON TO COLON

TO live *im Ganzen*, to experience in full the charm, the joy, the opportunity of life, has always been the aim of healthful manhood; but thus to live is over and over again to find that "what was once precious is become indifferent." Each new experience is enjoyed at the expense of its predecessor, each new interest supplants the one that went before. The traveller, especially the exploring traveller, is perhaps more inevitably conscious of this succession of interests than are men of any other category, for to him each new point of attraction becomes physically visible ahead as the old one fades away behind or dips below the horizon. Each goal attained becomes a mere mile-stone of the way. Also, when a journey is ended, and memory takes the place of sight, the mind no longer trudges on from successive scene to scene, but, isolating this or that vision of paramount beauty or interest, dwells upon it, or leaps with light speed from one to another,

A   I

never laboriously retreading the footsteps of connecting stages.

Authors of books of travel are thus all alike faced by one initial problem: Shall the writer take the reader with him along the road, or, like a lantern showman, shall he display only the choice moments and striking scenery of the journey? The latter alternative is the more attractive, but there is an insuperable objection to it: it takes no account of the fact that scenery—that is to say, the impression produced on the observer's mind by a scene or an event—depends not merely upon the thing beheld, but upon the nature of the beholder too, the mood in which he looks, the experiences through which he has passed, the preparation through which he has gone. If the Jungfrau Railway is ever finished, the view from the summit will produce upon travellers who mount by its long tunnel a very different impression from that received by a climber who laboriously fights his way to the top over long glaciers and snowfields and up steepening ice-slopes and the final ridge. A prize seized and possessed as the outcome of long and well-spent energy will be to its owner a much more delightful thing than a prize won in a raffle. It is the difference between a war medal and a five-shilling piece. If my readers care to feel even a semblance of what I have felt, they must, in some degree at least, travel the road with me. I cannot even leap with them from London to Bolivia, for the eyes that I opened on Bolivia's lofty plateau had traversed its far and near environment, and were equipped for interpreting the scene with something acquired on the way in the long days of land and sea travel thither.

2

It was on the 13th of July, 1898, that I sailed from Southampton by the Royal Mail Company's steamship *Don*, the same boat that nineteen years before carried Mr. Whymper to his famous journey of exploration in the Great Andes of Ecuador. Like him, I was accompanied by two Alpine guides from the village of Val Tournanche, Antoine Maquignaz and Louis Pellissier by name. Pellissier had never been from home before, but Maquignaz, in 1897, was H.R.H. the Duke of the Abruzzi's leading guide in the journey which resulted in the first ascent of Mount St. Elias in Alaska. I took him on the recommendation of his uncle, J. B. Aymonod, one of the most charming as well as one of the best mountain-guides, who accompanied Mr. E. A. Fitzgerald and me on our *Alps from End to End* journey in 1894. How Pellissier was enlisted I forget, or I would here record my thankfulness to the power that gave me so admirable a companion. Maquignaz is the son of Jean Pierre and nephew of Jean Joseph Maquignaz, two very famous guides, both members of the first party that ever climbed the Matterhorn from the Italian side, as readers of Whymper's *Scrambles* may remember. Jean Joseph, with Daniel, brother of Antoine Maquignaz, also made the historic first ascent of the Aiguille du Géant. My leading guide was thus a representative of one of the most famous guide families of the Alps.

Early in the afternoon of a lovely day our vessel cast off her moorings and steamed away down Southampton Water; the sun shone on white-sailed yachts racing before a merry breeze. A big North German Lloyd liner turned round beside us, picked

up passengers and mails from a tender, and was off
again, westward ho! Two hours later she was out of
sight ahead. Of all the chief ocean entries to England
this by the Needles is incomparably the finest, the
most beautiful, the great historic approach; what
greetings and farewells have saluted those white
blades thrust upward from the blue sea!

Four days of pleasant monotony followed, each a
little warmer than the one before. Such wind as
blew followed in our wake and scarcely rocked the
ship. All this time we were in the West Indies; for
it is one of the charms of ocean travel in a big liner
that the moment you have sailed you are in the country towards which you are sailing. In a yacht, wherever you go, you remain at home, for the home party
surrounds you; but in a public liner you at once form
part of a company most of whom belong to the place
of destination. An outward-bound P. & O. is a piece
of India; an outward-bound Cunarder is the United
States in miniature. Our Royal Mail boat was an
epitome of the West Indies. The moment we sailed
England became a memory to all; their holiday was
ended, they were returning to their respective homes.
At Barbados, the great West Indian junction, they
would scatter to all their islands, from St. Kitts to
Trinidad and south to Demerara. A few would come
on to Jamaica, and very few to Colon for Central America; only three or four were bound with me for Peru.
No sooner, then, was our English coast lost in the
summer haze than their talk was of the West Indies,
of the sugar industry especially, and of "bounties";
of fruit-growing, and the need of swift steamers to

pour the oranges and bananas and mangoes of Jamaica into the London markets; of local politics and problems, the need for retrenchment in public expenditures; of the negro and labor questions in some of their infinite forms; of land questions, of possible new industries, and what not.

Such talk with a number of men, each of whom knows by experience the difficulties of his own problem, is the best preparation for viewing their country, which swiftly gains actuality and ceases to be a mere figure on a map. Charts are produced, descriptions given, plans for the employment of one's time suggested, invitations hospitably tendered. Thus what a few days before was but a name takes form in one's mind as solid ground. The various islands begin to have each an individuality of its own. As one walks the deck with a fellow-passenger after the morning bath, or in the intervals of squash cricket or some other game, the stone walls of reserve fall down; the man tells his tale to a sympathetic companion—you hear of his home, in Scotland, it may be, of his store in Trinidad, or his plantation in Jamaica, of his difficulties, his successes, and his hopes. A week or two so spent expands life. The young men and maidens on board danced and sang every evening, and played games vigorously all day long, whatever the heat; cricket every afternoon, and shovel-board at intervals, the ancient "slide-thrift, otherwise called shove-grout," one of the "crafty games" rendered illegal by an act of Henry VIII. "for the maintaining artillery"

On the morning of our fourth day of warming air

and pleasant breezes I came on deck to find the cliffs of San Miguel, the largest of the Azores, close at hand. The island front was swimming in moisture-laden, sunny air, and girt by the white-maned horses of a turquoise sea. Boldly profiled cliffs of scarred red rock or steep tree-dotted slopes support the cultivated land—an undulating area of green and golden squares, vineyards, and cornfields. Deep wooded chines are cut into the swelling mass. Higher aloft ridges fringed with trees ran together into graceful peaks, or lost themselves in a soft roof of cloud which floated over the island. Down by the shore glittered white-walled cottages or farms. A larger splash of brightness away to the westward revealed the town and church of Villa Franca. An hour or two later this land of beauty and romance had melted away into light, through stages of increasing transparency, and so disappeared, long before dipping behind the horizon bounds.

Beyond the Azores came weather quite reasonably warmed through, a delight to experience after a background of cold English spring; yet, thank Heaven! our race was nurtured in east winds and gray skies, which drive men to keep moving, and make work essential to happiness. In the tropics work is a curse; in England and the other arctic regions it is a joy. On the eleventh day out (noon, lat. 14° 45′ N., long. 57° 11′ E.) we came into a dirty green sea, colored, I was told, by the mud of South American rivers; we also entered an area of splendid torrential showers, good to watch as they swept over the ocean. Next morning our anchor was punctually dropped at six o'clock in the harbor of Barbados, an island about as

6

large as the Isle of Wight. The omnibus steamers that come from different directions to meet the mail were anchored around, boats and launches were flying to and fro, while shrieking negro boys in their tiny home-made craft congregated about our ship to dive for coins. I made haste to land, in company with Mr. F. Cundall, the capable Director of the Jamaica Institute—a kind of offshoot of the English Science and Art Department. We jumped into a buggy without delay and drove out into the country.

I make no attempt to catalogue what we saw. The impression made upon me was overpowering and will last. The town was well enough, and its historical reminiscences would have sufficed to fill many days with interest, but these were insignificant behind the immediate sense of exuberant life, animal and vegetable. The ways simply abounded in niggers; their bits of cottages were everywhere; their babies swarmed like flies in Egypt. Nature provides a perfect setting for these white-robed throngs on the white roads flooded with sunshine. It was the flamboyant trees that completed my wonder, trees like acacias, but with scarlet flowers instead of green leaves. I suppose they have leaves, but it is the flowers that you see, a flush of glory overarching the roads and contrasting with the blue sky and piled-up towers of white cloud. There were palms waving beside them, and the white walls of houses and gardens flooded with Bougainvilleas in full bloom; and there were hibiscus, and I know not what more, all bursting with life and triumphing in gay efflorescence. There were orchards and gardens and sugar plantations covering every yard of cultivable land, for the population is too great for the land, so that not an inch can be left untilled. The pressure of population in Barbados, like the climate in Europe, forces men to labor.

As we drove inland we rose above the sea-level and obtained wider views. A beautiful garden appeared in a fine position. The house was embowered in the flamboyant trees. I made bold to drive up to it; it proved to be the residence of the Colonial Secretary, and the master gave us hospitable entertainment. I tried to take a photograph in natural colors* of the gorgeous vegetation, but the breeze would not permit a sufficiently long exposure. We drank our morning coffee on the terrace under the shadow of flowers, with a landscape of sugar-fields stretching away to the beautiful sea. The drive was continued through intricate lanes, abounding in niggers, and past barracks and drill-grounds down to the hotel at Hastings-by-the-Sea, where we lunched on flying-fish and mangoes, and rejoiced to be alive. A couple of months later came a great hurricane that blew flat all the trees and ravaged the gardens that were now looking so fair; but the same nature that destroyed will raise again, and ten years hence the destruction of yesterday will be unperceived.

The last hours of our stay in Barbados were spent in the club, among a group of captains and shipping agents, the local personification of that old and most respectable company, the Royal Mail, which seems to hold the West Indies in the hollow of its hand.

* Ives's process. The apparatus, which is not expensive, can be bought in London from the Photochromoscope Syndicate.

The talk was of harbor-masterships vacant, and who would get them; of the prospects of one man and the misfortunes of another; of how Jones was getting fat and Brown was drinking too much; of the parson's wife, who makes the best guava jelly in the world; and of a certain dozen bottles of Barbados rum lying hidden somewhere, that surpassed all other spirits ever distilled since the foundation of the earth. At last the company broke up and went aboard the various steamers already weighing their anchors. An hour later, when the sun was setting beneath a towering purple cloud with a great gold wing, three spots of smoke on the horizon showed where the scattering ships were gone.

From Barbados to Jacmel, in Hayti, is a run of 815 miles. At an early hour one morning we entered the beautiful bay, and the cutter was launched to land the mails. As an exceptional privilege, and after undertaking to be responsible for our own safety, Cundall and I were allowed to land. Few travellers in recent years have landed at Jacmel. The "Black Republic," whose birth was watched with an ill-founded enthusiasm, and whose history is a tale of steady decadence, cannot even keep order in the foul streets of one of its chief ports. Seen from the ship, Jacmel looks lovely, a specimen of tropical village of picturesque huts among graceful palms, surrounded by hills whose densely wooded covering has the velvety texture, even when beheld from a great distance, that differentiates tropical from temperate forests. I suppose there exists in the whole round world no island more blessed with natural beauty than Hayti. Its

bays, its beautiful hills rising to 12,000 feet, its incomparably fertile soil, its wealth of water, should
combine to make it the very garden of the earth; but
it is a garden inhabited by a people sinking back into
savagery and for whom there will be no salvation till
the white man has shouldered them again as part
of his burden. The day that the United States, having
brought order and prosperity to Cuba and Porto Rico,
adds Hayti and Santo Domingo to its growing empire,
will be the most fortunate that has ever dawned on
those unhappy regions since Columbus discovered the
island of Hispaniola.

Rowing ashore, we landed at a half-ruined jetty,
near which rose an ugly arch of triumph made of
planks in honor of the recent visit of President Heu-
reaux of Santo Domingo (since murdered). It may
have cost $50 to build. I am told that it figured in
the republic's accounts for some $30,000. Near the
landing-place was the town pump, only a foot or two
away from a stinking sewer. There was also a broken
electric light on a post. Beyond a paved street, rather
rougher than an average moraine, were some crazy
public buildings, made of planks nailed to a frame,
and roofed with corrugated iron; many of the planks
were loose and most were rotten. The filth of the
streets was indescribable; the few people about were
as degraded and dirty as any I ever saw. They looked
upon us with eyes of malignant suspicion. The
houses matched the people. There was no proper road
leading inland, but only a wandering track, which
amply suffices for all the trade that comes to this port.
If there were any energy or uprightness in people or

A PEASANT'S HUT, JAMAICA

ARCH OF TRIUMPH AT JACMEL.

government, Jacmel ought to be a thriving emporium of trade. But it is as good as dead. The degradation of the people is lower than in the days of slavery.*

The sight of Jacmel is one of the most horrible I ever beheld. If civilization's day is ever done, and mankind begins to rot away, it will die out like this. Whoever has seen Jacmel will be cured for life of the belief that self-government is any panacea for human ills. Under self-government Hayti has sunk from a thriving community to a foul blot on the face of the earth. However well self-government may suit some few white races, it is poison to blacks, and the man who takes it away from them will be their greatest benefactor. Under no system of slavery and despotism could the individual's state be more miserable than it is in Jacmel to-day. With joy we found ourselves again on board ship, which all day long sailed by the south coast of the island—an array of beautiful hills, fair valleys, and pleasant, undulating lowlands.

Next morning (July 29th) we came early in sight of Jamaica, and watched the Blue Mountains, dyed purple and gold in the glory of sunrise. While rounding Port Royal and entering the fair bay of Kingston, we talked of Rodney and Nelson. Cundall, with his wealth of local knowledge, peopled the scene for

* "In Haiti," says Henry Sandham in *Harper's Magazine* (August, 1899), "if you see a bridge, go round it; whenever you see a sidewalk, take the road. . . . I wish it were possible even to refer to all the evidence of the high state of civilization of this island only one hundred years ago that we passed in our climb up that mountain; aqueducts, bridges, houses, gateways, etc., to say nothing of sections of broad, well-paved highways, that must have been marvels—all destroyed when Haiti became a republic."

me with heroes of the past. Under his hospitable wing I spent the next two days in uninterrupted enjoyment. Between Kingston and Jacmel no more emphatic contrast can be conceived. Nature is the same in both; the difference is in man. The Jamaica negro is the best negro in the New World; such, at any rate, is the officially recorded experience of the contractors for the Panama Canal.* Though not an agreeable person, by all accounts, the Jamaica negro is a fairly good workman, and has other merits. I suppose that, like other negroes, he is a problem; but this book is no place for problems, nor was I travelling in the part of special Providence. Jamaica to me was a picture, a scene of abounding beauty and exuberant vegetable wealth. From Barbados to Panama the luxuriance of vegetation continually increased, and it was this preparation of the eye that made the Peruvian desert so appalling a contrast. For this reason only do I here briefly refer to a country that has

* " Dans ces colonies (les Antilles anglaises) la libération du nègre ne lui a pas fait oublier sa place naturelle, et s'il avait eu quelque tendance à en perdre le souvenir, ses maîtres de la veille, ses supérieurs d'aujourd'hui, auraient su le lui rappeler. La race s'est conservée intelligente et forte, et, en quelques années, de ces cultivateurs de café on (i. e., the canal engineers) a pu faire des mécaniciens et des chauffeurs capables de conduire des locomotives ; on a fait même des terrassiers chargeants aux grands wagons, ce qui représente un effort de travail considérable dans ces pays chauds. En résumé, cette catégorie d'ouvriers a donné des satisfactions relatives ; en tout cas, c'est la catégorie certainement la plus élevée de travailleurs qui soit venue s'employer au Canal. . . . Les ouvriers blancs, seuls, apportent, dans ce qu'ils font, la conscience du devoir à accomplir et la vanité de l'ouvrage bien présenté. Le nègre, avec son laisser-aller et son sentiment de maraudeur, n'est pas capable de cette notion."— P. BUNAU-VARILLA, Panama. Paris, 1892, 8vo, pp. 60, 61.

been completely described by generations of visitors and inhabitants.

My whole time was spent on the plain and slopes between Kingston and the Blue Mountains, in weather that was fine, though punctuated with thunder-storms. We saw the hills from the plain, as a purple wall piled high with white domes of cloud, a background to royal palms of Cuba and flamboyant trees; we looked down from the hills upon the plain, girt and framed by them, spreading away green and rich to the glittering sea. I shall never forget the view of the hills from the Hope Botanical Gardens—a foreground of fair lawns and chosen trees, where the orchid-house is a palm avenue, and where ferns grow with superb luxuriance. Nor shall I ever forget the panorama of the plain from the old barracks, now Reformatory, of Stony Hill, the crest of the road crossing the island from south to north; nor the gorgeous storm that stalked across it, coming down in great majesty from the mountains and vanishing over the sea. If I had a week in Jamaica again I would devote much of it to the various botanical gardens, where man asks questions and Nature makes reply. There are experimental stations in the hills and in the plains, large cinchona and orange plantations on suitable lands, grounds devoted to experiments with sugar, pineapples, and fruits of all sorts. It is impossible to overestimate the value of this work to the island. If sugar fails it, there is hardly a limit to its possible fruit production; but the native fruits are not good enough for export. Oranges, mangoes, pineapples need cultivation and improvement, and the way of doing this is shown for

the people at trifling cost, under the control of able
men of science. Such did not appear to be the opinion
of the elected members of the legislature, whose debate on the estimates for these very gardens I had
the opportunity of attending. They were for closing
as many of them as possible. They proposed to
abandon to destruction a plantation of 100,000 young
orange-trees. "What's the use of trying to improve
our oranges?'' they said. "They are the best in the
world as they are, growing *silvestre*, sown by the
birds. It is all waste of energy. Look at your cinchona plantation—what that cost. Let us close them
all and save money.''

A little of this kind of debate was enough. Cundall whisked me off to see his museum, where is a
library of books and prints dealing with Jamaica,
laboriously brought together by him out of the second-
hand booksellers' catalogues of the world. A glimpse
into the natural-history museum, with its beautiful
preparations of marine organisms and its remarkable
collection of local cretaceous fossils, was all that I was
allowed; then off to Gordontown in the hills, by way
of the Hope Botanical Gardens and a fine road zig-
zagging up a deep valley densely wooded with blossoming trees and creepers, and flowers below—a perfect
bewilderment of beauty, all reeking wet after one of
the frequent downpours proper to this time of year.
One could almost see things growing in the dampness.
We drove back to Cundall's house, with a flaming
gold sunset above the dark plain; and, after a dinner
of novel foods and fruits, spent a long, delightful
evening under the stars, with music of the trees and

the gentle, perfume-laden breeze. The last thing I remember in Jamaica was breakfast in the beautiful garden of an old Cambridge contemporary, beneath a gorgeous flamboyant tree with a royal palm above it and the Blue Mountains behind. The cool morning air was perfectly still; the low sun drew long shadows across the dew-spangled grass; humming-birds seemed to hang over the bushes like live flowers. In the midst of this paradise my friend talked of his longing for gray, damp, populous old home.

CHAPTER II

THE ISTHMUS OF PANAMA

ALL too soon for me we were aboard and away, sailing no longer westward, with the swell behind, but south, for two nights and a day of solid discomfort—typical weather for the Caribbean Sea. The almost empty ship was rolled about by the agitated waters. Deluges of rain fell, winds blew, and thunder crashed. The air was as heavy with moisture as it could be soaked. All on board were limp and many were sea-sick. Thus when we anchored off Colon, least attractive of ports, it seemed quite a haven of rest, though when the time came for shifting my baggage from boat to train it proved to be the very reverse. In no hurry to land, I sat for an hour or two with the ship's officers, to whose kindness I am much indebted, and talked with the many Colonians who came aboard on apparent business of one kind and another, but really to ask for ice. In the Republic of Colombia ice is a government monopoly. The supply for the Isthmus is made at Panama, and just now—horror of horrors!— the ice-machine had broken down; so the entire population, from highest to lowest, had to drink their cocktails tepid during three whole weeks! Revolutions have arisen from lesser misfortunes.

The site of Colon is by nature a rank tropical swamp. It has been partly reclaimed by the railway and canal companies. Most of it, however, is not reclaimed at all, and there the houses are built, like prehistoric lake-dwellings, on piles sunk into the black swamp, into which also the black, whity-brown, or yellow inhabitants cast the refuse of their filthy lives, so that the accumulation swimming or stranded below the houses is as vile and putrid as anything to be found in the worst back-eddy of a European sewer. "Colon unhealthy!" said a man to me, with modest deprecation. "Colon unhealthy! Do you think people could live like this if the place were not naturally one of the healthiest in the world? Now Panama and Guayaquil, if you like, . . ." It was always that way; no one would ever acknowledge his town to be unhealthy. "Yellow-fever! We've not had yellow-fever here for twenty years, but at Cartagena the workmen are dying like flies." I dare say at Cartagena they would have reported an epidemic at Colon.

An embanked promenade, with an avenue of cocoa-palms leading to De Lesseps' abandoned house, and a statue of Columbus protecting (good heavens!) an emblematical figure of America — these are all the sights of Colon. When I had seen them I returned to the ship, where my doings had been reported. "If that man goes on walking about in the sun, he'll be down with yellow-fever by evening," said some one of me; but it was no use foreboding; I was here to see things and intended to see them. After a frightful struggle my goods were all booked at the station and we were ready to start upon the most expensive journey for its length in the world, not even excepting the Mendoza Railway. From Colon to Panama the distance is about forty-five miles. The fare for myself, the two guides, and the baggage was over £10. At last the train started and we soon came upon the wreck of the savings of the good people of France. It was a pitiful sight. There were rows of dredges in the water, and fields of abandoned machinery on shore, much of it never even put together, more put together but never used, boilers, piles of rails and tram-lines, innumerable trucks with their wood-work rotted away, sheds full of engines, the whole invaded by tropical growth and standing on the edge of the rank swamp through which the railroad runs. Presently come drier patches where bananas grow, and palms matted with creepers. It was a disappointment to find all this soaking greenery hardly enlivened by a single blossom. By degrees the land became more solid and a hard mound or two emerged from the pools of lazily flowing waters that still predominated. The whole region had an abandoned aspect. It seemed as though vegetation overpowered animal life. Birds were few. Yet there must have been something to shoot, or the gun-carrying nigger I saw waiting about, up to his waist in water, would hardly have looked so cheerful. Imagination pictured the place full of things creeping and gliding. Damp, tropical regions always produce on me the impression that whoever made them made them to be the home of vegetation, and that man is out of place in them. The conditions are hostile to his habitation. He may come and look, but if he stays his active energies are sapped and he tends to vegetate himself.

Where the ground began to rise definitely we came to the station and village of Gatun on the famous (or infamous) Chagres River. The village consisted of a corrugated iron church and rows of plank huts with iron roofs, all evidently made to a set of patterns and imported from France—so many houses of one type, so many of another. It was all prettily enough projected, but multitudes of difficulties arose that were unforeseen in the hurry of reckless enthusiasm.

"The fundamental error made by De Lesseps and his associates," writes Colonel William Ludlow,* "was in basing the Panama plans and estimates upon the most favorable results obtained in the Suez constructions, without making adequate or any allowance for the radically different conditions. Suez was merely one hundred miles of level digging through sand, in a region where the rainfall is but an inch or two in the year, the climate comparatively cool and healthful, a large supply of native labor, and the mechanical resources of Europe at no great distance; but, notwithstanding these advantages, the work, planned on an estimate of $40,000,000, cost $110,000,000, on a reduced cross-section, before it was opened. The physical conditions on the Isthmus are the precise reverse of those in Egypt, and the cost of every item of work was enormously greater. A material increase was inevitable, even with the most careful and economic management. The scarcity and dimin-

* *Harper's Magazine*, May, 1898, p. 842, an excellent summary of "The Trans-Isthmian Canal Problem."

ished effectiveness of labor, losses from disease and sickness, the interference and burden of the heavy rainfall, would at least have doubled cost, and to these drawbacks were added political disturbances and local acts of violence, with a home administration of unparalleled extravagance.

The estimated cost of the whole enterprise was $210,000,000. In 1888, five years from the commencement of work, $300,000,000 were actually spent and only one-third of the work to be done was completed. The consequent failure of the company was due only in a small part to financial improprieties. Reckless impatience was the main cause of ruin. If a long experimental stage had been passed through first, and the conditions of the problem had been discovered and overcome one by one before work on a great scale was taken in hand, a very different result would have been arrived at. In fact, most of the $300,000,000 was spent experimentally, and therefore largely wasted. Even when the company went into liquidation, its remaining assets being some $70,000,000 (including the Panama Railroad), and some $15,000,-000 recovered from blackmailers, the new company, which continued the enterprise, had to spend most of its funds on the very experiments which ought to have been made before regular work was ever begun. It has, moreover, dredged the mouth of the Rio Grande and carried a deep channel three miles out to sea; it has also built a pier and port near Panama, and deepened the Emperador and Culebra sections. The original design, it must be remembered, was for a sea-level canal—a Bosporus. This was soon changed to a lake and ten-lock canal, and this has been varied several times, while the width of the water-way has been greatly reduced. Of course, the cessation of work in 1888, and the consequent scattering of the staff, many of whom had become immune from the local fevers, was in itself a great destruction of capital.

As the train carried us along, I noticed that the soil of the middle region was rich and red, and that the waters of the Chagres, flowing along in great flood, were thick with it. Heavy clouds drifted overhead; every moment we expected a new torrential downpour to redrench the sopping earth. Such storms are of daily occurrence in the rainy season; they raise the Chagres twenty or thirty feet in a few hours. A river like that is indeed a wild neighbor for a canal which has to borrow the river's bed in several places. Between Gatun and Bujio came low hills, with a few cane-walled, thatched huts in clearings, and some banana-groves and patches of indifferent cultivation, but nature retains the upper hand.

Bujio is a finer village than Gatun, with great wealth of corrugated iron, and in its neighborhood are acres on acres of wasted machinery lying about on the ground among trucks and numbered huts and bits of shaped iron and steel; and there is a street of stores where Chinese swarm, dressed in ugly European clothes. The air here was more reeky than ever, though a storm had recently passed over. The people came crowding down to the steamer just like any throng of Hindoos. Here was the Chagres River once more, flowing with swift current, while every flat place was under water. It is at this spot, according to most of the projects, that the great dam should be built to close the Chagres River and catch its flood in a lake which at the smallest estimate would be very large. Whether the dam would withstand the sudden pressure of the enormous floods which rise in this district is a question that engineers must answer. I believe there is some doubt about it.

Another field of abandoned machinery, more big dredges in the river, then the tropical bush began as before, deluged and covered up in creepers and saturated with wet. To continue cataloguing the flotsam and jetsam of the Canal Company is scarcely worth while. We passed whole villages of empty huts and more fields of machinery than I could keep count of. At last came really higher ground and fairly open country; that is to say, country that had been cleared and kept clear of bush, where the highest village, though most of the houses in it were empty, had a healthier and more livable appearance, and the air felt fresher than any we had breathed thus far. Near the station some kind of a fête was going on, to the accompaniment of a fife-and-drum band, while a cricket-match was being played by the negroes, and the ball had just been landed with a mighty swipe right into the heart of the neighboring bush. We thus came out on the top level and saw the famous Culebra cutting, which, to my astonishment, appeared practically finished. There were still three thousand men at work upon it, but all that remained for them to do was a relatively small deepening of the gigantic trench which yawned before us.

The descent to the flat plain, at the edge of which

the town of Panama is built, carried us through scenery in most respects similar to that passed on the ascent, though the hills were more picturesque, the slopes more rapid, and the valleys more precipitous. It is not on this side that the problem of the canal is difficult of solution. The two great difficulties, as everybody knows, have been to form a stable cutting through the rotten substance of the Culebra Hill and to deal with the flood waters of the Chagres River. The Culebra cutting is practically complete, and I do not think that any doubt remains as to the success of that gigantic undertaking, but the problem of the Chagres River is not yet solved. One of two things must be done—either a great lake must be made to catch the tremendous floods that come down in the rainy season, or the course of the river itself must be changed by carrying a tunnel through from the west, whereby the waters of the Chagres would be thrown off down the Pacific slope into the Bay of Panama. Which of these alternatives will ultimately be adopted I do not know.

CHAPTER III

A CENTRAL AMERICAN REVOLUTION

IT has been my good or ill fortune to visit Panama on three different occasions. Perhaps the most interesting of these visits was the second, made in the summer of 1890. A few days before sailing from London I had met a Colombian gentleman. "Is it true that there is a revolution going forward in your country?" I asked. "That is nothing," was his reply; "it is our substitute for cricket. Our young men must have their games." A month later I saw the game played. It proved to be not unexciting.

On the morning of July 24th we landed at Colon. Telegraph communication with Panama was interrupted, and the local newspapers were silent about the existence of military operations, but report said that Panama was besieged and was to be stormed that day. "Besieged!" snorted our Yankee skipper; "I have seen these disturbances. Two small bodies of opposing troops come in sight of one another. They fire their guns in the air and then they run away in opposite directions. That is a Central American revolution. You won't have any trouble." We climbed on board the morning train, which started as usual for Colon. I sat beside a French engineer of the Panama Canal, and was fully occupied for the two or three hours of the journey in observing the works accomplished or in progress, which he explained to me. Three thousand men are still continually at work, and the great Culebra cutting has been excavated down to the level of 45 metres above the sea. At Culebra the engineer left me, and a short time afterwards the train halted in the outskirts of Panama. We had heard no firing, and were skeptical about there being any fighting. Looking forward along the line, I saw a man wave his hat, whereupon the train advanced slowly. It entered a shallow cutting with a high bank on the right (Panama behind it) and a low one on the left. Looking up to the right, we saw a few armed men, and presently discovered that the whole length of that embankment was topped by a breastwork lined with riflemen, whose heads occasionally peeped over and looked at us. Three hundred yards or so away to the left in a scrub-covered swamp were an indeterminate number of men, the attacking force. Across the line a little way ahead was a road-bridge, which proved to be the object of attack. A few hundred yards farther ahead was the corrugated iron railway station, ending in a warehouse carried on a pier stretching out into the sea. We had not advanced many yards towards the bridge before a few shots were fired, the temptation of the heads peering over at the train probably being too much for the attacking force. They were at once replied to, and, before we realized what was happening, the train was between two lines of some 2000 fighting-men, separated by less than a quarter of a mile, and pumping lead at one another from Mauser rifles. A shell dropped near the bridge as we crossed below it. The men on our right fired over the train, but the cars were often exposed to the insurgents on our left, and bullets came over in a horizontal stream, the cars being freely hit. Down on the floor dropped the passengers with singular unanimity. "All come forward to the baggage van," shouted the guard; and forward they went along the corridor of the train, grovelling on hands and knees, the funniest sight imaginaable. There were old and young, men and women, priests, niggers, peasants, bagmen, globe-trotters, and what not. One very fat old negress blocked the way, and a yet fatter priest climbed on her, like one tortoise over another. Both got wedged between the seats. As a matter of fact, one place was as safe or dangerous as another.

In this condition the train stopped in the goods station, and every one was left to shift for himself. There were, of course, no porters or officials of any sort; there was nowhere for the passengers to go. Bullets were coming freely through the shed, and a few hours later our train was itself the main point of attack, the two opposing forces fighting between the wheels and through the windows. At present, however, the attack was only beginning to be pressed home. The passengers having local knowledge melted away in a moment, and we foreigners, a dozen men, were left like sheep without a shepherd. Under the impression that I was going towards the town, I walked along the shore and came out directly into the open, faced by a line of skirmishers, who gave me a warm reception. I doubled back with no undue delay and entered the American company's warehouse on the pier, wherein a great multi-colored mob were sheltering. Several individuals were wounded there in rapid succession. Every man I asked for geographical information was in no condition to give it, till I struck a young Jamaica negro, who professed to know the position of the American Consulate. By this time I had lost all trace of my fellow-travellers, who were somewhere in the crowded warehouse, so the negro and I sallied forth alone down a bullet-swept street and then around a corner. We passed carts laden with dead and wounded, bumping hideously against one another over the uneven road. The streets were practically deserted, but almost every house displayed a flag, English and American flags being commonest— any flag, indeed, except the Colombian. It looked as though some fête was about to take place. Through doors ajar and barred windows frightened faces peeped and withdrew. We passed two men firing their rifles this way and that, in a state of excitement, either drunk or running amuck. Bullets were always whistling overhead and pinging against the houses.

The American Consulate was full of refugees, for whom the hospitable Consul was at his wits' end to find food, none having entered the town for some days. Newly directed, I found my way to the house of Mr. Mallet, the English Consul, who most kindly received me. This house also had been struck by plenty of missiles, and I suppose that few houses in the town escaped. Later in the day my fellow-travellers told their story. After waiting on the pier under fire for an hour or two, they fortunately attracted the attention of a boat's crew of H. M. S. *Leander*, and were rowed off to a schooner out of the reach of danger, where they remained without food till the middle of the afternoon, watching the battle, which went forward on the beach and a short way inland before their eyes. There was no firing of guns into the air and running away. The combat was waged on both sides with the utmost bravery, the opposing forces being always at close range. Several times the insurgents charged the barricaded bridge and the intrenched railway embankment and station. Once they all but carried the position by direct assault. They could not turn it, for it was protected at one end by the sea and at the other by a pathless swamp. When evening came the position of the two parties was unchanged. There were unsuccessful night attacks, and firing went on almost all night.

Neither side had any ambulance arrangements worth mention. Asked for their ambulance, the insurgents produced two spades. Accordingly, Captain Fegan landed an ambulance party and a hundred men from H.M.S. *Leander* next morning, and a suspension of hostilities was arranged. The scenes in and about the trenches were of the most horrible description. Nearly one-quarter of the troops engaged on both sides were killed or wounded. The trenches were full of dead. The wounded had crawled into neighboring houses and hidden themselves under beds and in various holes and corners, where many of them had died. Nothing had been done for them. No surgical treatment whatever had been applied. The injured men displayed the utmost apathy. They neither groaned nor complained. One or two came to have bullets cut out, and stood apparently unconcerned throughout painful operations. Equally apathetic were the uninjured. They offered no help to the British tars, and even refused to lend a hand towards moving the wounded when asked to do so. No attempt had been made to collect, still less to bury, the dead, upon whom the tropical sun had been pouring down for a whole day. Fighting recommenced the second afternoon, and was continued all night again, but the insurgents' task was now hopeless. The government had received reinforcements at Colon, and it was a mere question of hours when they would arrive by train. Still, the insurgents continued the fight, hurling themselves against an impregnable position. Their two field-guns were tolerably well handled, but the defences were too strong. All night long the rain of bullets poured upon the town; the principal hotel was hit every few minutes, and the visitors lying in their beds had their windows broken or heard the bullets hammering on the walls.

On the third day the ambulance party again went forth. Before the morning was far advanced the insurgents, after receiving a guarantee that no one's life should be taken, made an otherwise unconditional surrender. The town immediately came to life. Though the inhabitants almost to a man sympathized with the insurgents, they hurried out into the streets wearing the government colors, and all was rejoicing and triumph. An amnesty was at once issued to all political offenders, and the revolution was at an end so far as Panama was concerned. The disorganized local authority was incapable of dealing with the problem of burying the dead. The wounded had been carried by the sailors to the hospitals of the Canal Company and the town, where, however, there was no accommodation except the floor for more than a small portion of them.

The dead still lay in the roads, the streets, the trenches, and beneath bushes where they fell. Ghastly sights met the eye on all sides—frightful things no longer recognizable as men. Thousands and tens of thousands of carrion crows came flying in from all directions and settled upon the field of battle. At night some attempt was made to burn the bodies with petroleum, but it was unsuccessful — indeed, only made matters worse. Next day the condition of things grew yet more disgusting and dangerous to the public health. A wind blowing over the trenches to the town rendered it almost uninhabitable. Next night a better-organized effort was made. Big fires were lit and well supplied with brushwood and oil, and most of the bodies were disposed of in a sufficiently grewsome fashion. There was nothing exceptional in this treatment of the dead. It is the South American revolutionary fashion. All over South America, where there have been battles, you find human bones lying about until nature does away with them. Sometimes, perhaps, as near Lima, you may meet with a monumental bone-house, where the skeletons have been gleaned and piled together, but that is the exception. The rule is to leave the dead where they fall, for the sun and the crows to deal with after their fashion.

During the week I spent at Panama and in its neighborhood, in 1898, I devoted most of my time to the investigation of the present condition and past history of the canal; and I concluded, as I believe every one concludes who investigates the matter, that the canal can be and will be finished at no very distant date and no very vast expenditure of money, and this whether

PANAMA CATHEDRAL

PALM AVENUE, PANAMA

the Nicaragua Canal is made or not. It is impossible to imagine that, when such an enormous fraction of the work has been completed, it will be allowed to go to ruin. If the worse comes to the worst, and the French Concession lapses and the works revert to the Republic of Colombia, it is obvious that the government will be willing to get them completed, at however low a price it may be necessary for them to reckon the work that has been done. I have not been over any part of the site of the Nicaragua Canal, but one fact about the region through which that must pass is, I believe, admitted by all—it is a region where earthquakes are very frequent. Now whether a lock-canal can be safely maintained in an earthquake region, no one knows. Possibly the locks might be frequently deranged or put entirely out of action. No such misfortune is likely to interfere with the locks of the Panama Canal, for I believe the Isthmus, in this neighborhood, at any rate, is free from earthquakes. Undoubtedly it would be well to have two canals, and that may be the outcome. But if there is to be only one, the short Panama Canal, which is now in so advanced a state of excavation, undoubtedly offers the best chance of success.

As a town Panama is greatly to be preferred to Colon, for Colon is nothing but a nineteenth-century settlement, while Panama has some of the dignity and picturesqueness of an old Spanish city. It has its churches, its large cathedral and fine houses, and is apparently a more important centre of trade. The hotel was haunted by a most entertaining crowd of old inhabitants, who, as usual, protested

against any reflections on the salubriousness of the
city.

"Yellow-fever, my dear sir? We never have it;
healthiest place in these regions; never had fever
in my life, and I've lived here fifty years come next
January. Now, for a pest-house, take Colon or Guayaquil. Those are foul places, where they have fever
all the time; but Panama is as good a place to live
in as there is in the world."

"But it's dull here," interrupted his neighbor.

"Yes," replied the other, "damned dull; but it is
better here than at other places, and if only the canal
were finished we should look up. Yes, sir; if the
United States took it up, we should finish that canal
in four years; and we would, but the Company wants
us to buy all its rusty machines at the price they paid
for them. No, sir; we don't buy a dead hog when
we want a live one."

These old fogies of the town were full of reminiscences; some of them were Forty-niners, and fine
tales they had to tell of their adventures in old days,
crossing the Isthmus partly by the Chagres, and
then by mules over the hills; and how many people
died by the way, and how many of those that they
had started with they never saw again. And then
there was the talk about the canal, and how money
had been poured out like water, and how the engineers and the contractors and the contractors' men
had died one after another like flies; of the waste
of life, waste of money, waste of everything, that
they had seen and battened on. But one and all
believed that sooner or later the canal would be

finished, and the great days of Panama would come again.

Time did not hang heavy on my hands, for I went out to see the canal, or drove through the beautiful Hospital Park, which overlooks the bay and its islands, and where the cheerful Mother Superior received us with utmost kindness, and sent for an English Sister to come and tell us about the place. If the French Canal Company had done nothing else than build this hospital, Panama at all events would have to remember it with thankfulness. Not far away is the enormous cemetery, which tells its own tale; and beside it is a hideous coffin-strewn patch of land, reserved for the Chinese, where the dead are left till their relatives, if they have any, can dig them up and take them back again to China.

Panama, in fact, is not really a bad place to live in; such, at all events, was the mature opinion of our consul, Mr. Mallet. It is feverish, of course, has its own very choice fever, and is liable to epidemics, but its situation is beautiful, on one of the loveliest bays in the world, dotted with islands which form salubrious holiday resorts. In the dry and comparatively healthy season the country behind the town is a splendid and easily accessible sporting-ground. There is alligator-shooting also to be had up the creeks, and the continual flow of travellers passing through prevents the stagnation which is felt in towns less immediately on one of the world's highways.

C

CHAPTER IV

PANAMA TO LIMA

O N the 5th of August we sailed away on the Pacific Steam Navigation Company's mail-steamer *Peru.* These steamers, which patrol the west coast of South America, never have to face a really heavy sea, and are therefore built in a fashion not possible for ordinary ocean-going boats. All the cabins open to the deck, so that you can lie on your deck-chair in front of your own door. Few lines of steamers have a more comfortable fleet, but the boats are by no means fast. They only travel about one hundred miles a day, including halts.

From the ship, lying a mile or two off the town, close to a pretty, wooded island, the view of the bay was very beautiful. To the eastward, a few miles off, were the site and ruins of Panama, which Morgan and his buccaneers cruelly pillaged and burned, after boldly marching across the Isthmus, in January, 1671. Hazy in the distance were the Pearl Islands, where in 1685 the buccaneers lay, under the command of Edward Davis, awaiting the Spanish treasure-fleet from Lima, with Dampier on board writing a journal. The Spaniards succeeded in landing the treasure betimes, so that the buccaneers had nothing to win by fighting; but if a battle had taken place, and the command of the South Seas had been, as it probably would have been, won by the buccaneers, an independent buccaneer realm would probably have arisen and the course of South American history might have been different.

As we sailed off, the Bay of Panama put on all its beauty. A gorgeous cirque of rainy-season clouds marshalled themselves around upon the hills—piled monsters, rearing aloft like a wave gathered for its plunge, sunshine on its brow and purple gloom in its bosom, or like a range of snow-mountains founded on the forest-covered hills. The Pearl Islands and the coast disappeared; the calm, opalescent sea and pale-blue sky above remained. A night of beauty followed, breathing soft, warm air. The pole-star trembled on the northern horizon, while the moon and her perfect reflection floated serenely in sky and sea.

The weather at Panama had been most indubitably hot—a steaming heat that sucked the strength out of a man—but before we reached Guayaquil (even the very day that we crossed the equator) the heat was gone, and I found that woollen underclothing suitable for a London winter was not uncomfortable on the line in the Pacific. Of course, when we came to Guayaquil and landed it was warmer again, but the sea down this western coast is always cool, owing to the Antarctic current. The coast of Ecuador. where we first saw it, was low and dull, lumpy land seen under a gray and overcast sky. Its historic interest, however, is great, for one cannot visit these lands without thinking much of Pizarro and his bold companions, men whose rare bravery will always cause their crimes to be less regarded than the marvel of their adventures. Little love though I bear to the Conquistadores, I found it impossible to look unmoved upon Puna Island, where Pizarro fought his first fight with the Coast Indians.

In three days and a half from Panama we anchored in the river of Guayaquil by night, and I landed early; not, indeed, in any eagerness to see the town, but all agog to climb the little mound of Santa Ana, whence on rare occasions giant Chimborazo is visible in all his greatness. I might have saved myself the trouble, however, for not the faintest sign of a mountain was in sight, only an extensive flat country, with a noble river more than a mile and a quarter wide winding through it, and some small hills rising in various directions. It was a picturesque view enough, but not what a mountaineer came forth to see. The point where I stood was, I imagine, the spot daily visited by Mr. Whymper, when he was waiting to start up-country for his expedition to the Andes of Ecuador, but I gather that he was no more fortunate in the matter of view than I was.

Descending the little hill, we tumbled into the back garden of one Brosel, who looked upon us with emphatic suspicion, an attitude of mind fully shared by his dogs.

"What do you come here for?" he said.

"To take your photograph," I replied.

"To take my photograph! But how can you do that?"

"I will do it with this box," I said.

"Well, that is a good idea! What do you want me to do?"

"Sit on that chair and put the dogs out of the way—all the dogs."

"Very good," he said, "but I must first go in and brush up."

He disappeared and came out again in a moment, like a quick-change man, in a new suit of store clothes. After no little discussion we posed him on a crooked chair on the hill-side, and all was ready for the act, when he jumped up and cried out:

"Stop! Stop! How much are you going to make me pay for this?"

"Nothing," I said.

"That's impossible," he said. "What will you get out of me?"

"I will get nothing out of you."

"But I think you will," he said. "You will be wanting something or you will not give me the photograph."

It was with difficulty that I calmed his fears and took the photograph.

The town of Guayaquil, like so many tropical cities, stands on a reclaimed swamp. One wonders how the people live in these places. I imagine in Guayaquil they would not live if the town were not periodically burned down. Fires destroy the rapidly accumulating filth. One such fire had swept away practically the whole town a year or two before my visit. The place was still in process of rebuilding. The new houses had quite a magnificent appearance. Looked at not too close, one might believe them to be splendid structures of stone. As a matter of fact, they were of split bamboo and plaster, with corrugated iron roofs, and you could stick a penknife through the walls. The poor people in the suburbs dwelt in wretched huts without walls, built upon piles, as in the slums of Colon. I asked a Guayaquil gentleman how he came to be alive in such a climate. "Alive!" he said. "In Guayaquil? Why not? It's one of the healthiest places in the world. Now Panama or Colon, or places like those"—*et cetera*. I began to know this tune.

A little distance south of Guayaquil begins the desert-coast region of South America, which continues uninterruptedly as far south as Coquimbo in Chile. The change from fertility to mere sandy wastes is made in a few miles, and nothing can be imagined more barren and desolate than is the shore thenceforward. There is little attraction to land at the ports on this forbidding coast. They are not proper ports at all, but only roadsteads, where the ship lies at anchor while dilatory people bring the cargo out on lighters, and officials invent excuses for wasting the ship's time. Now it is a bishop for whom one is kept waiting several hours; now some local functionary or some local functionary's cargo. In the Peruvian *mañana*-land such trifles are not worth considering. If gringos are annoyed, so much the better; no one else minds. Only at the north-Peruvian port of Payta did I care to land, while quantities of cattle and bales of cotton were being shipped. The cattle were brought out in flat-bottomed barges, about a hundred on a barge. One by one they were hoisted on board by a rope passed round their horns. The process was not devoid of cruelty. I am told that the beasts are driven down from up-country, and that they have no food, the last day at least, on the road. Neither are they fed on board ship. If the voyage lasts three days, hungry they go.

Payta is a dead-and-alive place, built of bamboo huts, where it only rains once in seven years, and where all the drinking-water has to be brought by train from the interior. Nothing grows in the neighborhood. Sand and gravel slopes behind the town lead steeply up to a flat, far-stretching desert-plateau called Tabalazo, on which lies a bed of recent marine deposits, containing quantities of well-preserved shells belonging to existing species. This dreary town was for the time enlivened by rumors of a revolution said to be beginning in the interior. A Peruvian man-of-war was lying at anchor, having recently landed some troops. A gentleman of influence, whom the government wished to remove from the scene of temptation, was hustled on board our boat, with orders to repair to Lima and stay there for the benefit of his health as long as the revolution lasted.

While lying off Payta we were boarded by various traders in so-called Panama hats, which, indeed, are not made at Panama at all, but only at a group of villages about fifty miles inland from Payta. Gone are the great days of the Panama hat—the days when a wealthy slave-owner would pay a hundred dollars for one of finest make; yet even now the genuine article is a far better-made affair than the best London shops would enable one to guess. It happened that one of our passengers was an experienced dealer in Panama hats, and he explained to us the difference in quality and the different kinds that were offered for sale.

"This hat," he said, "is worth five dollars, this ten, and this twenty. If you were to go to the villages you would no doubt find better ones, but it is seldom that they make the very best now."

I was wearing what I believed to be a Panama hat, which I had bought in London and paid a pound for. I handed it to him, saying, "And what is this worth?"

"Paris machine-made—one dollar," was his prompt and doubtless accurate reply.

There also came on board, and sailed with us a stage or two, numerous petty dealers in fruit and vegetables. This was the case not only at Payta, but at most ports down the coast, the bi-weekly steamer serving the purpose of an itinerant market for poultry and vegetables. The west coast of South America throughout the desert belt is about as dull a seaboard as you will find in the world. Such, at all events, was my experience of it. I had expected that the coast-range of mountains would be visible at least sometimes, and had pictured myself sitting on the deck of the steamer in the comfortable enjoyment of tropical heat tempered by sea-breezes, while the outlying ranges of the Cordillera passed before my view from hour to hour. Instead of this, all that I saw beneath a roof of cloud, and through an atmosphere thick with moisture or dust, was the sandy margin of the continent backed by bare slopes reach-

LADING CATTLE

A BALSA LADEN WITH PETROLEUM

ing up to hills of mean appearance, whose summits were frequently lost to view in the heavy sky. Only once was there a momentary glimpse of greater altitudes, or even a suggeston of snow. The nights were always cold; one was wet and foggy, too, the siren blowing for hours—the tropics forsooth! Monotony and insignificance were the general characteristics of the scene. Not indeed that the absolute barrenness of the desert coast had not a certain dignity of its own; the desert is always dignified; its mere emptiness suffices to endow it with a sense of breadth. But the ports and human settlements had a sordid appearance to my eyes. Not one of them possessed any picturesqueness or excited a trace of human attachment towards it as a place of abode. Each town, if these collections of wooden shanties with corrugated iron roofs can be called towns, bore on the face of it the fact that no human being would live there if he could help it. Eten, Pacasmayo, Salaverry—we anchored off them all in succession. They had their cheap iron piers where the lighters were laden, their railway stations for short lines running inland, and that was all. At each we lay a wearisome number of hours, impatient to move on; and, now that they are gone, none of them lingers in my memory as less dreary, less unattractive than the rest. The only incidents I remember in the voyage from one port to another was the sight of here and there a whale or a whaling-vessel "trying off," or a guano island, or rocks haunted by seals. But such slight excitements were few and far between, so that when at last, on the 15th of August, we anchored off

Callao, with four days to spare, I landed with no little satisfaction.

Nothing, I think, indicates more plainly the enthusiasm with which Pizarro and his companions set forth on their enterprise of South American conquest than the fact that, after sailing as they did for weeks and months down this forbidding coast, they still retained faith in the wealth of that unseen interior which in due season they landed to visit. The mere sight of so barren and apparently valueless a region would have determined the hopefulness of an ordinary sane man. But, I presume, the wonderful experiences of Cortez in Mexico had so worked upon the imaginations of his contemporaries that they saw gold everywhere, and would not have been surprised to find it lying about in solid lumps upon the most desert shore. Of course, at the mouths of the fertile valleys were large native towns, and the mounds which to-day contain their ruins are in some cases visible to a passing ship. Could we have landed and inspected these, the voyage from Guayaquil to Lima would not have been so dull.

We landed at Callao just in time to catch the evening train to Lima, while the sun, nearing the horizon, poured a flood of crimson orange light below the everlasting pall of cloud that at this time of year hangs over the coast region. Purple hills sloped up on either hand from the level fields of sugar-cane, maize, etc., which were divided from one another by adobe walls shining crimson in the sunset light. The walls and houses thus glorified seemed as though built of some priceless substance, but the glory was evanescent. Almost before the effect had faded we were in the capital town of Peru, where I was most hospitably entertained by Mr. Alfred St. John, the British *chargé d'affaires*.

Even to the eye of a casual visitor Lima is a decidedly impressive town. The latticed bow - windows, reminiscent of Moorish influences from the Far East, render the streets highly picturesque. The great old Spanish houses, with their arcaded *patios* and their galleries, sometimes enlivened by blossoming shrubs or trees, of which the passer-by gains a glimpse through the open *portes-cochères*, tell of the rich and splendid society of by - gone days. The cathedral and churches, if not architecturally beautiful, are at all events imposing; and the population that throng the roads show that if there is no longer an abounding prosperity, there is at least a tolerably high standard of average comfort. By all accounts the society of Lima is pleasant and refined. The ladies are said to be charming, and those best able to judge think most highly of the city as a place of abode. A passer-by like myself, the length of whose visit was measured by hours, had, of course, no opportunity for forming an opinion. What sights there were I made haste to see—the desiccated body of Pizarro in a glass box in the cathedral, a rather second-rate museum of Peruvian antiquities in a building erected for an exhibition, the Botanical Garden, and a few of the principal old houses. That which was once the abode of the Inquisition was now in the occupation of the French Minister, Monsieur Larrouy, of whose kindness to me I retain a warm recollection. The palace occupied by the President and his ministers is said to date, in part, at any rate, from the days of Pizarro, while in one of the court-yards there is a tree reported to have been planted by the conqueror himself. It goes without saying that the streets were dirty, ill-paved, and close. The sanitary condition of the town, I imagine, leaves a good deal to be desired. As a place to sleep in, Lima is by no means to be recommended. The cocks crow there with a frequency and vigor which I understand is regarded as an excellent sign by poultry fanciers, but is far from conducive to the slumber of neighbors. The police and watchmen are apparently under orders to warn thieves of their whereabouts at frequent intervals by loudly blowing on their whistles.

Next morning at an early hour I hastened to the railway station. The weather was depressing and drizzly, the roads muddy; all the people who were out were well wrapped up with shawls round their mouths. Thus I started to make the ascent to the crest of the Andes by the famous Oroya Railway, which, starting from sea-level, takes you in nine hours to an altitude somewhat higher than that of the summit of Mont Blanc. As we left the town by a valley leading inland, the low mists began to clear away and disclosed upon the hills a belt of metallic green lustre caused by vegetation springing up at this time of year where the mists rest. The valley produces rich crops of corn, sugar, cotton, and tropical fruits wherever artificial irrigation reaches. The irrigated area is very much smaller than it used

to be in pre-Columbian days.   Terraced fields, once
irrigated by now ruined aqueducts, stretch up the hill-
sides in all directions.   The terraces, falling into decay,
show how much larger an area was under crops in the
days of the Incas, and account for the dense population
which inhabited the numerous ruined villages that
are seen along the foot of the hills.   There is something inexpressibly sad in the sight of these abandoned
terraces, broken watercourses, ruined villages, and
signs of a vanished population.   The villages stand
at the edge of the cultivated land, just as they do in
Egypt; but if the irrigated flat ground recalls the valley of the Nile, the terraced fields reaching far aloft
awake vivid reminiscences of the mountain country
along the northwest frontier of India—as, for instance,
in Hunza, where the native population are living in a
stage of civilization that must bear no little likeness
to that of the Peruvians under Inca government.
The mist-nurtured vegetation did not go far inland,
but was succeeded by hill-slopes sunburned and apparently desert.

As we went inland the hills grew bigger and somewhat bolder in outline.   The valley bottom became
fuller of trees and bush.   Presently we left the dreary
roof of fog behind, and, at a height of some 5000 feet
above the sea, where the health resort of Matucana
is prettily situated, came out into fresh air and bright
sunshine.   Now the valley narrows, patches of snow
come in view ahead, knobs of rock protrude through
débris slopes, and cliffs and the great knees of the
mountains appear aloft.   The gradient of the rails
grows steeper; the engine pants, and, no longer fol-

lowing the bed of the valley, the line begins to wind its way up the side, taking advantage of every contour which enables a little altitude to be gained by corkscrew curves or other engineering devices. About 10,000 feet above the sea comes San Mateo, a famous resort for consumptives. And now the first symptoms of mountain sickness — *sorocche*, as they call it in Peru*—began to be experienced by my fellow-travellers. Most of them had brought some pet remedy, something to sip or something to smell, but I could not perceive that these nostrums were any more effectual than those patronized by Channel passengers as remedies for sea-sickness. One had only to look around the car to see how rapidly the complaint was invading the company. A great silence fell upon all. People crouched themselves into strange positions. They wrapped up their heads in shawls, or otherwise endeavored to find relief from their unwonted sensations. At first those who were less affected overwhelmed their companions with fruitless advice, but gradually the advisers themselves succumbed, and before long uncanny sounds were heard from all parts of the train.

The ascent became steeper. There were several zigzags, at each of which the position of the engine had to be changed from one end of the train to the other; and there were corkscrew tunnels and spider-legged bridges over narrow ravines, curves up side-valleys, and circumventings around protruding bosses —in fact, every ingenious contrivance for getting

---

*It is commonly called *soroche*, but I am told the correct Indian word is *soroc-che*.

ON THE OROYA RAILROAD

TERRACED HILL-SIDE

up hill by a steady grade of 4 in 100. The higher we rose the brighter was the sunshine and the fresher the air. Now and again the train was halted, that rocks fallen on the line might be cleared out of the way, such little accidents being of continual occurrence. At Chicla (12,215 feet) the valley opens and becomes for a while more level. At last we were above the highest of the terraced fields, where grazing-grounds take the place of former cultivation.

By the time we reached Casapalca (13,606 feet), I was distinctly conscious that we were no longer down at sea-level. A slight dizziness came over me, I felt a tension across the crown of the head, a disagreeable excitement, a tingling in the soles of the feet as though they were in contact with velvet, and I walked with an uncertain step. But all these symptoms were mild enough not to prevent my enjoyment of the journey.

We now passed great caravans of llamas, the first I had seen. They were engaged in carrying ore to the smelting-works of Casapalca. Beyond the grassy valley a small glacier - covered peak came in sight ahead, and soon we passed by rocks evidently smoothed in ancient days by glacier ice. Patches of snow were lying beside the line in the shadows; a hard frost chilled us to the marrow of the bones. I cannot say that I felt regret when we entered the summit tunnel and knew that we had reached the upward limit of our way. At the far end of the tunnel we came out again into sunshine, and the snow range of the inner Cordillera smote upon our eyes in all its silver splendor, while a beautiful glacier-covered mountain rose close at hand.

Mr. Ellis, the Permanent Way Inspector of the line, was awaiting me with a hand-car, composed of four wheels, a platform, a seat, and a brake. As soon as the train had started down eastward the hand-car was set on the lines to run us back to Lima. The air was so bitterly cold that I was glad enough to wrap myself in two thick *ponchos* provided by the foresight of Mr. Ellis. Gravitation was our engine; it gripped us in the midnight darkness of the tunnel, where, sightless, we felt the ground as it were sliding out beneath us. The wheels whirred. There was the sense though not the aspect of motion till the tunnel's eye came in view ahead, a mere speck of light revealing stalactite icicles on walls and roof. Larger and brighter it grew; like a bomb from a mortar we burst forth into day. Down we went—down and down. The kilometre posts flew by like a railing. We were swung around corners, and plunged into and out of the night of tunnels. These, when curved, as they frequently were, seemed to screw about us with a motion of their own Faster and faster we went; the landscape shot up on either hand. Some llamas strayed on the track, and we missed them by the breadth of a fleece. We dashed along the margin of giddy precipices and over unpaved bridges, through which one looked down into giddy depths. Bang! went the wheels against a stone fallen upon the rail. The car was flung into the air, but fell back safely upon the track. Mr. Ellis did not notice so trifling an occurrence, but I did, and have recalled it since with inward shuddering. At the V's we had to dismount, turn over the points, and then proceed in the opposite di-

THE SUMMIT OF THE OROYA RAILWAY

rection. If we had overshot the mark we should have leaped off the point of the line and flown down the precipice. Such an accident once happened, in days of revolution, to a trainful of soldiers. Some engineer, unaccustomed to the line, was told off to drive the train. He put it in motion without properly applying the brake. It rushed down with frightful velocity, and was almost immediately beyond control. The passengers realized their approaching fate, and raised a wild shout of terror as the train dashed over the point of the V and was smashed to atoms two thousand feet below. The handle of the brake was found flung across to the other side of the valley with a human arm still grasping it,

The changes of vegetation at different levels, slowly climbed through in the ascent, were much more conspicuous in the rapidity of our downward passage. The snow-patches and the green uplands were swiftly left behind. We passed through a belt of blue blossoms like lupines, and then a belt of yellow. The evening shadow climbed the hill. As we came down into the narrow gorges a roof of pink cloud hung overhead. We saw it in the intervals between tunnel and tunnel, the effect being specially fine at a place well named Infernillo, where a spider-like bridge, hung across from one vertical cliff to another, unites two corkscrew tunnels. The world was turning faster against us than we were rushing west. The brief twilight was soon over and solid night came on. Then the romance of this one hundred and fifty miles' switchback ride began, and fancy was turned free to dignify our flight with imaginary terrors.

D   49

There was no moon, but Jupiter and Venus, in close conjunction just over the edge of the black hill, were bright enough to cast a shadow. The Southern Cross was now and then visible ahead. The Milky Way shone brighter than I ever remember it. Meteors darted across the sky, and the hill-tops reflected flashes of summer lightning. Now and again we passed the house of some railroad employé, where a light shone and dogs rushed barking forth; but we hurried on unceasingly down and down, rejoicing in the furious flight. At Matucana the night was spent in a reasonably comfortable inn. Next morning the descent was continued, but the gradient and our consequent speed were less. The only remaining excitement was caused by the knowledge that a train was coming up in the opposite direction, travelling at a pace of twenty miles an hour. The quick twists and turns of the line rendered it impossible for us to see far ahead, and we might easily run into it if great care were not taken. We waited long in one or two sidings, hoping the train would pass. Finally, deciding to trust to luck, we ran down to a station where the missing train was drawn up at the platform, a solid hour and a half behind its time. The sun was hot through all this part of the descent, but on coming under the shadow of the coast cloud we were glad enough to put our *ponchos* on for the run into Lima.

CHAPTER V

LIMA TO LAKE TITICACA

TWO days later I was on board ship again, sailing away southward over the calm ocean. There were three more ports to stop at, each as uninteresting as those that had gone before; and there were more guano islands to pass. The coast remained as dull as ever in the thick air and gloomy sky. Off Pisco, where the cheap spirits come from, a countless number of pelicans, cormorants, and other birds were flying or floating over a great shoal of fish. It was wonderful to see the large pelicans dropping into the sea from a great height, with their curious sidelong dip, and always coming up with a fish in their ungainly beaks. Picture the long, dark, foreshortened mass of birds on the splashing water, the similar cloud a hundred feet or so above in the air; at one end of this a cascade of birds falling and diving with a great splash; at the other end the birds who had swallowed their catches rising again into the air and flying forward till they gained the front rank and dived again, thus producing an elongated oval which seemed to roll forward over the sea. The noise of crying and splashing could be heard from a great distance. Near at hand, the air was simply black with the profusion of bird-life. The divers and cormorants swam about on the surface and took ample toll on their own account. Such a sight amply sufficed to account for the guano islands.

On the 21st of August, just thirty-nine days from London, I was awakened at an early hour with the welcome information that we were approaching Mollendo. Kind friends boarded the ship to receive me when she cast anchor. Our baggage was dropped into one barge, myself into another, and we rowed away for shore. Fortunately the sea was reasonably calm; not that storms are frequent down this coast, but there is often a heavy swell, causing an immense surf to break upon the shore. At no time is landing an easy matter at Mollendo, for there is always a considerable surf, but the actual landing-place is protected by a reef of rocks very similar to that protecting the shore at Beyrout, on the Syrian coast. The boat was rowed through a narrow opening in the reef, the great white breakers foaming close on either hand. Though the rowers evidently knew their business, an inveterate landsman like myself does not pass such a place without experiencing some emotion. Inside the reef the water was, of course, calmer, but the swell penetrated there; and the rise and fall of the waves was such that, after coming close to the landing-place, we were more than half an hour before the opportunity came for jumping ashore. I landed breathlessly almost in the arms of the mayor of the little town, who officially greeted me with a welcome to Peru, and a warm expression of good wishes for the success of my expedition into the Bolivian mountains.

Mollendo is one of the cleanest towns I saw any-

where in South America. This is due to the energy
of the local board, elected by all the inhabitants of
the place irrespective of nationality. Mollendo is
thus very healthy, and serves as a sanitarium for
Arequipa and La Paz. Mr. V. H. McCord, the manager of the railway, took me at once under his wing,
and himself accompanied me by the train when he
had finished breakfast. Instead of striking straight
inland, the rails follow the coast for thirteen miles,
along a sandy flat, where the marks left by the great
earthquake wave of 1868 are still clearly visible. Turning up a valley, we began to ascend over a sloping
desert, which irrigation would fertilize if only there
were water to be had. The road winds about and
gains altitude without need for big cuttings, tunnels,
or bridges. In fact, if I remember right, there is only
one very short tunnel, and one, or, at the utmost, two
bridges on the whole length of the line from the sea
right up to Lake Titicaca.

At a certain level, approximately the same, I suppose, as that where I observed the same phenomenon
behind Lima, comes the belt where mists are frequent,
and where, accordingly, at this time of year some
vegetation can grow. The slopes were pleasantly
green, and there was here and there a fragrant white
flower with strong perfume like a tuberose. Here
in the damp season cattle are fattened in large numbers for the Iquique market. The fertile Tambo
Valley came into sight, below to the south, with a fine
view of hills at the head of it, piling themselves up
and up farther inland, the buttresses of the continent.
Looking back in the other direction, the surf-edged

sea was still visible. The view marvellously developed as we rose above the undulating green foreground to a crinkled blue, purple, and yellow desert, that stretched away down on the one hand to the ocean, and up on the other to the high mountains, where the great volcano Misti (18,650 feet, railway survey) came in sight.

A little over three thousand feet above sea-level we emerged on an almost flat pampa that seemed to cry aloud for irrigation. There does, in fact, exist a perennial stream which might be turned on to it by a short tunnel; but such is the uncertainty of titles to land in this country that no capitalist would be rash enough to venture his money in the enterprise. The green belt was left behind, and the rippled white desert stretched around, with black hills rising from it—the first specimen of the volcanic mountain landscape of which I was afterwards to see so much. A larger desert pampa followed, higher up, flooded by great lakes of mirage; and here came into view, away to the northward, the great mountain whose true name is Ampato, but known at Arequipa as Coropuna. Its altitude, as measured by the railroad surveyors, is 22,800 feet. I never saw it save from a great distance, but the enormous glaciers that flow down and envelop all sides of its dome-like mass prove it to be a peak of great height. I should not be surprised if an accurate measurement found it to be higher than the highest peaks of the Argentine Andes. Misti and its larger neighbor, Chachani,* were full in view

* Nineteen thousand feet (railroad survey). The astronomers at Arequipa state that this peak is probably about 20,000 feet high.

THE PAMPA OF AREQUIPA

ahead, their summits crowned with considerable accumulations of winter snow.

The desert was now dotted all over with heaps of sand, self-piled on a crescent-shaped base, the convex side of the crescent facing the prevalent wind. These heaps of sand slowly march across the plain by the simple process of the wind blowing the sand up the outer slope of the heap to the top, whence it falls down the inner face. When one of the sand-heaps reaches the edge of the railway line, it has to be dumped over on to the other side by a gang of navvies. There it reforms its crescent shape and proceeds upon its slow journey. The crescents are of various sizes, averaging perhaps some twenty-five yards in width. Above the fields of sand-heaps, at an elevation of 5000 feet, the railway enters a region of mounded stony hills, where it winds up to the edge of the deep-lying canyon of a river whose waters fertilize the oasis of Arequipa.

Descending to the river, we soon ran into Arequipa station, as the lowering sun picked out, with blue shadows and ruddy lights, the fine ridges and gullies that seam the Misti's graceful cone. McCord hospitably put me up in the station-house. There were several bullet-marks in the walls of my room, scars of the last revolution. The sofa in the sitting-room had a tragic interest, for under it an unpopular officer was run to earth and shot by the revolutionaries. As I was unpacking my things a smart shock of earthquake occurred, causing the place to rattle and quiver as though a heavy freight-train were passing. In Arequipa no one pays much attention to earthquakes, for they are of daily occurrence and the houses of the town are specially built to resist them.

The four days I was compelled to wait in Arequipa for the weekly train that goes up to Lake Titicaca were a pleasant interlude. The climate of Arequipa is exceedingly treacherous for a new-comer. The place is 7550 feet above sea-level; the nights, therefore, at this season of the year, are bitterly cold, though by day the sun has great power. It is easy to take a violent chill, and pneumonia is a very common and fatal disease.

Had I not been occupied with much unavoidable business, it would have been pleasant and not difficult to have made the ascent either of Misti or of Chachani. Misti is very easy to climb; mules can go to the summit, where stands a small meteorological observatory equipped with self-recording instruments, a dependence of the Harvard College Astronomical Observatory at Arequipa. Every fortnight a man goes up to bring down the observations and set the instruments. Chachani has likewise been ascended. Mr. Wagner, of the Cailloma Mine, whom I had the good fortune to meet at the Arequipa Club, informed me that he found among the old papers at the mine one dating from the time of the Spaniards, which stated that the summit of Chachani was the burial-place of an Inca. A plan of the tomb was appended, with a point marked on it indicating the position of treasure. After repeated attempts, Mr. Wagner succeeded in reaching the summit of the mountain from the north, and did, in fact, find the remains of the building. He took

THE OUTSKIRTS OF AREQUIPA

some native workmen up with him and made excavations on three different days. Portions of the skeleton of a woman were revealed, and some wooden cups and spoons, and fragments of pots. The old plan proved to be correct in its main outlines, and the point indicated for the treasure was identified without difficulty; but it was evident that a previous treasure-seeker had been there, for the grave had been disturbed, and anything of value it ever contained had no doubt been rifled long ago. He told me that the pavement and walls of the grave were of granite, a rock which is found near the base of the mountain below the volcanic superstructure.

To a new-comer from Europe the town of Arequipa is very interesting. It arouses strange reminiscences of the Old World, with a novel touch added by the craftsmanship of the local Indians. A group of craftsmen, however minutely directed by a foreign architect, will inevitably leave traces of their own character upon their work. Thus, in the chief streets of the town, the one-storied façades of the thick tufa-walled houses are designed with pilasters, cornices, and other architectural members of classical or renaissance tradition; while the sculptured details, sometimes very rich in effect, are rough and almost barbaric in style. The by-streets are, of course, dirty and pervaded by most unpleasant odors. At night the whole place is loud with the shouts of intoxicated men and the voices of barking dogs, like the jackals of the East. The passer-by obtains brief glimpses into slummy drinking-dens and dimly lit places of amusement, where a low population of half-breeds takes such recreation as it is likely to desire. To walk at night to one's lodgings, as I often did, was a sufficiently unpleasant experience, unless one adhered to the main street.

In the midst of the city is a great cathedral, shaken down more or less frequently by earthquakes, and now in process of rebuilding by local talent. It is large, and not architecturally unimpressive, though in a wild fashion of its own. The towers are almost riotous in design, as indeed are old Spanish-American church-towers generally, yet it is impossible to deny that they have a certain splendor and dignity. The interior of the cathedral is whitewashed and spacious, with some rude but effective carving in suitable positions. High mass was going on when I entered. For orchestra there was a cracked piano, jerkily erupting airs from "La Fille de Madame Angot." One boy and one man, standing together at the extreme west end of the church and shouting all they knew how, were the whole choir. Workmen were sawing wood and hammering nails in the aisle while the service proceeded, and incense was ascending in clouds by the altar.

I likewise visited the Jesuits' church, the interior of which must have been striking when there were six side-chapels, with great altar-pieces reaching to the vaulting, all carved, painted, and gilded in the most gorgeous Spanish style, with figures in niches, painted, enamelled, and dressed up to life, some of more than average excellence. Unfortunately, these fine decorations are now considered old-fashioned, and three of them have been removed, though some

AREQUIPA PLAZA

AREQUIPA CATHEDRAL TOWERS

one told me that they were not destroyed but only transferred to a country church, the name of which I did not learn. My presence was evidently obnoxious to the verger. He pursued me with scowlings and mutterings, and slammed the door behind me on my departure, gringos being almost as obnoxious to the ignorant Catholic lower orders of Peru and Bolivia as Christians are to fanatical Mohammedans.

One afternoon I had the loan of a slight, spirited pacing pony of charming disposition. In company with a kind friend I rode out to visit the observatory. The ponies were wonderfully sure-footed, as indeed was necessary, for the tracks they had to travel over were of the most rugged description. But the ride was delightful. It led through the enchanting semi-Oriental suburbs of the town and by positions commanding beautiful views. In aspect Arequipa, as one looked down from a distance upon its white stone walls, its many cupolas, and its all-pervading trees, strongly resembled an Eastern city. At the observatory I was most hospitably received, and all doors were opened to me. Mr. Clymer and his fellow-observer showed me their fine instruments. I was, of course, especially interested in the admirable equipment for celestial photography, for which this observatory is deservedly famed. They also described to me the ascent of Mount Misti, which both of them had made on more than one occasion, and they gave me, among other beautiful photographs taken from the summit, the one which I have the pleasure, with permission, to publish here.

At seven in the morning of the 25th of August,

the train at last started which was to carry us to the shores of Lake Titicaca. A railway official came down to see me off and cast an eye over the train. He detected a dirty friar who had filled the place of two travellers with his baggage. "Take it out and get it registered," he said. The man protested, at first truculently, then grovellingly. "Out you go, then, baggage and all. It's too bad," he said to me; "in this priest-ridden country we have to carry priests for half-price, and these barefoot Johnnies for nothing, and the barefooters give more trouble than any other passengers. They are always going up and down as though they were the busiest people—a mean, filthy, idle lot."

The sun was yet low; a smoke-cloud hanging over Arequipa indicated that the town had breakfasted. Misti and Chachani, on either hand, seemed to swim in the glowing air. Green fields spread wide on either bank of the river, till the desert resumed its sway, and cactus and spare brown plants were all the vegetation that remained in sight. The soil consisted of volcanic ejections of gray and pink mud, with large, angular rocks embedded. The whole area through which we were passing was cut up into small hills and shallow, winding valleys, all equally desert. Clouds now settled heavily on the high mountains, and all the view we had was backward over the sea-like pampa. About thirteen thousand feet above sea-level came a land of tussocky grass, supporting sheep, llamas, and a few horses. Now the car began to smell of some nasty camphorated drug that the passengers were sniffing as a remedy for mountain sickness. Silence had long ago descended upon the people; those who could disposed themselves to slumber. Even the two dirty friars stopped the gossip with which they had entertained each other all the way, and only a babe gave vent to its feelings in ceaseless yells and screams. Presently another baby began to howl in chorus. The higher we got the more undulating and uninteresting was the scenery of the bleak and bare region. A fog descended and blotted out all view. On the top level the only growths were the moss-heaps called *yareta*, a resinous growth largely used for fuel, and grass tussocks growing round the edges of the moss-heaps. Patches of snow were lying about, dimly seen through the mists. Droves of llamas, great flocks of sheep, and a few cattle came vaguely into sight and faded away. Once or twice we saw wild vicuñas, so well accustomed to the passing of trains as to take no heed.

At half-past two we were on top of the pass (14,666 feet), and I was pleased to find that on this occasion I experienced none of the disagreeable sensations that assailed me on the Oroya railroad a few days before. There was no view either from the pass or during the first part of the descent, which was made in fog and driving snow over an immense moor. Two lakes came by, in a wild, abandoned-looking region, admirably suited to be a home for Thebaid hermits, but quite wasted on a worldly age. Plenty of ducks, of three different kinds, frequent the waters. At Maravillas (13,000 feet) snow gave place to rain. A ranch on one side of the line and smelting-works on the other seemed forbidding abodes in the raw day.

Down we went by steady incline. At the cold hour of sunset we came out on flat ground, occupied by barley-fields, but once covered by the waters of Lake Titicaca. Abandoned terraced fields ringed the hillsides all about, but darkness swallowed them up, and when we reached the port of Puno (12,540 feet) and went on board the little steamer *Coya*, the cold night had already come on.

CHAPTER VI

LAKE TITICACA TO LA PAZ

THE Scotch engineer made me comfortable, and in conversation with him the time passed pleasantly. He told me of the troubles they had had with the boats, which were brought up in sections years ago and had to be put together on the shore. Maintenance and repair must be accomplished without any of the usual facilities, but such is the energy and intelligence of the European engineering staff that everything goes well. When traffic increased. and a larger boat was needed, one of the steamers was actually hauled up on the shore of the lake, cut in half then and there, and a great addition made to its length by adding a new piece in the middle. Of course, in times of revolution it is the aim of both parties to obtain possession of these steamers at the earliest moment, and many an exciting adventure has happened upon them. Bullet-marks can be traced all over them, and they have been the scene of bloody combats. "Many's the man I've seen shot on this deck," said my friend. I wish I might here retell some of the tales he told me.

When morning came the coldness of the night was proved by the ring of ice surrounding the shore.

It was the opening of a calm and brilliant day, as good fortune had it, for the waters of Titicaca are usually stirred to tumult by contending winds that rush down the surrounding hills without warning. Thus the steamer passengers usually suffer terribly from a combination of sea and mountain sickness of so overpowering a character that even the best sailors seldom escape; and the stokers and crew, who should be habituated, if habituation were possible, are by no means always free from the complaint.

Of all lakes in the world this one, the largest in South America, named Titicaca* in the ancient language of the country, is in many respects the most remarkable. Its altitude, according to the railway survey, is 12,516 feet above sea-level. In the rainy season it rises about five feet higher. Its area is over three thousand square miles, half the size of Lake Ontario, fourteen times the size of the Lake of Geneva. It is over one hundred miles in length, and averages thirty miles in width. Twenty streams empty into it. The Rio Desaguadero very slowly flows out to Lake Poopo, fifty leagues away to the southeast, from which there is no surface exit. The level of the surface of both lakes has sunk within the historic period. Three hundred years ago the margin of Titicaca was near the ruins of Tiahuanaco, which now lie over six miles from the water's edge. At an earlier date, when the

---

* *Titi karka, Titi ccacka, Titi ccan-na* are early spellings of the name given in Padre Baltasar de Salas's MS., *Historia de Copacabana* (1618-1625), printed in the La Paz Review, *La Brisa*, Vol. I., No. 2 (October 31, 1898). *Titi! Caca!* is commonly said to have been a war-cry.

A BALSA ON LAKE TITICACA

temple was built, it stood upon an island. At an earlier but still recent geological epoch the southern limit of the great inland sea was in about latitude 27° S.

Before the boat started I made short excursions along the shore to investigate the native boats called *balsas*. They are made of the great Titicaca rush, very neatly bound together, just as they used to be made in the days of the Incas. They are not, of course, very long-lived things, for when once the rushes become well sodden the boats are waterlogged, and have to be drawn up on shore and left for many days or even weeks to dry before they can be used again. In these crazy craft the Indians, nevertheless, navigate the great lake, and even cross it from side to side. There were plenty of birds in sight — gulls, coots, various ducks, and some herons, besides smaller birds. The low lands and hills round the shore were all sunburned and sorrowful, apparently sparsely populated, but the multitude of abandoned terraced fields now visible in the daylight were proof, if proof were needed, of the greater population that once dwelt on this high plateau. From December to May, which is the rainy season, the land is green, and produces a harvest of barley, potatoes, and other hardy growths. Now all the hills were yellowy brown, a golden frame for the blue water.

Our steamer passed down a canal cut in the shallows, and so out into a bay. At its south horn is Taqueli Island, very useful, at times of revolution or general election in Peru, for the temporary exile of persons obnoxious to the party in power. As

E

the steamer rounded the island and entered the waters of the great lake, Mount Sorata came into view eighty miles away, perfectly clear, apparently rising out of the waters themselves. Nothing was visible but its snow-covered upper portion, which shone with great brilliancy in the bright day. To behold thus plainly and from so remote a distance one of the chief goals of our expedition was rare good fortune. It would be difficult for a reader to imagine the excitement we felt as we gazed upon the mountain through our telescopes and canvassed the possibility of an ascent. All day long it was before us, gradually coming nearer and revealing more definitely the intricacies of its great northwestern face. The more we looked at it the more we admired the beauty of its appearance and the less we liked it as a mountain to climb. It is a very complex mass, with high snow plateaus below the snow *arêted* summit towers, drained by ice-falls and steep *couloirs* cut in its cliff-rimmed base. The northern peak, the true Illampu, is finest in form, a rock-walled mass seemingly vertical on all sides save where it is buttressed by narrow rock ridges. North of Mount Sorata the range drops to a long, almost flat, line of hills about 16,000 feet in height. Southward the range extends away and away, a straight line of snow mountains thoroughly Alpine in appearance. Perspective makes them sink one beyond another till Cacaaca appears like a rival to Sorata, and as fine or even finer in form. From hour to hour the snowy range, of which Sorata is the northern end, revealed itself, one peak after another appearing above the waters and gradually joining itself to its neighbors.

Far away to the north, and belonging to a different mountain system, there stood another great peak, apparently the unmeasured Asongati, which I only saw on this occasion. It had every appearance of being about as lofty as Mount Sorata.

The mountain system in Bolivia is rather complicated. Hugo Reck,* whose classification has been followed very generally, divides it into five parts:

1. The Coast Cordillera.
2. The Cordillera de los Andes or Western Cordillera.
3. The Cordillera Real or Bolivian Andes.
4. Isolated ranges lying between 2 and 3.
5. Ranges east of the Cordillera Real.

For practical purposes, however, it is best to divide the whole into two main and approximately parallel ranges, the Western Cordillera and the Cordillera Real, between which lie lakes Titicaca and Poopo and the high plateau or Puna. We crossed the Western Cordillera on our way up from the sea by train; the Cordillera Real was now before us. These two ranges are said to separate from each other in latitude 14° 40′ S., where is the pass leading over from Titicaca to Cusco, and to reunite, or at least approximate, about latitude 24° S. Though the eastern range in its whole length may be correctly termed the Cordillera Real, that proud designation was undoubtedly gained by the splendid snow-covered stretch which is terminated to the north and the south by the two world-renowned mountains So-

* Hugo Reck, *Geographie und Statistik der Republik Bolivia.* Petermann's *Mittheilungen*, 1865. With map.

rata* and Illimani, sixty-four miles apart. Locally the snowy part of the range is called Cordillera Brava, but this designation seems to be falling into disuse.

With our attention concentrated upon the distant mountains, the nearer lands and hills received less notice than they deserved, and it was with surprise that I found the famous Titicaca Island close at hand. We passed close along its western shore, and then through the narrow Tiquina strait that separates it from the peninsula of Copacabana. This island of Titicaca and its neighbor Coati, the islands of the Sun and of the Moon, are said to have been the original home of the Incas, as all who have read Prescott's *Pizarro* know. It was on Titicaca Island that Manco Capac (*Mallcu Kcapa*) and his wife Mama Oello Huaco (*Marmi Ojllata*) arose, the legendary founders of Inca civilization. It was the people of these islands, and possibly of the neighboring mainland, that gradually extended their power over the inhabitants of the plateau. Afterwards sweeping northward, they founded the great city of Cusco, whence their empire spread to remote and now not definable boundaries. Later researches have thrown much doubt upon the correctness of this popular history.† The ruins of the great Inca buildings on these two islands were visible from the boat, and as I passed I promised myself to make a special pilgrimage to them. But fortune was averse, and I left Bolivia without seeing them

* This peak is generally, but incorrectly, called after its second summit, Illampu. The name of the highest point is Ancohuma or Hank-uma.

† For a brief *résumé* of the results of modern research, see A. H. Keene's *Man, Past and Present*, Cambridge, 1899.

again. Just as we were approaching the strait which gives access to the inner lake, known as Vinamarca, the sun set, bathing the snow mountains in violet gloom before the on-coming of the windless night. Then the moon shone bright and beautiful upon the waters. At eight o'clock we anchored off the Bolivian port Chililaya,* having thus reached our destination in forty-four days from London.

At an early hour next morning, Mr. N. E. Bieber Managing Director of the Yani Gold Mine, to whom I had a letter of introduction, came on board and greeted me. Thoroughly *au fait* with the ways of the port, he made arrangements for landing my goods and sending them off by cart to La Paz. A number of native Aymara Indians carried the things ashore, each man wrapping a box up in his *poncho*, and supporting it on his back just as my coolies used to do in Kashmir. This was my first contact with the pure-breed Indians of South America. All the men were dressed in the same fashion, wearing trousers split down the back of the leg from the knee downward, with some kind of loose linen lining which flapped about through the slit; a European shirt, and perhaps a waistcoat, covered their bodies, but their chief garment was a great blanket of some brilliant color, such as crimson, with strips of green or yellow at the ends; a hole cut in the middle admitted the head, while the loose ends flapped down all round. A *poncho* is to an Indian what a mantle was to an Irishman in the days of Edmund Spenser. "When it

* One hundred and eleven miles by steamer from Puno.

raineth, it is his pent-house; when it bloweth, it is his
tent; when it freezeth, it is his tabernacle. In summer he can wear it loose, in winter he can wrap it close;
at all times he can use it, never heavy, never cum-
bersome." For head-gear the Indians usually wore
a sort of close-fitting woollen nightcap with flaps
over the ears, and over that a round-crowned, rather
narrow-brimmed felt hat. They were all phenomenally
dirty. The hardness of their lives and the severe
climate of this high plateau on which they live were
manifested by their deeply furrowed, weather-beaten
faces, burned brown by the sun and cracked by the
cold winds.

A so-called tilbury, which had been telegraphed
for in advance, was awaiting us. It proved to be
an ordinary light American wagon drawn by four
mules. Like all the La Paz tilburies, it was old, and
inspired little confidence in its capacity for holding
together any length of time. The harness was no
less antique than the machine, and was patched up
with pieces of cord, and bore the signs of many a
rough-and-ready repair.

With much shouting and cracking of his whip,
our driver got his sorry team in motion, and off we
went at a brisk pace, with a stray donkey cantering
ahead. Two more tilburies were starting at the same
time. Wherever the road was wide enough the drivers
raced against one another, wildly screaming. Mine
was the slowest team, and we were soon left behind.
That was my luck throughout this journey. Whatever train I took was the slowest of the week. The
five ocean steamers I voyaged on were each and all

A TILBURY

the slowest of their respective lines. The road wound over some low mounded hills, and descended with a sharp zigzag on to the plain. Just at this point, a week before, one of the tilburies lost a wheel; the vehicle rolled over down the slope, killing one of its occupants on the spot and dangerously injuring the other. The whole of our drive from the lake to the edge of the La Paz basin lay along the high Bolivian plateau, here called the Puna. This plateau, lying between the coast and inner Cordilleras, stretches southward for several hundred miles at about the same altitude. In many respects, as will hereafter appear, it reminded me of Tibet. At the time of my journey it was held in the bonds and drought of winter, so that, but for the old furrows of last year's ploughing and the brown stubble visible here and there, one would have imagined it to be a mere desert. One or two insignificant streams were passed, expanding into occasional ponds, the surfaces of which were so stoutly covered with ice that they had to be broken before the horses could drink. The air was bitterly cold, and, until the sun had climbed fairly high, we suffered considerably from chill. At 12,500 feet above sea-level the climate must always be severe. The natives' habit of wrapping up their heads in shawls or *ponchos* is easily accounted for. Pneumonia is the commonest and most fatal disease in the high parts of Bolivia. Few people live to any great age there. Even in the town of La Paz, which lies in a hollow and is well protected from most winds, old people are rare, and a man seventy years of age is pointed to as a phenomenon.

When the small hills of Chililaya had been left

behind, the great mountain range on our left became visible, Mount Sorata being thirty miles away, rather behind us, Cacaaca almost as far ahead, and the nearest mountain, between the two, about twenty miles off, while great Illimani was seen from time to time in the distance, fifty-five miles away. Detached hills, those of Peñas and Palcoco in particular, rising like islands out of the plain, sometimes shut off parts of the higher range, but in the main we saw it throughout the day as a long white wall rising at the top of a series of gentle slopes cut up by deep valleys. It was a beautiful range, but owing to the clearness of the air seemed very much closer to the road, and therefore smaller than it really was. Naturally our eyes were riveted on it, and at every pause we directed our telescopes upon the different peaks and discussed the probabilities of ascents and the routes to be taken. The side of Sorata which was now displayed to us was evidently a better side for attack than that seen from Lake Titicaca, and a great glacier descending from the foot of the highest peak, in direction almost due south, offered a route by which I decided to attempt the ascent when the proper time came.

The road was a good enough track, dusty and heavy, but fairly level, so that by changing horses every couple of hours we were able to make a good pace. At first we met few people, but after passing the points of junction, first with the road from Achacache and afterwards with that from Pucarani, it became lively enough. We passed many small farms, and saw larger villages, and even towns, some distance away. Almost every man we met was an Indian;

they travelled sometimes singly, carrying loads, but usually in parties of half a dozen or more, driving laden caravans of donkeys or llamas, and sometimes pigs for the market. The donkeys were small, and bore large loads, usually sheaves of *cebada*—that is to say, barley cut before it is ripe, and dried with the corn in the ear. This is the principal crop of the Puna, and forms an admirable fodder for mules and donkeys. A continual stream of caravans thus laden pours from all the country round into La Paz, and on the return brings back such small merchandise as the villagers consume. The poverty of the people was obvious enough; when I was afterwards informed that the agricultural wage is only from about two-pence to threepence a day, I was not surprised.

As the day advanced the bright sunshine and the crisp air became most exhilarating; the freshness of all the sights and novelty of the scene even awoke the interest of Maquignaz, who seldom allowed the calm of his indifference to be disturbed by the strangeness of his surroundings. Before noon white clouds began to mount from the hot valleys on the far side of the Cordillera, and showed themselves over the crest of the range; this we afterwards learned to be a daily phenomenon. In fine weather at early morning the range is generally clear, but long before sunset great masses of clouds that come up from the hot, damp east, pouring over every pass, bury the mountains out of sight and often drift down to the plain, bringing occasional thunder-storms with them. In the months of June and July, I believe, this eastern cloud does not appear, but in 1898 it came regularly throughout

August, September, and October, gradually increasing
in size and in the frequency of the storms to which
it gave rise. In November and the succeeding months
it settles down on the country as a rainy season, lasting
until the following April or May.

Thus hour succeeded hour, and we became more
and more thickly enveloped in dust till there was no
difference between the color of our faces and our clothes.
We grew tired of the bumping, tired of the uniformity
of our surroundings. Before the afternoon was far
advanced the sense of novelty had entirely worn away,
and even I was feeling bored with the monotony of
our movements. To make matters worse, a long,
gentle, upward slope reduced our pace and hid all
view ahead. When I least expected it, the leaders
dipped over the edge of the rise, turned sharp to the left,
and as the carriage followed them we found ourselves,
without warning, on the edge of a cliff (called *La
Bajada*) which dropped some 1600 feet to a great
basin, that looked for all the world like the crater
of some enormous volcano—a basin ten miles or so
in diameter, with a valley leading up from it towards
beautiful Cacaaca, and another stretching downward
to a remote distance. Below us, like a mosaic pavement, lay red-roofed La Paz, a much greater city
than I had imagined, while twenty-five miles away
rose the glorious isolated snowy mass of Illimani.
This view, wonderful at any time, produces an indescribable effect upon all persons coming newly to
La Paz, so suddenly does it burst upon the unpre-
pared vision of the traveller. The whole of this great
basin and the ramifying valleys that debouch upon

it have been excavated by the agency of water from the vast alluvial mass out of which the high Bolivian plateau is built. A great inland sea, whereof Lake Titicaca is but a small remnant, once stretched to the foot of the Cordillera and hundreds of miles away southward of La Paz. It was slowly filled up by the denudation of surrounding mountain ranges. Once or twice volcanic discharges, from some vent the position of which is not ascertained, were cast into the waters, as is evident from the two or three bands of trachytic tuff displayed by the great section down which I was now looking. It is the immensity of this great excavation, which is visibly in process of enlargement at the present day, and the barrenness of its freshly carved walls, that impress an observer. Save in the neighborhood of La Paz, in the bottom of the great hollow, where artificial irrigation can be carried on, there is hardly a trace of fertility, except, I suppose, in the rainy season. All the forms are those made by an apparently torrential flow of water, which cuts deep gullies and eats back by *cirques* into the cliffs, bringing down landslides and mud avalanches in great masses. Yet, except in the traces of its action, there was no sign of water; all was dry and baked and bare.

To bring a railroad from Chililaya to the point where we now stood, which is called the Alto, would be a perfectly easy thing to do, but to drop it down to the town would be far from a simple matter. The road is well laid out in zigzags, down which the tilburies are galloped at a fine pace. There are steeper paths for mules and donkeys, while llamas still use

the world-old tracks which were trodden by their predecessors centuries before the Incas ever rose from
obscurity. Quitting the carriage, I ran down the cliff
by the straightest way and entered the outskirts of
the town alone. They were not in any respect like
European suburbs, nor could one have mistaken them
for the suburbs of an Oriental city. It was impossible,
however, not to feel that, in type, the surroundings of
the way were of great antiquity. There is a certain
Spanish varnish on the surface, and the larger buildings and towers, seen farther off in the midst of the
town, obviously remembered Spain; but the Indian
suburbs bore on the face of them the marks of an
ancient tradition, a habit of life old as the East, yet
other. It was not refined, however picturesque. The
mud hovels by the road-side were oftenest drinking
booths, where the signs of intoxication were flagrant,
and the folk looked degraded and dirty; yet their
costumes, with all their bright colors, made the roads
like a flower-garden.

CHAPTER VII

LA PAZ

LA PAZ, seen from above, looks flat; when you get among its streets, it is difficult to stand on the steeply inclined pavements. Where the paved way began I rejoined the tilbury; the man whipped up his horses, and we flashed along the ways at a dangerously swaggering pace, amidst a volley of cracks from the whip. People jumped aside and only just succeeded in escaping our wild rush. How we bumped and rattled! I looked every moment for the wheels to fly into disconnected spokes; but nothing happened. After swirling round one corner after another, a final dash brought us into the great square of the town, the Plaza (named "16 de Julio") lacking which no South American city could respect itself. We drew up before the door of "Guibert's Hotel," a really admirable hostelry to find in so remote a place. A moment later I was installed in excellent rooms, well furnished and thoroughly European in aspect, with a view from the windows across to a cathedral, and with all signs of civilization around. Had it not been that the lip of the Alto's cliff appeared high up on the sky-line, and the dust of the Puna was thick upon me, I might have found it easy to imagine that all the experiences of the day had been a dream, and

77

that I had come to this town, as one usually comes to civilized places, by train. Before I had had time to don the garments of civilization, the hospitable gentry of La Paz came to greet me with the cocktail of welcome. One and all offered me their help and did their best to make me feel at home at the very moment of arrival; nor from that moment until the day I left Bolivia did I experience at the hands of the people of La Paz anything but the utmost kindness, the grateful memory of which will not leave me until the end of my days.

The first work there was for me in La Paz was to settle relations with the climate, or rather with the altitude, for the hotel in the Plaza stands 11,945 feet above sea-level, and it takes time to habituate one's self to living day in and day out so far above one's usual altitude. Having already spent a week at Arequipa and on the way up, always more than 7000 feet above sea-level, and for the best part of three days from 12,000 to 14,000 feet, without experiencing the smallest discomfort, the last thing that occurred to me was that I should find the altitude of La Paz at all disconcerting. But the day after my arrival I awoke with headache and a general feeling of sickness, which increased as the hours went on, so that there was nothing to do but to go to bed again and stay there. I attributed my woes to the hospitality attending my arrival, but when the doctor came he assured me that I was only suffering from the normal inconvenience which besets new-comers, the redoubtable *sorocche*, or mountain-sickness, and that I should get over it sooner or later. As a matter of fact, it

CONGRESS BUILDING, LA PAZ

passed away in twenty-four hours. Englishmen, familiar only with European altitudes, generally labor under the delusion that they have never experienced any effect from diminished atmospheric pressure, because they have never been mountain-sick. They ascribe such fatigue as they may have felt near a mountain-top entirely to the work done in climbing. But if they could be moved to La Paz, for however short or long a time, they would soon perceive that they were not at sea-level. The streets of the town being steep, all the inhabitants, when they come to walk up-hill, demonstrate by the rapidity of their breathing and the slowness of their gait that they too are affected by the diminished atmospheric pressure. Many persons can never become habituated to the altitude, and are more or less ill during the whole course of their stay. This is particularly the case with children and persons of advanced age. In my opinion the diminution in atmospheric pressure affects men to an appreciable extent at far lower levels than is generally believed. Because a man is not conscious of the effect, it does not at all follow that no effect is produced upon him.

South America, as is generally known, is a great country for horse-racing. Even at La Paz races were of frequent occurrence. I was informed by sportsmen, thoroughly acquainted with racing at many different levels, in Chile, Bolivia, and Venezuela, that every thousand feet above sea-level tells markedly upon a horse. Thus, taking Valparaiso and Santiago, in Chile, as instances, the race-course of the latter being some 2000 feet above that of the former, a horse trained at Valparaiso is found to be unable to win a race at Santiago against an equally good horse trained there. On the other hand, a horse trained at Santiago and brought down to Valparaiso is in perfect condition for racing there. Again, the lengths of races which a horse can run have to be reduced as the altitude increases. At La Paz the greatest length that a horse can gallop is about 500 metres, and that is a severe strain upon any animal that has not lived at La Paz for months before the race. While I was there a very fine horse was brought up from Chile and was allowed to race within a week or two after his arrival. The horse was perfectly sound, but the strain was too much for him and he died the day after the race. It may be said that horses are more sensitive than men to differences in atmospheric pressure, and doubtless a man can climb many thousand feet higher than he can take a horse. I have not myself seen horse or mule capable of carrying a man over easy ground at a higher altitude than about 16,500 feet, where they almost uniformly break down. This was certainly true in South America, and, if I remember rightly, at about that altitude, travellers crossing the Karakoram Pass between Yarkand and Kashmir are obliged to dismount from their ponies, and, if they ride at all, transfer themselves to yaks, though I have been told that in Sikkim horses carry travellers to an altitude of 18,000 feet. The facts, however, which seem to be proved by the experience of South American racing men, are that some diminution in physical vigor is produced in a horse at even so low an elevation as 2000 feet above sea-level;

that this loss becomes more apparent at 4000 or 5000 feet, and that at 12,000 it is very marked indeed. What is true even of a horse in a high state of training is, in my opinion, likewise true of all men, though perhaps to a less degree. From sea-level upward, as the air becomes rarer and the supply of oxygen less, the strength of man diminishes. Though this diminution may not be perceived, except as the result of minute and careful experiment, and the man himself may be unconscious of it, it none the less occurs.

This diminution of strength is quite apart from the disease which we call mountain-sickness, and the South Americans *sorocche* or *puna*. That seems to me to be an illness corresponding in kind to sea-sickness, to which some persons are more prone than others, and most people can get over. It is caused by a nervous derangement. It comes on suddenly, accompanied by headache, vomiting, or other well-marked symptoms; it does not necessarily overtake the patient at the moment of his arrival at a high altitude, but may assail him even as much as a week after he has begun living high above sea-level; it may pass away in a few hours, or it may last for many days, but ultimately it goes, in the case of normally healthy persons. Having once disappeared, it does not return unless the patient has in the mean time descended to a low level and spent some considerable time down there. If my surmise is correct, we must conclude that mountain-sickness is not in itself a bar to high mountain climbing, and that time cures it. But the steady diminution in strength which accompanies increasing elevation is a permanent disability.

It naturally affects strong men less than weak ones, seeing that they have the larger reserve of power to draw upon, but it abstracts from the strength of the strongest just as it does from the strength of a weaker man. One who can climb 5000 feet in a day without special fatigue, starting, say, from 8000 feet, will experience greater fatigue in climbing the same number of feet if he starts at 12,000 feet, and still greater if he starts at 14,000 feet; so that in making a high mountain ascent, requiring several days, if we assume the work each day to be of equal difficulty, the stage of ascent will have to be made shorter and shorter.

This diminution of daily range will prove to be one of the most serious impediments, perhaps the most serious, to the attainment of the highest altitudes on the surface of the earth. Unfortunately for adventurous mountain explorers, the higher they rise the greater are many other factors of difficulty with which they have to contend. The cold at night increases very rapidly above 20,000 feet, and at anything like 24,000 feet it becomes a very serious matter indeed. Almost equally wearing to the system is the power of the sun by day, which, shining through the thin air, scorches the life out of a man in an appalling fashion. The difficulty of transport is another increasing impediment, for the higher you climb the less easy it is to find porters who can go with you, and the smaller are the loads they are able to bear. Lastly, the danger arising from bad weather is multiplied in almost geometrical progression the higher you go. These points will receive illustration in the course of my narrative.

Sorocche thus deprived me of my first day at La Paz, though not so suddenly as to prevent me from setting inquiries on foot for mules and other essentials for the formation of a caravan. The remaining three days of my stay were fully occupied. The baggage had to be unpacked and repacked, a store-room hired for it, various calls paid, and letters of introduction presented. Don Manuel Vicente Balliváin, President of the Geographical Society of La Paz and an honorary member of our own Geographical Society, was able and generous to serve me in every way, and was a cyclopædia of information as to all matters connected with his country. By him I was taken to the Meteorological Observatory of the Jesuits, where I compared my barometer with their standard, and found the two to be in close agreement one with another. The Fathers kindly undertook to read their instrument at frequent stated intervals during the days of my absence on mountain expeditions, and this agreement was faithfully carried out. The prefect of the department offered to place an officer of the *gendarmerie* at my disposal to look after my caravan and smooth down difficulties for me in out-of-the-way places. From a contractor, Coro by name, I hired the necessary mules. He likewise supplied me with one Avelino Villanova for *arriero*, a quaint individual, who would have been a mine of "copy" for this book if I could have understood the tenth part of what he said. He was a Sancho Panza come again —"paunch-bellied, short of stature, and spindle-shanked"—of honest, rather stupid, but right merry countenance, who took the troubles of life with grinning resignation, and bombarded adversity with proverbs. Like Sancho, he could neither read nor write. He rode a beast, to all appearance an ass, though he swore it was a little mule. His weak legs flapped against its flanks as though they had been pendulous from the beginning. His knees had been stretched into the same plane as his body by the wide saddles on which he had passed his days, pursuing errant mules from year's end to year's end, and trying to keep them in the way they should go. Every five minutes he dismounted to rearrange a load, thus abandoning his mule, and often forced to pursue it long before a recapture was accomplished—verily a soul-torturing existence; yet he had preserved an equal mind throughout it all and remained content with his lot, and even proud of it. If he retained any ambition, it was not to rule an island, but to become the owner of a few more mules beyond the two which represented the savings of a lifetime.

The first work we had to undertake was the ascent of Illimani. The mountain stared us in the face, when the weather was clear, down every main street in the town. Indeed, it is more closely associated with La Paz than is any other great mountain known to me with any considerable city. I can only compare it with Mont Blanc as seen from Geneva; but Illimani is nearer, and imposes itself upon La Paz far more emphatically than does Mont Blanc upon the Swiss city. Generally speaking, it is found that mountains attract little attention from the people who live within sight of them. But the Indians of Bolivia, long before the coming of the Spaniards, seem to have paid much attention to the great peaks of the Cordillera Real. To begin with, they are all named, not with general names applying to the range merely, but with individual names belonging to the single peaks. A stranger, unacquainted with the Aymara tongue, finds it impossible to discover these names and to identify the peaks to which they belong, while to the Bolivians the nomenclature is uninteresting. It is only the Indians who care about the mountains.

In the Alps, before the days of mountaineering, there were hardly any named peaks. The whole range of Zermatt Mountains was simply called Gletscher Mons, or, in the local *patois*, Monte Roese, now corrupted into Monte Rosa. A Latinized form of the same designation, Mons Silvius, was locally corrupted into Cervin. It was only much later that these general names were respectively attached by travellers to the particular peaks now known as Monte Rosa and Mont Cervin or the Matterhorn.

In Bolivia, in the days of the Incas, as I have said, and perhaps much earlier, the individual peaks had attracted the attention of the natives and figured in their legends as the abode of divinities. Illimani, it appears, was honored either as a god or the abode of a god by the people dwelling in the La Paz valley and on the flanks of the mountain. This traditional respect for the peak survives to the present day, though with diminished force. One of the principal streets of La Paz is named Illimani Street. An easily recognizable picture of the mountain forms the signboard of an establishment for the sale of alcoholic drinks, which seemed to be well patronized; and the people in general manifest in many other small ways their interest and pride in the mountain. Whoever should prove to them that it is higher than Aconcagua would earn their hearty gratitude. It was elicited, in response to diligent inquiry of those best calculated to form an opinion, that the remoter side of the peak was that by which an attack would most likely be successful.

I was by no means the first to attempt the ascent. Pentland and Gibbon tried it, but did not get very far up the actual mountain, though they crossed high passes both north and south of it. Mr. J. B. Minchin, whose acquaintance I afterwards made at Oruro, climbed to the edge of one of the glaciers on the west side, but, being alone, wisely declined to venture up the ice-fall. General Pando, now (1900) President of Bolivia, likewise once made a plucky assault on the great mountain and reached a high elevation. Monsieur Wiener, at the time French Representative in Bolivia, made an ascent from Cotaña Farm of a peak to which he gave the name Pic de Paris. Unfortunately, I was not able to identify it conclusively. What was more to the point for us than this ancient history was the information that Mr. Bandolier, of whom I shall have more to say hereafter, was actually at that moment encamped on the side of the mountain and contemplated attempting the ascent. If we had been inclined to delay, this news would have hastened our proceedings; but the shortness of the climbing season urged us to the utmost rapidity of movement.

In the afternoon, when we were in the midst of packing, there rolled into the room a small and self-important personage in uniform, who gave his name as José S. Espinosa. He was apparently in a high state of satisfaction, for he clapped me on the back, sat down on the best chair in the room, helped himself to cigars, and proceeded to harangue me at some length in Spanish. I had not the least idea what he said, my Spanish being in the most rudimentary condition, and I was well pleased to see him presently depart. Unfortunately, as will appear, that was not the last of him. Next morning he turned up at the hour of starting and asked for money. I then discovered that he was the *gendarmerie* officer who was to be my companion, and I at once detected trouble ahead. The mules arrived not more than an hour late, and a number of persons came to see our caravan start and wish us luck on the way.

The Bolivian mule-saddle is a wonderful affair; it appeared to consist, on an average, of some dozen sheepskins in various stages of dilapidation, among which a wooden frame was buried. There were no convenient angles, as in the Californian saddle, for the attachment of cords, and, indeed, baggage was only held in place by a convolution of ropes which injuriously constricted the beast. But what the system of loading lacked in wisdom was to some extent made up for by the skill of our *arriero*, who had a way of tossing over his ropes in peculiar loops and knotting them with great cleverness. It was always amusing to watch him load one of his unwilling animals. He would cozen it into the delusion of capture by throwing a mere rope's-end over its neck; then he would wrap his head up in a shawl and proceed to pile on his collection of sheepskins. The next step was to hitch two heavy pieces of baggage, looped together like panniers, across its back. With these for foundation, other goods were piled on, and then the whole was roped up. At each pull of the cord the man grunted, and so did the beast, in apparent sympathy, while every action was accompanied by some more or less humorous comment, addressed either to the mule or the by-standers. My guides justly considered themselves to know something about loading mules, for each was a mule-owner, accustomed to drive his beast of burden down from his village home with a load to the railway station at Chatillon and to bring it up again, such being the daily work, except in the climbing and harvest seasons, of the peasants of Val Tournanche. They therefore had many criticisms to make upon the mules, their loading and their treatment; and I have no doubt, now that they are at home again, they have more to say about the mules of Bolivia and Chile than about the people, or even the mountains.

CHAPTER VIII

LA PAZ TO COTAÑA.

A T last all was ready. Bidding farewell to my
agent, Señor Granier, a Bolivian of French extraction, whose assistance was most useful to me, I
gave the word to start, whereupon one of the baggage
mules began violently bucking, mixed his load up with
the others, kicked Pellissier's beast, and set up a little
pandemonium. Simultaneously the *gendarmerie* officer
began demanding an advance of money, and a quarter
of an hour was spent in quieting men and beasts before
we fairly got under way. By ten o'clock order was
temporarily restored and we were filing down the street
in sight of a crowd of on-lookers. I never commenced
an expedition with less sanguine expectations; I had
no confidence in my native companions; I had not the
ghost of an idea of the geography of the complicated
valley system that lay between La Paz and our mountain; I could not speak the language; I was ignorant
as to the character of the supplies that might be available, or where and how it would be possible to enlist
porters for carrying our baggage up the slopes of the
mountain. Thus it was with not a few forebodings
that I rode along the cobble-stoned street in the cold
morning air. In a few minutes the town was left
behind, and the road passed through a short, deep

89

cutting, which had doubtless been worn down into the dry alluvial hill by ages of traffic. On suddenly emerging from it, Illimani stood up before us in clearness and splendor. The sun was shining on its white crest and on the group of parallel glaciers that drain down its western slope. Maquignaz rode up beside me and seemed for the moment as hopeful of success as he was always determined to succeed. "What a splendid mountain!" he cried.

"Do you see a route up it from this side?" I asked.

"Who can tell?" he answered. "But let us come near the snow, and, one way or another, we shall assuredly get up."

In the course of my wanderings I have driven caravans of horses, ponies, donkeys, of camels, and of heathen coolies of different races, but it so chanced that this was my first experience of mules in quantity. It is generally understood that mules are not urged to continuous exertion by blows, but by strong language, towards which their understanding is as alert as their experience of it is profound. Strong language brings back the wanderer and urges on the faint; so I was informed. I approached my mules remembering the story of Billy the Pike in Clarence King's *Mountaineering in the Sierra Nevada*, one of the finest books on mountain-travel ever written. Billy had been congratulated on his powers of language. "'Swear?' repeated the Pike, in a tone of incredulous questioning. 'Me swear?' as if the compliment were greater than his modest desert. 'No, I can't blaspheme worth a cuss. You'd jest orter hear Pete Green. *He can exhort the impenitent mule.* I've

THE GUIDES LADING A MULE

AN INDIAN WEAVING

known a ten-mule team to renounce the flesh and haul thirty-one thousand through a foot of clay mud under one of his outpourings.'" I had swallowed this story whole with relish in London; I chewed the cud of it in Bolivia.

The exit from the great basin of La Paz is by the narrow valley of the La Paz River; this, like the basin itself, is delved out of the deep alluvial deposit, whose gray and brown substance, cut up into queer shapes and continually eaten into by the torrents of the rainy season, forms the barren sides of the gorge. The section reveals horizontal beds of shingle, sand, and clay, with a few layers of fine volcanic tufa, which may have come from the Western Cordillera. Now and again, where some stray leakage from an irrigation canal damps the soil, a tiny oasis of fertility springs up. One such spot close beside the road was rich with ferns and multitudinous flowers just beginning to show blossom; but for the most part the surroundings in the bright sunlight were practically bare of vegetation. So much the more did they throw into bright relief the groups of Indians in their colored attire who came in quick succession along the road, carrying towards La Paz the products of the fertile lower regions. Many of them this day were carrying rose-bushes, planted in old petroleum tins, to the La Paz flower-market; for the people of La Paz are very fond of flowers and pay much attention to their gardens. I noticed that the Indians who came up the valley were of a different type from those we had passed on the Puna, and that they wore a somewhat different costume.

A mile or two below the town comes the village or suburb named Obrajes, where many of the inhabitants of La Paz have villas; for Obrajes is not only lower and more sheltered, and thus has a less rigorous climate than La Paz, but is well supplied with water, and has some flat and very fertile ground suitable for gardens. Here were peach-trees in blossom, and cactus hedges, which a few weeks later were covered with beautiful wax-like flowers of the most delicate hues; and there were graceful willow-trees to give shade, and quantities of lupines growing wild on ground that is flooded in the rainy season. The gardens were full of fruit trees, and though the houses were merely built of mud, and looked ill-cared for and devoid of comfort, yet the place had an attractive air, and the affection of the inhabitants towards it was easily understood.

Crossing the mouth of the Calocota Valley, which will be described hereafter, and then crossing the almost dry bed of La Paz River itself, we passed along the right bank and entered a narrow defile, where the traces of the powerful denuding action of the rainy season became very apparent. There were the dried-up remains of great land-slips and mud avalanches which had fallen in previous rainy seasons. Higher up the scooped-out hollows could be identified, from which had descended the rounded heaps of débris now resting on the bottom of the gorge. A little lower down on our right hand came a great cliff of alluvial deposit, cut up all over its face and at its top into spires of the kind known as "earth pyramids." These were by no means the first earth pyramids we had come

THE LA PAZ VALLEY

across, for the edge of the La Paz basin is freely decorated with them, and they are common, as might be
expected, wherever the great alluvial deposit is cut
away into cliffs and subjected to the action of heavy
rains. Alpine travellers are acquainted with earth
pyramids in the Val de Bagnes and in the neighborhood of Meran. I had seen them on a large scale near
Lamayuru, in Western Tibet, but I never saw or heard
of such a remarkable development of this formation
as is shown in the La Paz Valley. Luckily our path
led by steep zigzags straight up the cliff, and I was
thus enabled to investigate the pyramids in detail.
I found on arriving at the top that the whole surface
of the ground for a great distance was cut up in this
fashion, so that the path wound about among strange
spires of earth in the most devious fashion, almost
like the track of climbers traversing a complicated
ice-fall. There were, in fact, deep crevasses cut far
down into the muddy substance, and shafts like glacier moulins, and scooped-out caves, and great hollows with narrow necks like bottles—all the work
of torrential rain-storms during four months in the
year. A more weird region it would scarcely be possible to conceive, though, of course, the cut-up surface
was of no great width—a hundred yards or so—merely
fringing the top edge of the cliff.

I presently discovered that the portion of the alluvium we were now traversing had a different origin
from that of the great mass out of which the La Paz
basin has been scooped. The facts appear to be as
follow: At a remote epoch the whole area of country
lying between the two Cordilleras, from latitude $14°$

S. southward for about 13°, was a great inland sea.
It is probable that this region was not then elevated
so high above the level of the surface of the ocean
as it now is. This inland sea had no exit eastward
corresponding to the present La Paz Valley. Its
basin was gradually filled up with débris produced
by the disintegration of the surrounding mountains,
the whole area being meantime elevated and gradually dried, so that the inland sea shrank to its present
dimensions. Later on, by a process to which I shall
have occasion to refer hereafter, the La Paz River
cut, approximately to its present dimensions, the deep
trench in which I had just been travelling, and down
which my way was to go to the foot of Illimani.
Then a relatively small lake, which may have been
formed by a land-slip damming up the valley, as the
great Gohna Lake was formed not long ago in the
Himalayas, bursting through its dam, carried down,
in the form of a mud-avalanche, an immense mass of
débris, which filled up the bottom of the La Paz Valley from the neighborhood of Obrajes downward,
a distance of about eight miles, to a depth gradually
diminishing from two hundred feet to not more than
forty, where it ended. This mud-avalanche, when it
freshly came to rest, resembled a glacier lying in a
valley-bottom. The La Paz River in process of time
cut a canyon through the mud-avalanche, so that to-
day only portions of it are left. The earth pyramids
I have been describing are on the face and along the
edge of this canyon.

For a mile or two our way lay along the top of the
old mud-avalanche, evidently a very fertile piece of

ROAD UP EARTH-PYRAMIDS IN THE LA PAZ VALLEY

land; the road was lined on both sides by a close hedge of cactus, and there was a prosperous little agricultural village where I noticed some orchards of prickly-pear. In due season we descended by another steep set of zigzags to the river-bank, where a halt was made to water the mules, three and a half hours from La Paz. We now returned to the left bank and mounted high up the steep slope. The valley was no longer cut in alluvial deposits, but in the rocky substance of the hills, against which bits of the mud-avalanche were plastered here and there. For half a mile or so the path was of a rather giddy description, cut into the precipitous slope. We kept encountering donkey-caravans coming up, driven by Indians, and there was always a struggle as to who should get the inside; for though, after the manner of mules and donkeys, the beasts preferred the outside edge, their drivers were in no case indifferent to the advantage of yielding that situation to the other party. At last we came out on another large flat area of mud-avalanche and had no more precipices to negotiate. It was evident that we were descending to a substantially lower level. The air felt oppressively dense; the heat, falling directly from the sun or reflected from the bright slopes around, was most oppressive, and neither the guides nor I were yet in hard condition. We saw a big country-house or *hacienda* not very far ahead, surrounded by fields and fruit-gardens, and we nourished hopes that this might be the place for lunch; but there was still an hour or more to go, and our only consolation was that for some distance the road was good enough for a canter, as up to then it had not been. Putting spurs to the mules, we raced gayly to the little *tambo* of Carrera.

Thus far our officer had only been objectionable in a mild fashion. He annoyed me, indeed, in the very outskirts of La Paz, by stopping a countryman bringing oranges to the market, and, as far as I could make out, though he denied it, robbing him; he also endeavored to force upon me his undesired conversation, and then sang at the top of his lungs the most cacophonous ditties.

"You don't sing?" he said to me.

"No," I replied, "I don't."

"I do," he said, "all the time—like this," and off he went. But arrived at the *tambo* he was in great form. He routed out the old lady who kept the store and gave his orders like a king; uncorked the beer, and divided the sausages and other simple foods that the little hut afforded, offering what he pleased to any one who came to look on, and helping himself before me or anybody else. Evidently, in his opinion, the whole expedition existed for his enjoyment, and he proposed to plunder it at his leisure. For the moment, owing to my small command of Spanish, I was obliged to let the matter pass and await developments. The *arriero* came up with the baggage-mules and proceeded to feed them. On preparing to leave I was charged for the mules' fodder, though it had been an item in the contract between me and the mule-owner that he should pay for their food. I therefore resisted the charge, and informed the *arriero* that he must pay, not knowing that his master had carefully sent him off without a coin in his pocket.

A DONKEY CARAVAN IN THE LA PAZ VALLEY

THE LA PAZ VALLEY

Accordingly, I rode away, and so, presently, did he, driving off the mules and leaving the good woman to whistle for her money. Later on, of course, I saw that she received her due at the mule-owner's expense.

During the remainder of the day we continued the descent of the valley, soon leaving the last remnants of the mud-avalanche behind. We passed one or two oases, where side streams, distributed by irrigation canals, brought fertility to the arid soil; but for the most part our way lay down the barren trough, with great bare slopes, fantastically denuded, rising steeply on either hand and shutting out all distant view. The road was usually bad, lying in fact among the actual bowlders of the now dry river-bed, but occasionally there came smooth fans of hard-baked mud, like an adobe floor, at the mouth of side valleys, and here it was possible to advance more rapidly. Our plan was to spend the night at a *hacienda* called Millocato, but the hours passed by one after another, the evening came on, and Millocato did not appear. Just at dusk, indeed, we reached a building which proved to be the *tambo* of Huaricana, but I had been especially warned not to stop there, for it is infested by tertian-fever. On we pushed accordingly, as quickly as the tired beasts could go, but black night overtook us, and still there was no house in sight. To make matters worse, it now appeared that neither our officers nor the *arriero* had ever been down the valley before. At last I saw the glimmerings of a light in the distance, and, riding towards it, found Indians, who directed us to the desired goal. A number of barking dogs and inquisitive Indians

surrounded us at the door, where the major-domo of
the place received us, and gave a somewhat grudg-
ing permission to enter.

We found ourselves in a large court-yard surrounded by a series of one-storied mud buildings,
whereof the one next to the gate was assigned to us.
They were all of the same kind, some used for store-
rooms, others for abodes, very dirty and unattractive to a person newly come from Europe. The chamber we were to occupy was swept out (it had previously
been occupied by the cattle), and we were allowed to
ensconce ourselves and our baggage there. The
officer put his things down in one corner and asked
what we were going to give him to eat and drink. I
showed him our teapot and condensed meats and
biscuits, whereupon he snorted and disappeared.
That was practically the last we saw of him that night,
but presently we heard him shouting and singing in
the major-domo's establishment over the way, and an
hour or two later, when he made a sudden inroad upon
us to carry off his baggage, I observed that he was
in a highly festive condition. His songs grew louder,
and other noises came from his neighborhood, as
though he were knocking things about and advancing
through various stages of intoxication. Whenever
I woke up during the night he was still at it, and I
was informed next day that he had consumed no
less than five bottles of the cheap spirits of the country.
Anxious to be early on the road and take advantage
of the cool of the morning as long as possible, I was
up betimes. Then the trouble began.

First the *arriero* came for money, stating that he

must have six dollars for the night's entertainment. Two would have been too much. Then the drunken officer, whose debauch was not yet concluded, came with the major-domo to demand more dollars to pay for what he had consumed. He addressed us truculently, and then wandered away, rolling about the court-yard in a condition of great excitement and haranguing all and sundry. Needless to say he was not too firm upon his feet, and in the midst of his eloquence he frequently collapsed upon the ground. He had been sent to see that we were not cheated, but he took this first opportunity of threatening the major-domo with his everlasting displeasure if he allowed us to go unless we paid him a considerable sum—a large percentage, doubtless, for his own pocket. The poor major-domo came to me and explained that he was in terror of all *gendarmerie* officers, as they had it in their power to do him a great deal of harm. There were one or two other Bolivians in the place, but they all cowered away in dread of the drunken official. Presently the court-yard began to fill with Indian farm-laborers coming to their day's work. The officer turned his attention to them, and proceeded to make a pretence of drilling them. They had to shoulder mattocks, present, etc., to his word of command. It was one of the funniest things I ever saw—this small, strutting personage, with his flushed face, thick utterance, and uncertain drunken paces, rollicking about in front of the dismayed Indians, explaining to them how they must stand and what they must do, and falling over from time to time in the midst of his eloquence. To make matters worse, he was armed with a carbine and kept threatening to shoot. After much trouble I succeeded in getting the mules loaded up behind a corner, where they were not in view, and sent them away with the *arriero*. I also sent off an Indian to La Paz with a letter explaining the situation. On myself endeavoring to start, the officer and the people of the place, whom he overawed, opposed my departure, and the officer, in order to establish his position, made bold to declare that, so far from being under my orders, I was under his; that he had been sent to watch me and interfere with my movements, and that he called upon the Bolivians to support him and prevent me from going farther. With the inconsistency of a drunkard, however, he forgot this a few minutes later; so, watching my opportunity, I jumped on my mule and rode away, whereupon, I am informed, he mounted his animal and started off in pursuit, but he hadn't gone a hundred yards before he fell off. He smashed his carbine, cut his forehead, and hurt himself in other ways. The people of the farm found him in this plight and put him back to bed, where he remained for the best part of the next two days, and thus relieved us of his unwelcome company. On our return to La Paz his superiors offered me every satisfaction for the misbehavior of this fellow.

When it became clear that we were free of our troublesome companion, the pleasures of the day began. The air was soft, the bright sunshine gilded the crest of the mountains, and the grandeur of the scenery could scarcely be surpassed. We trotted gayly along the valley bottom, over a mud flat whitened with a

THE LA PAZ VALLEY ROAD

NEAR HUARICANA

saline efflorescence; then came again into stony ways, where our pace was necessarily slow. At Esquina de Pongo we passed the mouth of a deep side valley, leading straight towards Illimani, up which, as we afterwards discovered, lies a better route towards the mountain than the one we took. It was, in fact, by this valley that we descended. Blissfully ignorant of all such geographical details, for our *arriero* had not the dimmest idea of where we ought to go, we pushed on down the valley, and in a couple of hours came to the richly cultivated oasis named Tirata, where the track passed along the edge of a large sugar plantation. The contrast was striking between the tropical luxuriance of the foreground and the barren hill-sides rising all round.

Below Tirata the valley narrowed to a gorge and the scenery waxed more wild. Steep cliffs approached one another from both sides, and the bottom was reduced to a narrow stretch, covered with rounded, water-worn bowlders difficult to travel over. Once or twice we had momentary glimpses, up some side gap, of the snows of Illimani enveloped in cloud, but overhead the sky was clear and the sun shone down into our trough with scorching power. The heat was, in fact, overwhelming, and the very rocks seemed to be ablaze. Conversation ceased; we pushed along, each in the solitude of his own suffering. At noon there came a deeply shadowed cave, wherein we sheltered awhile to lunch. It was a hollow excavated by water, for during the rainy season the whole width of the gorge down which we had come is flooded with a great torrent and rendered inaccessible to man. Caravans descending from La Paz must then take a different route, circulating round the slopes of the mountain by devious and difficult tracks instead of following the valley itself. Here I found it easy to imagine myself back again in the barren gorges of the Kashmir Himalayas, and even the few Indians who came by were not unlike the natives of those Asiatic fastnesses. But the travelling population was small, and we did not encounter more than half a dozen persons during the day. The losels and scatterlings who people the tracks of Asia, going long foot-journeys on business or pilgrimages, or merely drifting from place to place, find no parallel in South America. I missed the nomad's greeting and the traces of his tent or camp-fire. The orbit of an Aymara Indian is small, and the men one meets by the way are evidently not going far. It is otherwise in Asia, where countless wanderers link together the remotest parts of the great continent.

Two hours lower down our troubles came to an end at the beautiful farm of Lurata, where we could quit the deep hot hollow and turn up towards the cool heights. The desert bottom was exchanged for a zigzag track among beautiful vineyards, and soon for a gently sloping pathway along the edge of an ancient canal, conducting the waters of Illimani to the roots of the vines. We afterwards made the acquaintance of the wines of Lurata, and found them highly meritorious, strong red wines of much body, somewhat resembling port in character. Great bushes of cane grew beside the watercourse, and many trees, as yet bare of leaves, for springtime was only

just at hand. Gaunt cactuses covered the uncultivated slopes above the farm. The heat diminished
as we rose; the sun, drawing to the westward, cast
shade upon the path. The view widened, and soon
there came in sight a large area of orchards ahead,
surrounding houses and a church. Birds chirped
and fluttered about, flocks of green paroquets of the
kind called Lobitos screamed among the trees, and
multitudes of pigeons flew about. The track widened
into something like a road, which ended in a beautiful
avenue of eucalyptus-trees, leading to the *hacienda*
of Cotaña. On dismounting at the gate I found to
my surprise that we were expected. Señor Guillen,
the manager of the estate, came down through a cack-
ling flock of white turkeys to greet us, and, carrying
me immediately into the house, introduced me to his
family and the friends he was at the time entertaining,
the nephew and grandson of the prefect of La Paz.
Luckily for me, Señor Guillen's son and the prefect's
grandson could both speak English. The ground
floor of the house consisted of store-rooms and offices
for the servants. The first floor contained all the
dwelling-rooms, and was approached by a wide brick
staircase which gave access to a broad arcaded ve-
randa. The double row of well-proportioned columns
gave a stately appearance to the façade, and the whole
house, standing in the midst of tall eucalyptus-trees,
had quite a fine appearance. The rooms were large,
though rather out of repair, the walls covered (as
commonly in Bolivian country houses and inns) with
prints cut from English illustrated papers, mostly
about twenty years old.

CHAPTER IX

THE FERTILE SLOPES OF ILLIMANI

THE next day was spent in this charming place. Cotaña may be taken as an example of what in Bolivia is called a *finca*—that is to say, an organized country estate, which may be compared with a mediæval English manor. A *finca* is a social unit, and, as far as I could learn, its organization mainly descends from pre-Spanish days. The land belongs to a proprietor, and so, in a sense, do the Indians dwelling upon it; but the proprietor's ownership is subject to a multitude of rights possessed by the Indians. They cultivate the owner's land, he providing the necessary seed; each Indian, in return for his labor, yearly receives a certain amount of land for his own use. A *finca* Indian will do things for his proprietor or his proprietor's representative which he will do for no one else. It would have been impossible for a stranger like myself to have hired Indian porters for such unusual employment as I proposed to them. Only through a *finca* proprietor could that be done, and then with difficulty. He could not compel them to go with me, but he could use his influence to persuade them to do so.

Of course, without land, an Indian must practically starve, so that he is to that extent at the mercy of the

COTAÑA

finca proprietors. On the other hand, the owner of a *finca* depends on his Indians for labor; if they were to desert in any numbers, his property would become valueless. The only system of agriculture the Indians understand is the prehistoric system of their forefathers, and I believe it is practically impossible to introduce improved methods, for the natives are intensely conservative, and become difficult to manage if any of their customs are interfered with. Physical force is not available to keep the Indians in order. They are controlled by tradition, the authority of the priests, their own absolute ignorance, and their poverty. As Maquignaz said: "The white folks give employment, and so are the masters. It is the same here as it is everywhere. Poor folks must find some one to pay them for working. The whites are the only people who can do that." In the Bolivian towns there are resident police, and a small body of *gendarmerie* is maintained, which can be sent to refractory villages if necessary; but in a poor country like Bolivia it is impossible, under present circumstances, to police the scattered Indian population. They must be kept in order by moral suasion, and can only be coerced on rare occasions. When a local disturbance arises a special force is drafted in to deal with the refractory village. It seemed to me that the white people live in some fear of the Indians. When the enormous predominance of the native element is considered, such an attitude is by no means unnatural; in fact, a traveller can only regard with astonishment and admiration the manner in which the millions of Indians are actually kept in

order by the small white population. It is sometimes
asserted that the Bolivian Indians are, to all intents
and purposes, slaves. That may be true, but if they
are slaves they are certainly not enslaved by force,
nor are they kept to their work by physical compul-
sion. No attempt seems to be made to raise them
in the social scale. The present generation is doubtless as ignorant as any under the dominion of the
Incas. But in a quiet way time passes and men live
their lives not unhappily, though with occasional
intervals of anxiety. Of course, the immense possible productivity of the soil is mainly wasted under
this system. In some parts of the country a field
is only cultivated once in four years and lies fallow
for the other three, while in other parts a turn comes
even less frequently. Seeing the farms, as I did,
before the commencement of spring, they appeared
to be of immense size, for there was nothing to show
which fields had been cultivated last year and which
had lain fallow; but, as a matter of fact, the efficient
size of a farm, in any single year, leaving the orchards
out of count, is from one-third to one-eighth of its
apparent size, only a small fraction being at any one
time under cultivation.

I was informed that Cotaña was once the property
of an Irish lady. When I was there it belonged to
Don Lisimaco Gutierrez, at that time Minister of
Finance. His deputy was Señor Guillen, my host,
whose son, Señor Ezekiel Guillen, agreed to accompany me with the Indians, at all events up the lower
slopes of Illimani. This was very good luck. Word
was sent up to a higher village that suitable men

should be sought. As nothing is done in a hurry in these parts, there was time to spare. In the morning I was taken over the orchards of Cotaña and shown the great plantations of peach-trees, all then in blossom, and the orchards of custard-apples, granadillas, oranges, lemons, and vines. The whole place had been laid out with an eye to landscape-gardening. Charming arbors were erected at pretty points of view. Under the shadow of splendid trees we found a brick-lined swimming bath, excavated in the ground, with a little bathing-house built beside it and a streamlet flowing through, an ideal place for a plunge. I afterwards learned that such a swimming-bath is a common adjunct to the fruit-growing *fincas* of Bolivia. Most of the fruits are allowed to grow as they please, with little cultivation, the peaches, for instance, not being grafted; it is only the custard-apples and the granadillas that are sent to the La Paz market for sale. Peaches and grapes are the chief product of the estate. The latter are made into wine and the former into a very low class of spirit, largely consumed by the Indians. Machinery worked by water-power for crushing the peaches occupies a large shed; the still is erected in another close by.

In the afternoon we went out shooting and made a mixed bag of pigeons and partridges; but when the heavy clouds, which had been covering Illimani and had prevented us from even discussing a route up the mountain, began to break away, all other interests faded before the glorious vision that was slowly unrolled. At last the great cliffs, sharp ridges, and snow-crest stood forth clear beyond the foreground of blossoming peach-trees. I thought I had never beheld a more beautiful sight; but it was far from reassuring to a mountaineer, for the whole south-west side of the mountain here disclosed was frankly unclimbable. The upper snow-field is entirely cut off from the lower slopes by a great cliff, quite vertical all round the top edge, where the glacier-cap breaks away and discharges itself in avalanches at all points. The northwest side of the mountain, visible from La Paz, though not easy, was certainly possible of ascent; this side seemed impossible. However, Señor Guillen, who had lived all his life at the mountain's foot, encouraged me by declaring that round the corner of the mountain, to the right, I should find a very different aspect of affairs. There was a valley there, he said, which seemed to lead very high, and by it he conceived the snow-field might be attained.

Illimani, as we now came to know it, is a very broad mountain mass with many summits, each of which in the Alps would be considered a different peak. As seen from Cotaña, the highest point is at the extreme left end. It was already evident that any gully there might be round the corner to the right would only lead up to some point on the upper snow-field two or three miles away from the true summit. I pointed this out to Guillen, and he acknowledged that it was true; but, in his view, as long as one got on to any part of the top, what more could one want?—right-hand end or left-hand end, it was all one—nor did he at first grasp the idea that there was anything to be gained by reaching the mountain's very top. I foresaw that, however easy the gully might be, this question of distance would be the great difficulty of the climb; but there was now no option, as the whole intervening face was frankly inaccessible. If the ascent was to be made from Cotaña at all it must be made by the hidden gully. Failing that, we must climb by one of the northwest glaciers visible from La Paz. It was not reassuring to observe that much new snow had recently fallen, and that the winter snow still lay down to a low level. From a climbing point of view the mountain was only just beginning to come into condition. What I had yet to learn, however, was that in the high regions of Bolivia winter snow is brought, in the long dry months of July and June, to a degree of hardness seldom paralleled in other mountain ranges, while in summer all the snow that falls remains soft and rotten. The clouds, having once departed, returned no more that day. A night of bright moonlight followed, in which the mountain shone like silver, with every detail almost as clearly visible as in sunshine.

On the 4th of September young Señor Guillen escorted his guests and us to the higher farm of Caimbaya (11,800 feet). It was a delightful ride up a good path, which now crept beneath overarching shrubs, now plunged into delicious dells, now boldly circled round broad open slopes, or mounted steeper inclines by rapid zigzags. The scenery of the green alp, sloping up to rocky walls and ridges with high snows beyond, had quite a Swiss character. The farm-house of Caimbaya was a very simple two-roomed affair, standing beside a walled court-yard with four eucalyptus-trees growing in the midst, the highest trees of any size on the mountain. The Indian village was picturesquely grouped round a church on a knoll, backed by Illimani's splendid *cirque*. Paroquets flew about in chattering flocks, and so did the beautiful little pigeons which exist in such multitudes in this neighborhood. The manager of the farm, José Amestoy by name, was a most intelligent and kindly fellow. Guillen said that he was of Indian blood; if so, he is proof of the capabilities of Aymara Indians for civilization. He was a skilful mechanic, a good sportsman, and had a better understanding of the geography of the country than almost any one else I met. He was well read, considering his opportunities, and knew the legends of his own people. He had practical knowledge of the mineralogy of the neighborhood. He could understand a map, had a good general idea of the different countries of the world, and was so far acquainted with modern inventions as, for instance, to have heard of photography in natural colors, and to be capable of understanding the process by means of glass screens of three primary colors.

Desirous of not wasting time, I immediately sent the two guides off towards the precipitous face of the mountain to see whether they could find any direct way up, while I climbed a detached hill, named the Place of Flies, from the summit of which a good general view might be expected. The ascent was made in a couple of hours, and well repaid the trouble. It led me through the village and the higher fields, and then up grazing lands all scored with ancient tracks. Obviously this was land that had been trodden by human feet for generations and centuries. There were traces of old irrigation aqueducts no longer used, and countless ancient terraces, while on the actual summit of my hill were the foundations of ruined buildings and numerous graves, some recently excavated. From this commanding eminence the whole basin of Cotaña was in full view, and the hollow of the long La Paz Valley sweeping in a great curve round the mountain's foot; beyond arose the barren slopes stretching up and up to the desert hills fringing the high Bolivian plateau. Southward stretched away the lower continuation of the great Cordillera, which rises beyond Illimani to one more snow peak, the "Three Crosses,"* and then stretches away in steeply foreshortened perspective as a range of bare rocky peaks, with slopes of barren débris reaching nearly up to their summits. Between the top of Illimani and the bottom of the La Paz Valley the long slopes were divided into two great grassy basins, like the upper parts of funnels, each narrowing below into a gorge. I stood between these two great basins on the hill-top, so that when I faced the mountain one of them was on my right hand and the other was on my left. The basin of Cotaña was the one to the right, and by that we had come up; to the left was the basin and valley of Salapampa, by which we afterwards commenced our descent. The little depression between my hill and Illimani was the pass we rode over when returning to La Paz.

As to the route up Illimani, nothing was to be learned

---

* Or "Five Crosses." I heard both names used.

from this point of view. I was merely confirmed in the conclusion come to at Cotaña, that there was no probability of success in an attempt to ascend by the cliff, a confirmation which the guides enforced when they came back to me late at night. Their story was that they had crossed the little pass I have just referred to, and had traversed up towards a gap in one of the side ribs, which they had reached with some difficulty. Passing round this rib they came, to their astonishment, on the ruins of an ancient village, with burial places and some abandoned terraced fields and broken aqueducts. They said the only way to reach this village was by a quite difficult scramble. Higher up, they said, the rocks were cut away into a cliff which was overhung at the top by the perpendicular edge of the upper snow-field, and even if the rocks could be climbed it would be impossible to surmount the last ice-wall.

CHAPTER X

ILLIMANI: THE LOWER SLOPES

NEXT morning (September 5th) all was ready for our final start. Only four Indians could be persuaded to come with us; but they sufficed, and we rode away in good spirits. For an hour or two the ascent led up old, well-trodden paths, among shrubs, and then over a tawny green alp. The mules soon gave evidence of suffering from the thinness of the air; they halted at frequent intervals, and all behaved alike, taking several short, quick breaths in rapid succession, then three or four slow, deep ones, after which they were ready to go on again. Exactly such I have found to be the manner in which a man recovers himself from special exertion at high levels. If at any moment one has put forth an unusual effort, an overmastering giddiness attacks the head; one is compelled to halt and take a series of very quick breaths. The giddiness passes, and with three or four long breaths a normal speed of respiration is arrived at. The paroxysm of discomfort being removed, one can then go forward leisurely on one's way.

The topography of Illimani is so complicated that, at the risk of repetition, I must describe more particularly the route which we were taking. When we were on the summit of the Place of Flies the previous day, the mass of the mountain rose before us in a wide cliff; the right-hand end of the mass was in the nature of a great buttress of rock culminating in a rocky peak which hid the rest of the ridge abutting on the mountain itself. The highest point of this ridge is the snow-peak I afterwards climbed and named the "Pico del Indio." Behind this buttress—that is to say, farther on round it to my right—lay the gully so often referred to and up which our route ultimately went. The proper right or southwestern side of this gully was formed by the buttress I have just mentioned; its left or northeastern side consisted of a great wall of rock, some two or three miles in length, above which were visible the *séracs* or broken icy edge of a glacier, which I called the Caimbaya Glacier. It stretched to the crest of the Cordillera south of the high peaks of Illimani, and was separated from all those peaks, and the snow-field supported by them, by the Pico del Indio. At its lower end the Caimbaya Glacier is discharged by ice-avalanches over the wall of rocks into the gully, and these avalanches reform below into a relatively small snout, actually situated in the gully. Formerly the glacier descended to a much lower level, and its ancient moraines may still be traced almost down to the village of Caimbaya. It retreated stage by stage, and left a series of other terminal moraines at different altitudes, many still quite distinct.

The grassy slopes up which we rode were the slopes at the foot of the great buttress, and I was informed by the intelligent manager of Caimbaya that this was the way taken by M. Wiener on the occasion

ILLIMANI AND THE PIC DE PARIS FROM ABOVE CAIMBAYA

of his attempt on the 19th of May, 1877; he likewise informed me that M. Wiener and his Indians climbed the actual rocks of the buttress, and that some of them reached the rocky peak which was visible from all parts of the Cotaña Valley. If this account is correct, that rocky peak must be the Pic de Paris, but M. Wiener's published description, though I am unable to understand the whole of it, seems to me to imply that he went up the gully rather than the ridge, and climbed the rock-wall pretty much where we climbed it; but what he did, having arrived at the snow-field above, what peak he chose and how he got up it, I am altogether unable to ascertain. It seems certain that a high elevation was arrived at, and I hope that at some future time it will be possible to say exactly where that elevation was situated.

In various places the dry grass showed signs of having been burned. I afterwards discovered that the habit of the Bolivian highlanders is to burn portions of the upper alp every year on St. John's Day, an occasion of great festivity, when all the villagers turn out and fire the grass in mutual emulation. An hour and a half's slow riding brought us to a flat plateau, where the Indians suggested that we might camp. In fact, an hour and a half's work was about their idea of the amount we could reasonably expect them to do in a day. The proposal not being favorably entertained, we went on, and were driven by the form of the hill-side to swerve to the right, where the only possible line of advance was by a narrow foot-path along the side of an *acequia* or irrigation canal, doubtless of very ancient date but still kept in good repair. On the water brought by this canal the farm of Caimbaya entirely depends. The canal was some eighteen inches wide by perhaps a foot deep, so that the volume conveyed by it was not very great. Imagine, therefore, our surprise when we discovered that it practically conveyed the whole of the drainage of the great Caimbaya glacier. We afterwards found by observation, all along the Cordillera from Illimani away to Sorata, that the amount of water yielded by the Andean glaciers is extremely small, the very largest of them never yielding during the months I was in the country a drainage stream of anything but the most exiguous dimensions. The fewness of ice-avalanches that fall from the *sérac*-edged cliffs of Illimani and the other mountains is likewise probably due to the same cause, the fact being that here, as on Mount Kenya, in Equatorial Africa, the melting snow and ice of the glaciers is absorbed into the air by evaporation instead of flowing away in the form of water. During the rainy season, the real summer of Bolivia, avalanches may be more frequent, and the snow may melt with more rapidity; but in the spring months—August, September, and October—very little melting seems to take place.

A brief inspection sufficed to show that it would be quite impossible for the mules to accompany us farther. Argentine mules, driven by such an *arriero* as we had on Aconcagua, might have been brought along, but Bolivian mules are far less skilful and their *arrieros* are less daring. Here, accordingly, the loads were deposited on the ground and the beasts of burden sent away.

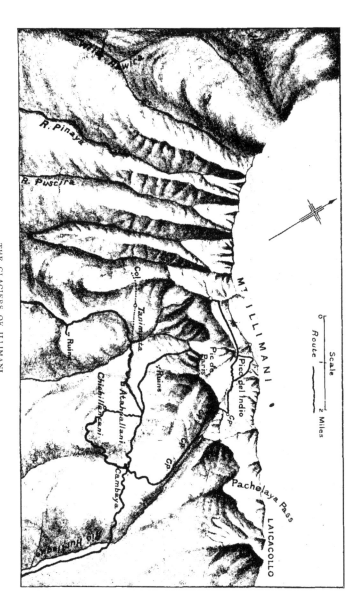

THE GLACIERS OF ILLIMANI

Trouble with the Indian porters now began. There were four of them, and there were eight loads; it was necessary, therefore, to make double journeys. They were slower even than Baltic coolies in loading up, and they were equally anxious to halt every few yards of the way; while, as they cared nothing about us and were comparatively indifferent to money, our means of urging them on were restricted. At any moment they might have thrown down the loads and left us in the lurch. It was only the presence of Guillen, who could speak their abominable language, that enabled us to persuade them to advance at all. The canal proved to be boldly engineered across what was in places a sheer cliff; the path beside it was often completely encumbered with shrublike growths just coming into leaf. It led for about a mile round the remainder of the buttress, and so conducted us to the foot of our gully. Here a broad slope, perhaps a couple of miles wide, stretched steeply up into the heart of the mountain, narrowing as it rose. We mounted it some 500 feet, already, in our untrained condition, conscious of the enervating effect of the diminished atmospheric pressure. Unfortunately, the Indians refused this last ascent, and we were obliged to return and camp at the level of the head of the canal, on a soft patch of grass among a picturesque group of bowlders, the altitude being about 14,000 feet.

Next day we only succeeded in pushing camp 2000 feet higher, such was the dilatoriness of the porters. The way led up slopes of tussocky grass and then up the crest of an old lateral moraine. All suffered greatly from the altitude, much more indeed than two or three days later we suffered upon higher levels. Lack of condition had something to do with this, but still more I think the fact that we were in one of those enclosed positions which seem always to be more trying at high levels than are open snow-fields or even broad walls of rocks. Some excitement was caused by the sight of eight mountain-deer, to which we gave pursuit, armed with a shotgun and a revolver. They headed up the gully on one side of the moraine; we stalked them by slowly scrambling up the other side. Finding that they were pursued, instead of taking to the rocks and going upward, as chamois would have done, they turned back near the top of the glen. One of them passing us at close range was easily laid low. With a rifle we might have secured two or three others, for their pace was slow and they seemed bewildered at being caught in the upper part of the gully. Evidently they are not to be regarded as good climbing animals. The Indians, who were too lazy to hurry with the loads, were glad enough to watch us stalk; they left the luggage scattered about on the hill-side and hurried up to see the sport. Many hours afterwards they brought our goods together, just in time for camp to be pitched beside the moraine a little before sunset.

On the 7th the ascent of the gully was continued by mounting along the crest of the moraine beside the glacier's snout. The splendid rocks, furrowed by ice *couloirs* and crested with glittering *séracs*, were on our right hand and the ridge of the Pic de Paris on our left. The view was thus very restricted in width, but backward, from the elevation now attained,

THE FLANK OF ILLIMANI

we overlooked a great area wherein, all day long, we watched a sea of clouds that swept up the La Paz Valley from the hot eastern regions, hiding the lower levels from our sight and almost but never quite enveloping us. Such cloud effects, of which during the next three days we beheld many examples, were magnificent. Out of the white sea there mounted, under the uplift of hot air currents, great towers of cloud, which rose, like the smoke-discharge of volcanoes, high into the air, then nodded forward and overhung as the upper winds took them. Huge caves and cloud avenues were thus formed, wherein dark-blue shadows gathered, and here and there in their deep recesses some high mountain-top would perhaps peep forth, a mere foundation-stone to a gigantic mist castle.

During the day the Indians were more troublesome than ever; they refused to carry any but the lightest loads, so that three journeys were necessary instead of two. It was only by descending and re-ascending with them that we were able to get them to work at all. Ultimately they raised our things, not more than 600 or 700 feet, to a point close to the foot of that part of the wall of rocks on our right where a practicable line of ascent seemed to be situated, and where, against the sky-line, was no longer a line of impending *séracs* but only a snow-slope, safe and apparently easy to mount. The camping-place was within 300 or 400 feet of the top of the gully's débris slope, in a situation dangerously liable to be swept by falling stones. I undertook to dig out a tent platform under the shelter of a huge lump of rock stuck in the slope, to set up the tents and prepare food, while the Alpine guides, each carrying a heavy sack, climbed the rock wall to the snow above. They returned with the assurance that the rocks could be climbed without great difficulty. They had experienced much fatigue in climbing, as I had in digging out the tent platform, but their energies had been well invested, while, in Maquignaz's opinion, mine had been wasted. "You have dug out the tent platform," he said, "in exactly the wrong place. As you have put it, the tent will not be protected from falling stones, but rather more exposed to them than if it were out in the middle of the *couloir*. We must begin all over again and make a new platform, closer beneath the big rock." We accordingly set to work once more excavating with the ice-axes and building a wall of support with the larger fragments loosened. It was a toilsome business. All work this day was toilsome, and even the smallest exertion necessitated an interval of repose. Pellissier, who was physically the strongest of us, when sent off to fill a small bucket with water from a rivulet a hundred yards away, found it necessary to rest four or five times in that little distance. Yet our altitude was only about 16,500 feet above sea-level.

As bad luck would have it, the next day (September 8th) was to be a fête at the village of Ussi near Caimbaya. The Indians, all agog to be present on that occasion, left us as soon as they had brought the baggage up to the tent; but they promised to send up others to take their place. Late in the evening there did arrive an old man and a boy, who stated

INDIAN PORTERS

FROM THE TOP OF THE ROCKS, ILLIMANI

that others had agreed to follow them on the following morning. The boy, a round-faced, laughter-loving fellow, was more like a Burmese than an Aymara Indian; and the old man had a long, tragic face, strangely like the late Robert Louis Stevenson. They had never slept in a tent in their lives, and both were delighted with the experience. The boy laid himself down under his *poncho* and a mackintosh sheet, with his head sticking out of the tent door, and giggled with delight for hours.

CHAPTER XI

ILLIMANI: THE ROCK-WALL

THUS far there had been no real climbing to do, but only grass, moraine, and fatiguing débris slopes to ascend, nor would it have been difficult with good porters to reach this point in one day from the farm. Now, however, more serious work was at hand, so that the question of weather became all-absorbing. At La Paz I had been told that the month of September was usually a month of continuous fine weather, which might even last on far into November. But experience has taught me that few people dwelling in a mountain country pay any attention to the weather on the mountains. If they have clear skies and absence of rain at the place of their abode, it does not occur to them, even when they see clouds on the mountains, that the weather may be very bad there. So I was disappointed but not surprised to find that though La Paz enjoyed a large measure of fine weather in September and October, it was very different at levels where a mountaineer works. The weather on Illimani had been unsettled all the time I was in the country till the day we left Cotaña; then it had grown fine, and though there had been plenty of clouds sweeping over daily from the hot east, the days we had spent in the gully would have been favorable for climbing. Now, however, a change seemed to be at hand. Clouds gathered earlier each day and the upper level of the great cloud-bed had a tendency to rise. It was, therefore, essential to prepare for spending several days, if need be, on the snow-field above the rock-wall, so that a considerable amount of provisions had to be carried up.

With the dawn came no porters. We packed up camp, dividing the baggage into two parts, one to be left behind on the platform, the other to come with us. The latter contained two tents, warm fur sleeping-bags of reindeer-skin, cooking apparatus, provisions, and instruments. We waited, but not a human being hove in sight. At nine o'clock we decided to proceed with only the man and boy who had spent the night with us. All, therefore, had to carry a more or less heavy load, and our progress was correspondingly slow. Señor Guillen faithfully adhered to us and shouldered his burden like a man. Twenty minutes were spent in crossing the gully diagonally over the loose stones and reaching the foot of the rocks. The Indians regarded the cliff with dismay, for it was undoubtedly steep, and soon proved to be far from easy. The whole of this part of the ascent is about equal in difficulty to that of the ordinary routes up any of the harder Zermatt mountains, such as the Matterhorn, Gabelhorn, or Dent Blanche. Zigzag we went, following convenient ledges. Every few yards the Indians were for turning back, but the rope was put on and they were included in the string. This gave them some little confidence till a more difficult scramble came, when, with one consent, they cast themselves loose and sat down. I leaned forward from the top of the difficulty and held forth small silver coins to them, to come up and possess. The bait was taken, and things were easier for a few yards above; then another difficulty came, and was surmounted by the same rudimentary expedient. Thus, by the attraction of money and by hauling on the rope, we engineered our timid porters slowly upward. Far below, the four Indians could now be seen coming up, who were to have been our porters. But when they perceived where we were they shouted something to our men, turned tail, and disappeared. After about two-thirds of the wall had been surmounted there came yet another steep, indeed, almost perpendicular, chimney, such as we had already negotiated; but this one was thickly embellished with ice. It proved to be the last hard place, but nothing would induce the Indians to attempt it. Their cup of dread had been steadily filling; here it overflowed. They dropped their loads, cast off the rope, and fled. Two hours later the screams of joy which announced their arrival at our deserted platform came wafted up to us, along with the booming of the guns fired off for the fete at Ussi.

The morning had been fine, but clouds now enveloped us, and glad we were of it, for the heat of the sun was most debilitating. By hauling the loads up with ropes in difficult places, and by carrying them in easy ones, we came out at last on the snow near the proper right margin of the Caimbaya glacier, with a low rock-wall close on our left hand. On the snow beside these rocks, at a height of about 18,500 feet,

A HEAVY LOAD

we pitched the tents with solid satisfaction. The outworks of the mountain fortress were now passed; it only remained to deliver the assault on the final peak. Noon came when we reached the camping-place, and the sea of cloud lay far below us. For out-look our camp was admirably planted near the edge of a lofty mountain-shelf, with a short snow-slope in front, and then the sudden plunge of the cliff. We overlooked the low range of mountains that divides the La Paz Valley from the high Bolivian plateau, and saw the great desert, ruddy, sunny, and arid, stretching away to an immense distance, with the faint cones of the volcanoes of the Western Cordillera (among which Sajama was easily identifiable) rising beyond it. There was a marvellous play of color upon the desert, which seemed almost afire with sun-light, glimmering through the dusty atmosphere. The great depression of the La Paz Valley swept round to the left under its flood of cloud, dividing us alike from the desert and from the continuation of the Cor-dillera.

Once, no doubt, the Cordillera was continuous from Illimani southward. By some means an im-mense gap, which sinks to a level of 3000 or 4000 feet above the sea, has been cut through it, so that the La Paz River, which rises near the base of Ca-caaca, on the west slope of the range, and flows down through the town of La Paz and by the way we had come, receiving all the tributary streams from the west slope of the mountains as far as Illimani, ulti-mately passes right across the Cordillera by this im-mense gap, and, flowing away eastward, drains into a tributary of the Amazon, and thus empties into the Atlantic. How was this gap produced? How were the waters that ought to have gone, and once went, to the Pacific, captured for the Amazon and the Atlantic? Three answers to this question have been suggested. According to one, the great inland sea, whereof Titicaca remains a shrunken remnant, at some moment of unusual fulness burst its way through the range by some convulsion of nature whose character is not further particularized. This explanation is unsatisfactory, for there is no way by which a lake can burst through a mountain range or any great obstacle except by overflowing the lip of the cup and cutting down a channel through the obstruction as it overflows. For this to have happened there must have existed between Illimani and the mountain of the Three Crosses a low depression no higher than the possible former level of the waters. Here a waterfall or cataract must have been formed, which poured over the main watershed of the continent, and, gradually cutting it down, worked its way backward to the present edge of the La Paz basin. It is scarcely possible to invent a less probable explanation.

Another suggestion is that, before the Andes were crinkled up from the flat earth, there already existed a river, occupying approximately the track of the present La Paz River, which, as the range was slowly elevated, continued to flow in its old bed, and kept cutting that bed down and so maintaining its existence, while the range continued to rise on either hand. It is said that there is geological proof in the Alps of the persistence of pre-existing rivers flow-

PREPARING TO CAMP ON ILLIMANI

ing across the range, which maintained themselves throughout the whole period of its elevation. How this can have been I am at a loss to understand, for an examination of the rivers in Patagonia and the conterminous portion of Chile, where earth-movements are now taking place, shows that a very slight earth-movement is sufficient to break a river in half and cause the waters of its upper part to flow in the opposite direction to that previously followed by them Such an explanation seems most inappropriate to this trans-Andean gorge, for the upper part of it is cut out of the great alluvial deposit, evidently fallen into the lake from the slopes of the range itself, which could not have been deposited if the lake were at that time being drained away to the eastward. It is obvious that the river gorge had only invaded this alluvial deposit since the drying up of the lake; that is to say, that the gorge has eaten its way backward from many miles below La Paz almost to the foot of Cacaaca in quite recent times. If we presuppose the existence of an ancient river that crossed what is now the Andes before the range was elevated, it must have been a very short torrent, whose head was somewhere about the village of Huarikana, and it is impossible to believe that a little stream not more than thirty miles in length should have been strong enough to keep open a depression right across that gigantic range during the period of its elevation from an altitude of 3000 to over 20,000 feet above the sea.

The true explanation, as I think every person much acquainted with mountain gorges will agree, is that the mountain range was once continuous right across from Illimani to the Three Crosses, and that the normal processes of denudation acted upon it as they have acted upon the Himalayas and all other mountain ranges. The east side of the range was always more precipitous than the west, for the simple reason that the great damp area of the Amazonian forest stretches away from its foot and pours moisture against the mountain-wall on that side. The vapors condense into clouds, clouds fall in rain and snow, and the eastern face of the Andes is thus very rapidly denuded. On the west the amount of precipitation is, and probably for a very long period has been, much less than on the east; while the form of the country, with its succession of ranges of hills, which have risen from the sea with the rising of the land, or been generated by volcanic ejection, has hindered the denuding processes, so that the Cordillera Real throughout its whole length has been more vigorously broken down on the east side than it has been on the west. In consequence of the long action of these forces the eastern slope is almost a cliff, while the western, from snow-level down to the plateau, consists of long, gentle slopes thickly covered with débris.

A river whose upper waters are supplied by a steep mountain must continually eat its way back into the mountain. If the mountain rises to the level of perpetual snow the action of eating back proceeds still more rapidly, for the rocks are disintegrated by frost, cast down by avalanches, and if they fall onto the surface of the glacier are carried forward by it and dumped down at its lower end, where, tumbling into

ON THE TOP OF ILLIMANI

HIGHEST CAMP ON ILLIMANI

the river, they are rolled about and gradually reduced into a form transportable by water. Rivers and glaciers thus eat their way backward, not to any appreciable extent by grinding down their beds, but by merely transporting the materials which fall into or onto them from steep places. It follows that, other things being equal, this eating-back action will be more vigorous where precipitation is greatest. In the case of a big mountain range, precipitation will tend to be greatest in the neighborhood of the highest peaks. It may incidentally happen that in the same neighborhood, owing to the greater vigor of earth-movements, rocks may be more faulted or liable to fracture. Thus it is near the largest peaks that the most vigorous eating-back action of rivers or glaciers is to be expected. Allowing the process of eating back to operate on a mountain-range for a sufficient length of time, if it is more vigorous on one side of a mountain range than it is on the other, it is a mathematical certainty that one of the streams will sooner or later eat its way right through the range, just as the La Paz River has done. Having done so, it will extend its conquest and will capture the waters from the other side one after another and bring them down to add to its own volume.

This the La Paz River has done; it has cut its way right across the Cordillera Real near one of its highest peaks, and, continuing then more slowly, yet with considerable vigor during the rainy season, it has eaten its way back and back, and has captured one stream after another that formerly went into the great inland sea. Every year the upper edge of its basin is visibly eaten away farther and farther, and if no earth-movement occurs to disturb the process, the day is in sight when it must reach as far back as the position of the waters of Lake Titicaca. A similar process, as we shall hereafter see, is going forward at the north end of the snowy range near Mount Sorata, where the Mapiri River is likewise engaged in cutting its way back through the range, only in this case the process is not so far advanced and the great alluvial deposit has not yet been reached. In the Karakoram Himalayas, as I have already more than once pointed out, an exactly similar action has taken place, the successive ranges being there cut through by the Indus and its tributaries, in each case close to the highest elevation of the particular range. Here, again, it has been suggested that the river system existed before the mountains were elevated.

Throughout the whole area of the Asiatic mountains as yet surveyed — through Tibet, along its southern edge, throughout the kingdom of Kashmir, and along the great earth fold of the Hindu Kush —the phenomena of capture can be shown to have determined the course of almost all the rivers, great and small.

Such were the reflections that occupied my mind as I surveyed the view from our lofty perch while the guides slept in their tents after preparing and consuming our mid-day meal. Señor Guillen, however, finding himself in the great snow world at whose feet he had been born and brought up, could scarcely contain his impatience long enough to halt and drink a bowl of soup. Bred at 12,000 feet, he felt the effect of diminished atmospheric pressure less than we did, while his healthy farming-life no doubt kept him in good condition. He seemed absolutely to revel in the newly opened world of snow; he ran about like a chamois on glacier and rocks, seemed anxious to plant his foot on every surrounding eminence, and gazed about in every direction. Dangers did not exist for him; he smiled at our admonitions, and mocked at the mention of hidden crevasses. After lunch we saw him no more for hours, until, towards sunset, yells from the guides called me forth, and I beheld our companion calmly descending the glacier from far above, straight towards a perfect labyrinth of crevasses, open and closed They hurriedly put on the rope and went forth to save him from what they considered certain destruction, but he bore a charmed life and came back in safety, wondering what all the fuss was about.

CHAPTER XII

ILLIMANI: THE FINAL CLIMB

BEFORE two o'clock the next morning we had left camp and were winding our way up in the darkness among great yawning crevasses. A single candle in a pocket-lantern was our only light in the great solitude of the abode of snow. Ffteen miles away, across the valley of the La Paz River, another twinkling light was visible, shining through the window of a remote farm-house. That was our sole link with the world of men. The night was not cold (only 21° Fahr.), but the snow was hard as rock, and we made rapid progress. Once Guillen fell into a crevasse, but being roped, we pulled him out unhurt. The stars were shining in the clear sky and there was no trace of cloud to be seen, yet at frequent intervals weird flashes of electricity broke around us, unaccompanied by any sound, as though a search-light had been flickered over us from some distant lighthouse. Whence these flashes came and whither they went I could not perceive. They resembled rather an emanation from the snow-field, or a phosphorescence glimmering along its surface, come and gone in the twinkling of an eye. The old moon rising over the snow-field at length rendered the lantern superfluous. Mounting steadily upward we ap-

THE SKIRTS OF ILLIMANI'S GLACIERS

proached the water-shed ridge, and two and a half
hours from camp stood upon it, the very crest of the
Cordillera Real, and looked down an appalling precipice of at least 14,000 feet into the black depths of
some valley of fertile Yungas. It was still night.
Gloom enveloped us. Blanched snow and black
crags appeared dim and ghostly near at hand, but
the dim and vague horror of that almost fathomless
plunge into the dark gulf at our feet was one of the
experiences that it has been worth living to know.

During all this part of our ascent there had been
on our left a great mountain exactly between us and
Illimani; I called it the Pico del Indio, for a reason
to be presently explained. We knew that a snow-
plateau lay between it and Illimani, and we had
hoped to gain this plateau by passing round the
back of the Pico del Indio. Now, however, we learned
to our regret that the tremendous Yungas cliff rendered any such circumvention impossible, while the
corresponding cliff on the Cotaña side equally pro-
hibited a turning movement. The intervening peak
must be climbed over, and we must begin by going
up the steep and narrow ridge on which we were
then standing—no easy matter, as we could see even
through the gloom of the night.

A boss of hard, transparent ice, the size and shape
of a walrus, stuck out of the ridge and had first to
be surmounted. Steps were cut in it with much de-
liberation, and we raised ourselves to the crest above,
one foot over the fathomless precipice, the other on a
steep slope with a gaping crevasse a few yards down.
Slip which way we might it would be sudden destruc-

tion, and to slip was easy in this darkness and cold. The last stride was about as theatrical a performance as I can remember, for the ice even in the steps was as slippery as a frozen pond. Here Guillen decided to turn back. He said his curiosity was satisfied, and he had a pain in his foot. It turned out to arise from frost-bite, for the cold up here was intense, probably twenty degrees lower than it had been down at camp. How Guillen got down alone I don't know, but he went; and he arrived the same day in safety at Caimbaya, to our no small relief, and advantage too, as will appear   Above the boss of ice were steep rocks, up which we felt our way in the darkness, for the moon was now gone behind clouds. Farther up the ridge an enormous ice cornice barred the way, and could neither be circumvented nor climbed over, as dawn enabled us to ascertain. There was no alternative but to cross the whole steep south face of the Pico del Indio to a gap in the ridge on the other side, by which, as we knew, access to the high snow-plateau could be attained. The face was a great slope of ice, fortunately covered by a thin layer of well-frozen snow that adhered firmly to it, and into which steps could be cut. But for this film of snow the traverse, which occupied over two hours, would have taken four or five hours, and been infinitely dangerous into the bargain.

The day was at hand. All along the crest of the mountains and clouds in the east flamed the crimson glory of the coming sun. The brighter illumination only served to make more plain the solemnity and splendor of our surroundings. The ice

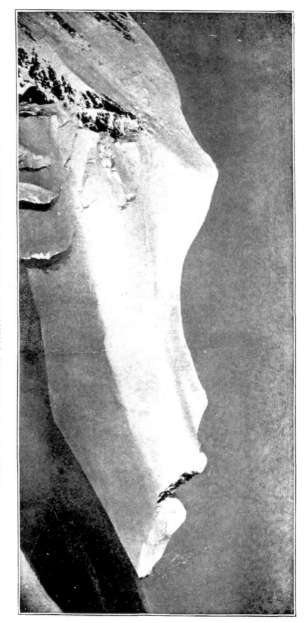

THE CULMINATING SNOW-FIELD OF ILLIMANI FROM THE PICO DEL INDIO

slope itself was one of the steepest I have ever stood on. A few hundred feet below it was cut off into a vertical cliff, overhanging in places, and by its feet lay the piled ruins of the ice avalanches which often fall from it. There must be no slipping here. The day increased, the sun came, and we slowly advanced; but how slowly the distance diminished between us and the western ridge I cannot describe. Click, click, click, went the axe, hewing out a step with painstaking care. Each had to be large and well-shaped. It was hard work. Half-way across, Maquignaz fell behind, and Pellissier took his place. Little was said. The steps were made as far apart as was safe, and the stride from one to another was an effort. At last the desired saddle was gained, and we could throw ourselves down and rest awhile, more than 20,000 feet above the sea, with the culminating peaks of Illimani now full in sight, rising beyond the snow-plateau, of whose existence we had been assured but which we now first saw—a vast, unbroken, undulating expanse, waving away to four snow-white peaks and the saddles between them. The highest peak was right opposite, and the way to it was obvious; we must gain the saddle beside it, and then follow a snow-ridge to the top, the saddle in question being the depression visible from La Paz immediately to the left of the highest summit.

After a few minutes' contented rest we descended a gentle snow-slope of about 400 feet to the level of the plateau. The Pico del Indio was behind us and Illimani ahead. By rare luck the snow was in good condition, so that we scarcely sank into it at all. Over large areas it was hard as a wooden floor. Now, of course, we felt, as any man must feel at such an elevation, the weakening effect of diminished atmospheric pressure. We had no headaches, nausea, running of blood from nose and ears, or other violent symptoms, but all were greatly reduced in strength. When the long, slow ascent beyond the level of the plateau began, the light load that strong Pellissier had to carry was almost too much for him. The remainder of the ascent was a featureless grind, and all suffered severely. Puffs of wind brought occasional relief There was not a crevasse, scarcely an inequality of surface to vary the way. The rounded snow summits shut off distant views, and were not interesting objects to look at in themselves. After three hours of slow, continuous plodding, the inclination ceased, and we stood upon a flat, wide saddle, from which there fell away at our feet the steep descent facing La Paz We threw ourselves down for a few moments to rest and eat. We were nearly 21,000 feet above the sea. For view there was behind us the great plateau, with snow-ridges to left and right, leading up to white peaks; ahead, a tumbled cataract of ice seen through gaps of changeful clouds, with now and then a glimpse over the wide Bolivian desert far away to north and west.

The ascent recommenced. Slowly, very slowly, we mounted the wide and easy snow-ridge, conscious only of heart-breaking toil and entirely possessed by a fixed determination to get the work done. The lifting of each foot in its turn was a tragic effort. Presently everything became unreal and dreamlike.

I fell into a semi-comatose condition, but plodded on
all the same. Twice I came to myself with a start;
I had been walking in something very like sleep. One
apparent summit was succeeded by another, but the
true one came at last. "Monsieur, à vous la gloire,"
said Maquignaz, as he moved aside for me to stand
first upon the highest point of snow. The altitude
was 21,200 feet.* It was half an hour before noon.
The moment was one of satisfaction, in that our toil
ceased; but we had no sense of triumph, nor was there
breath enough left in any of us for an exclamation
of joy in the hour of victory. Nothing was said or
done for several minutes; we just sat down and rested.
But five minutes later we had recovered, and were as
comfortable as at sea-level, so long as we neither moved
nor attempted to do anything, though I had lost my
voice and the others were quite hoarse. The cane flag-
staff we had brought up in sections was planted in
the snow and a little Union Jack set waving; but,
alas! none but ourselves could see it, for most of the
lower regions were buried in a sea of clouds, and La
Paz in particular was hidden. A flag-staff erected
in snow will not stand many hours. This one fell

---

* The measurements of the highest point of Illimani are as follows:

	FEET
Pentland	21,181
Pissis	21,355
Reiss	21,040
Minchin	21,224
Reck	21,339
Conway	21,015
Mean	21,192

137

before clear weather returned, and never showed itself through the telescope of the Jesuit Fathers at La Paz, who looked out for it at the first opportunity.

Notwithstanding the fog below, the view was impressive, for we stood out in clear air and brilliant sunshine, with towering clouds and snowy peaks near at hand. The peaks, draped in broken ice, were magnificent. The southward continuation of the Cordillera likewise lifted itself into sight, but of Mount Sorata and the northern range we saw nothing, while only patches of the Bolivian plain were seen through gaps in its nebulous covering. The descent was easy enough till we came to the foot of the Pico de Indio and had to reascend. There I thought my heart would burst, so excessive was the toil. Twelve short steps and a halt, twelve more and another halt, and so on, with deep breathing betweenwhiles to recover the power of motion. It was a dreadful hour, but it came to an end, and we could throw ourselves down at last on the mound of rock by the little snow-saddle and cast a last look back upon our conquered giant.

My hand touched something soft and clammy lying on the rock beside me. What could there be of that sort in such a place? I picked it up. It was a rotten piece of Indian woollen cord, swollen to the thickness of one's wrist. Maquignaz, to whom I gave it, unfortunately lost it on the way down. Tradition at Caimbaya asserts that many years ago an Indian desperately dared to invade the secret places of the great god Illimani. He was last seen from

ILLIMANI FROM THE COHONI ROAD

ILLIMANI AND THE PICO DEL INDIO FROM ABOVE THE HIGHEST CAMP

below, seated on this point where now we sat. He never came back to the abodes of men, for the god turned him into stone. That there is some foundation for the tale is proved by our discovery of the piece of rope; so I named the peak beside this place Pico del Indio.

We decided to complete the descent by another and more direct route, going straight down the long slope at our feet instead of crossing over the face and doubling back down below. The slope, which was of ice, covered with good snow, was steep, but less steep than the one we had crossed, and the snow was fairly thick and firm We went straight down, one only moving at a time, an axe always firmly planted into the slope and the rope paid out round it. It seemed as though the bottom would never come, so long and featureless was the sloping way. The snow became softer, and we began to fear that it might bodily slide off the ice and take us down in an avalanche; but it held. Another trouble ahead was the great *berg-schrund*, or crevasse, at the foot of the slope. We could see that there was one, but of its size or where to cross it we could see nothing, for the upper edge hid the lower. By good luck we struck it at a point—and, as it turned out, almost the only point—where it could be jumped. Then we were on leveller snow, strewn with ruins of ice avalanches. We picked a way through them and in and out of larger crevasses than I have elsewhere seen. The bridges over them were great hill-sides in themselves. By winding about, the labyrinth was at last threaded, though not without many errors and returns. More than once I feared that the night would overtake us before we had found a way through. Clouds, like mountains upon mountains, were gathering about us, casting gloom upon the tortured ice-torrent in whose thralls we were enmeshed. Thunder pealed forth to right and left, and the echoes rolled about in the deep solitude of the hollow places of the hills At length all difficulties were left behind, the main glacier was reached, and the morning's upward tracks rejoined. At half-past five we were in camp, and at six, it being already night, I was fast asleep in the sack of reindeer-skin which had so often sheltered me in Spitsbergen against Arctic cold.

Next morning (September 10th) found us hungry, for we had eaten little on the previous day, but otherwise well content with the world and with ourselves. It is true we were painfully sunburned; even Pellissier's seasoned hide, proof against reflected sunlight from European snows, had not been able to resist the tropical sunshine. All of us were, moreover, almost rent asunder by a violent whooping-cough. It proved to be a mere symptom of altitude, for we lost it on descending to Caimbaya. It returned again whenever we approached the 20,000 feet line, whether on Sorata or afterwards on Aconcagua. None of my party experienced it in the Himalayas, nor have I ever read or heard of it as experienced by other climbers at high altitudes.

The sun rose in great splendor over a calm, level sea of cloud, stretching away from our feet like a shining silver pavement. Snow had fallen on the tents in the night, but there had only been eleven degrees of frost and no wind. The group of the Three Crosses stood out like a violet island from the brilliant sea of clouds. There were no Indian porters to help us with the baggage, but we had found a fragment of paper in the tent, containing the information that Guillen had passed the evening before, on his way down to the farm, and that men would be sent up to meet us next morning. We knew that they would never climb the wall of rocks, so there was nothing for it but to pack up the baggage and get it down as best we could. We bundled as many things as possible into one of the big reindeer sleeping-bags, and wrapping the others around, corded it up with a mountain rope and wheeled it like a barrel to the edge of the cliff. We chucked it over just where an ice *couloir* stretched down to a snow-slope that almost reached the level of the next tent platform. The bundle began to roll, and then to take longer leaps, till about half-way down it burst open like a rocket and scattered our possessions in every direction. The sections of tent-poles flew about in wild confusion, and so did the cooking apparatus and every other small object; but they got down hill, all the same, and came to rest scattered about upon the snow-slope, where we ultimately recovered them. Little permanent injury had been done; only the fur sleeping-bag was rent open, and would require to be well clouted before it could be used again.

Arrived at the tent platform, we were glad to find that all the baggage we had left upon it had been carried down. Here again was a note from the admirable Guillen, stating that we might be sure of

Indians coming to this point, though he anticipated
trouble in persuading them, as the great fête continued. We lay for a long time in the sunshine, enjoying the pleasant breeze and lunching on the con-
tents of some self-cooking tins—that is to say, tins
containing Irish stew, with a little spirit-lamp so
attached that all you have to do is to cut the tin open,
tear off the soldered ribbon, apply a match to the wick,
and wait ten minutes for your hot lunch. Ultimately,
leaving the rest of our baggage on this tent platform,
we ran down to the foot of the gully, where we met
two Indians coming up, and saw two others farther
down on the way. Traversing the path by the canal,
we came out on the little flat meadow and found our
mules awaiting us.

Before half-past two in the afternoon we reached
Caimbaya, and met the Indian manager in the *hacienda* yard among his mules and horses, sheep, pigs,
poultry, dogs, and wondrously tame birds. He rushed
up to greet me, but suddenly halted, crying out with
amazement, "Cristo della Madonna! what boots!"
a remark generally made to me in one form or another
by every new acquaintance on the mountain-side.
In truth, the boots I was wearing were boots indeed.
The German captain of the ship by which I voyaged
down Smyth Channel was never tired of looking at
them; and when I left the ship at Sandy Point he
shouted after me that, as he would arrive in London
before I did, he would see that a dry-dock should be
ready for their reception. Mountaineering readers
may remember that our greatest difficulty in the high
ascents we made in the Himalayas was the inten-

THE DESCENT OF ILLIMANI

sity of the cold before sunrise, which took all sensation from our feet and brought us to the verge of frost-bite; so that we found it necessary to give up all attempts at climbing at high levels before the break of dawn. Even then, on Pioneer Peak, every member of our party came so near to being frost-bitten that we were obliged to stop, take off our boots, and rub one another's feet for half an hour to avoid that calamity. A similar difficulty was experienced by Mr. Vines on the upper slopes of Aconcagua. I was therefore determined to avoid, if possible, this particular trouble, for to be reduced to wait till the coming of the sun before commencing to ascend is, especially in the tropics, to reduce the climbing-day to very brief dimensions. I was fortunate enough to find in Norway a pair of goat-hair stockings of immense thickness, almost as thick as one's little finger, such as are worn by ski runners in the cold winter of the North. These stockings, with a leather covering, suffice to keep the feet warm in very great cold; but at high altitudes, owing to the diminished vitality from which all men must suffer, the body is far less able to resist cold than it is at sea-level in Arctic winters. Not satisfied, therefore, with these stockings, I wore within them a pair of Shetland wool stockings and a thin pair of socks besides. It is not, therefore, surprising that enormous boots were necessary to cover feet thus enveloped. The boots I used were of the kind described in my Himalaya book, made at Zermatt, with very thick soles, three thicknesses of leather over the toes, two over the body of the foot, and one over the ankle. Such foot-gear was, of course, very weighty;

but I became accustomed to it, and never regretted it, for in the result I was the only one of the party that entirely escaped frost-bite. It is scarcely necessary to remark that every one of us had been severely sun-burned on Illimani, though much of the ascent had been made when the sun was hidden in clouds. If we had not noticed the fact ourselves, the extraordinary eagerness of everybody at Caimbaya to show us our faces in the looking-glass would have conveyed the information.

CHAPTER XIII

RETURN TO LA PAZ

IN descending the La Paz Valley on our way to Cotaña we had passed, an hour or so below Millocato, the point of junction (named Esquina de Pongo) with the important side valley that drains the great Palca basin, intervening between Illimani and the basin of La Paz. To this Palca Valley we shall hereafter return Our descent from Caimbaya was made by crossing below the face of Illimani and going down direct to Esquina de Pongo, instead of returning by Cotaña and the route of our ascent. Starting about 8:30 A. M., after a good breakfast, we mounted through the village of Caimbaya to the low grass pass already referred to. It was a glorious day; Illimani, absolutely clear from base to summit, stood up before us, a splendid mountain. Below its cliff lay in green fertility the wide *cirque* that forms the head of the Salapampa Valley. Our way was to lead us a little distance down to the farm of Atahuaillani, and then, by a wide descending circuit, round under the face of Illimani and down the opposite side of the Salapampa Valley. If we had been better informed we might indeed have ascended the opposite slope of the valley, and so, passing the farm of Tanimpata, have gained a second grass pass immediately at the foot of the

K   145

great south *arêta* of Illimani's highest peak. Crossing one or more grassy ribs of the mountain, we should have descended in a couple of days into the Palca Valley, and so by the Alto de Animas have gained La Paz by a very interesting route. In fact, this line of travel is one that any future visitor to these mountains should by no means fail to traverse. Half an hour from Caimbaya we stood at the door of the little farm-house named Atahuaillani. We knew that Mr. Bandolier, whom I may best describe as the Flinders Petrie of prehistoric Peru and Bolivia, was making this farm his temporary abode, while excavating ancient villages and burying-places on the flanks of Illimani for the New York Museum. During the course of our preliminary explorations we had come across several such burying-places on the actual summits of the lower hills, and had found two ruined villages and their abandoned but still recognizable terraced fields in a position most difficult of access, just at the foot of a glacier, proof of the pressure of population in pre-Columbian days, rendering necessary the cultivation of every yard of land that could be reclaimed and watered. Even the position of the canals that brought glacier-water to the fields could be traced.

As we entered the court-yard of the farm Mrs. Bandolier was upon the steps. She greeted us heartily and went to call up her husband, for it was still very early. Both united to insist that we should spend a few hours with them, and I was nothing loath. Seldom in my experience has time passed more delightfully. I wish I could make this excellent couple visible to the reader. The Museum for which they work, and have worked for many years, may well be proud of them. Their lives are absolutely devoted to the science they pursue. Cut off from the world, without servant or companion of any sort, isolated in the midst of superstitious Indians, who regard their work as dangerous to the peace of the neighborhood, and expect daily vengeance to descend upon their villages from the ghosts of outraged ancestors, they pursue, nevertheless, the even tenor of their research, helping one another in every detail, each the other's only friend. To converse with such brave, alert, intelligent friends about their work, about the country, the natives, the mountains they know and love so well, was a rare privilege.

Mrs. Bandolier cooked our breakfast on a petroleum stove (and an excellent breakfast it was) while her husband answered my volley of questions. "Were the ancient dwellers on Illimani Incas?" I ignorantly asked. "I don't know. I have no theories. I know nothing about Incas. All I know is that throughout Peru and Bolivia there were ancient inhabitants, for whom I have no name—prehistoric Peruvians, if you like. These people left remains which exist, and descendants—the Indians we see about us. The remains show that there were great varieties of local habit and custom—whether the result of racial variety or merely of different conditions of life, I don't know. What we do is to investigate the remains and discover facts; we record the facts and leave inferences and generalizations to other people. There are not facts enough discovered yet to warrant very general inferences. Some day there may be, but it will need much more excavation first. Our investigation is two-fold. We dig into the ground, and we dig into the minds of the living people. The Indian to-day is very little altered by European influence. He carries a thin varnish of Christianity, but below it are all the pre-Columbian beliefs and superstitions practically entire. The difficulty is to get the people to talk. For example, the Indians here worship Illimani as a god; but they would not acknowledge to you that they did so." Thus he talked for four hours, from the wealth of his experience, and if he slackened for a moment, another question would release a new fund of reminiscence and laboriously acquired knowledge. I was surprised to find him full of admiration for the ancient Spanish laws dealing with the treatment of Indians. I gathered that the failure was in administration, not in legislation. "Anyway," he said, "the general ignorance about Spain and her colonies in the old days is colossal."

Bidding farewell to our kind hosts, we followed one of the grandest view-commanding mule-tracks I ever saw. It descended amid an ever-increasing wealth of vegetation, circling round a vast basin in the hills, just below Illimani's southern cliff. Our peak was always visible far aloft, for the day was perfectly fine. It juts up like a tower from this side, apparently inaccessible save by wings. Shrubs just bursting into flower, and some of most fragrant scent, over-arched the track, and the high snows glimmered through them. Water tumbled and sang down the gullies between the arms of the mountains. We

ILLIMANI FROM THE COHONI ROAD

crossed the tracks of one or two mud avalanches.
The swing round of the *cirque* carried us farther and
farther out from the bosom of Illimani. On a little
bare field, beaten flat like some dancing-floor in a
Himalayan village, a party of natives in gay attire
danced round and round in a circle to the simple
music of pipe and drum—a little air endlessly repeated:

A gentle breeze hummed in the tall dry tussocks
of grass. Thus at the end of our encircling traverse
we gained a promontory at the mouth of the *cirque*
and had one look back from the top of a granite mound,
that seems as though it had been placed where it is
in order to command the most majestic view possible
of the great mountain. So the heathen inhabitants
thought, for on it are ruins of what may have been
an open-air temple, and there are graves in and about
the sacred enclosure. After a brief halt we turned
the corner, and our mountain was hidden from view.
It is probably this last view of it that I shall longest
remember—the Pic de Paris on our right, the summit
on the left, and the great curving cliff between, reaching up at one point almost to the top of the Pico del
Indio.

I have already mentioned that the upper snow-field
is mainly drained away by avalanches that fall over
this cliff. Most of them descend to a low level, where
they rapidly melt away, but the avalanches that fall

from between the Pico del Indio and the Pic de Paris reform below into a small glacier which there fills a mountain *cirque*. The great crevasses which we found so
difficult to thread on our descent from the Pico del Indio
were situated just above this *cirque* and were formed by
the ice giving way and preparing to fall over the cliff.
It was easy to see from the point where now we stood
that the cliff above the little glacier was being rapidly
eaten away into the mountain. Not only does frost
constantly peel off the face of the rock, but the enormous
avalanches that fall down it smash and abrade the
surface, so that the face of the cliff is continually planed
away. The débris that fall from it would pile themselves up at its foot were it not for the little glacier below,
which receives them on its surface or into its mass, and
gradually carries them down and dumps them over
its foot in the form of terminal moraine. The glacier,
small though it be, thus becomes a potent agent in
breaking down the hill-side, for by preventing the formation of a débris slope, which would protect and ultimately cover up the cliff, it enables frost and avalanches
to continually eat away the cliff itself and so to carry
it back and back, just as the cliff over which Niagara
falls is continually cut back by action of the water. It
is easy to see that the process has been going on for a
long time and that to it the formation of the great cliff
of Illimani is due, for not so long ago a glacier occupied
the whole of the basin round whose sides we had been
riding, the path being carried entirely over moraines or
ice-worn rocks. By this means the ridge that joined
the Pic de Paris to the Pico del Indio has been broken
through, so that now a part of the snow-field, which

once drained down the Caimbaya glacier, is drained
by avalanches into the Salapampa basin.*

From the mountain-temple a long, dull descent followed, with nothing in sight but low desert-hills to
the west, furrowed by torrents descending in the rainy
season into the La Paz Valley. It was a view of the
unclothed world. Just at sunset we turned a corner
and looked down upon the strangely picturesque Indian
town of Cohoni—a large and tightly packed assemblage
of mud-houses roofed with thatch, planted one above
another on the steep hill-side. The streets proved to
be narrow, precipitous, and intricate. It was hard to
find the way through, and we were in a hurry, for
night was at hand and we still had far to go. Beyond
the town came apparently endless steep zigzags, deeply worn into the hill-side by the tread of countless
generations. Thousands of feet below we saw, by
the last gleam of daylight, the fields of the farm where
the night was to be spent. Darkness rapidly came on.
The crest of Illimani, again in view, palely glimmered
after all else was shrouded from sight. We had to dismount from our mules and feel for the way. There
was no moon. The bright evening star alone gave
light. The air grew sensibly warmer and thicker as
we descended. Dense vegetation flanked and roofed
the way. A tall broom with a large blossom, common
in South America, filled the air with rich perfume. It
gave place to high canes, and I know not what other trop-

---

* This is a concrete instance of the invasion of a longitudinal by a
side glacier in the manner explained in my paper "On an Exploration, in 1897, of Some of the Glaciers in Spitsbergen," *Geographical
Journal*, vol. xii., p. 144. August, 1898.

ical vegetation. The night grew blacker and blacker. We could not even see our hands before us. There was a sound of water below. By grovelling on the ground and feeling we discovered that the path was again following the edge of an abyss. I walked along it, tapping with a stick as a blind man taps the edge of a curbstone. Presently I felt wood and found a bridge, and beyond it the continuing path. At last we came among barking dogs, and lights of a *hacienda* glimmering through trees. The name of the place was Taguapalca. Its owners extended to us a kind hospitality.

Before pursuing our way next morning we were conducted over the orchards, where coffee grows and fruits of every sort for the La Paz markets—figs, grapes, oranges, olives, custard-apples, granadillas, lemons, peaches, bananas, chestnuts, and many other kinds which the reader might not recognize by name. They grew in rich profusion, but are cultivated with little art, nor was there any of the tidiness we are accustomed to associate with good gardening. The effect, however, was most picturesque, thanks to nature's profusion, and to the splendid hills, peeping in through every gap in foliage and flowers. In a corner of the garden was a grove of giant olive-trees, the largest I ever saw, casting so dense a shade that the group of seats beneath them form a cool retreat in the hottest weather. Near at hand is the usual swimming-bath, filled by a stream of ruddy water. A pretty summer-house stands on a jutting promontory with vertical sides, pushing forth from the trees. It commands a strange view of the desert hills and valleys by which this oasis is surrounded. Filling our saddle-bags with fruit for the way, we bade adieu to our kind hosts and set forth before the sun was high. Descending over the débris of many mud avalanches, we soon entered the La Paz Valley at Esquina de Pongo, and thence rode back to the city by the way we had come.

CHAPTER XIV

PREPARING TO ASCEND SORATA

THE ascent of Illimani fortunately accomplished, there was in our minds but one idea—to attack the other and probably higher great mountain of the Bolivian Cordillera Real, Mount Sorata. I call it Mount Sorata because that, among other names, is sometimes applied to it, and is the most convenient designation. Sorata, as we shall see, is the name of a town at its foot, and the whole mountain mass at that end of the Cordillera may be well enough thought of as the mountain of Sorata. Regarded from a European Alpine point of view, Mount Sorata is a group of peaks, like the Mont Blanc group, each of which, if much attention were given to the group, would equire a name of its own. The natives in pre-Columbian days had already distinguished two of these peaks by name and legend. One was the actually culminating-point, a noble crest of snow They call it Ancohuma, I am told; the word as pronounced to me sounded more like "Hankuma," but I adhere to the received spelling. Mr. Bandolier tells me it should be written *Hankouma*, and that it means "white water." The other and more remarkable peak is a great buttress of the former, not, in fact, quite so lofty, but, when seen from Lake Titicaca or from the Sorata Valley, far more imposing—a majestic rock tower, not unlike the Matterhorn, although vastly greater, built up of precipitous dark cliffs and ridges, whereon the clouds drift and play in wonderful complexity. I never saw a peak more gloriously decked with clouds than was this one. The Incas, I believe, worshipped it as a god, and named it Illampu. For this name many derivations have been suggested. Mr. Bandolier says that the name should be written *Hilampi*, and that it means "with his brother," implying, quite correctly, that it is the lesser of a pair of peaks. Padre Baltasar de Salas, writing in 1618-1625, spells the name, "Inti-llampu," which means I know not what, but *Inti* is the word from which the name *Andes* is supposed by some to be corrupted. Mount Sorata is popularly called Illampu in Bolivia nowadays, and Ancohuma is called the south peak of Illampu. I prefer to restore to the individual peaks their proper designations, and to apply to the whole mountain the designation Mount Sorata.

When driving from Lake Titicaca to La Paz over the high Bolivian plateau we had noticed that the most promising way to attack the peak was by a glacier that descends southward from Ancohuma, which I afterwards named the Ancohuma glacier. The lower part of it was apparently much crevassed, but there seemed to be a high snowy plateau above, leading to the foot of the final peak. The peak itself was evidently precipitous, but we hoped it might improve on acquaintance; at all events, this was the route we decided to attempt. Such a decision is in Bolivia the smallest part of a climber's trouble. The mountainous parts of the country, which are almost exclusively in-

habited by Indians, cannot be traversed in the free
fashion possible in most mountain regions. The traveller who went with two or three companions, and set
up his tent wherever seemed most convenient to pass
the night, would be liable to find himself raided by
Indians, whose suspicions, and perhaps terrors, are
aroused by any action on the part of white men to
which they are not accustomed. To roll up a tent and
leave it with other baggage indifferently protected on a
hill-side, as in mountaineering must sooner or later be
done with a heavy camp, would merely invite theft.
Wherever a mountaineer goes in the Bolivian mountains his movements are sure to be carefully watched,
and there is no chance of his hiding his property where
Indians will not find it. The only way, therefore, to
approach any of the great mountains is to do so with
the assistance of some considerable body of the natives
themselves. All the Puna Indians belong to one of
two categories: either they inhabit a *finca* or they are
what is called pueblo or village Indians. A *finca*, as I
have already explained, belongs to a proprietor, but the
pueblos are *Comunidades* — village communities belonging to the inhabitants themselves. A *finca* is
governed and administered by the major-domo representing the proprietor; a pueblo is administered by
an official named the corregidor, who represents the
government and is under the sub-prefect of the district.
Pueblo Indians pay tribute for their lands and work in
common; they appoint their own alcalde, who regu-
lates the partition of crops and other domestic questions.
It appears that the Pueblo Indians are less under control
than the *finca* Indians; at all events, the traveller is

more likely to be well received if he goes to a *finca* armed with a letter of recommendation from its proprietor than if he goes to a pueblo with merely an official letter to the corregidor.

Thus, having determined in a general way upon the route I desired to follow, it was necessary to find some one who could tell me what *finca* was best situated for a base, and then to procure an introduction to its owner, and get from him a letter instructing his major-domo to supply me with Indian porters, and give me whatever assistance I might require. If there had been in existence even a moderately good map of the mountains, this would have been no very difficult matter; but as no such map existed, it was by no means easy for me, with my limited command of Spanish, to explain what I wanted in La Paz, without either the mountain or a map to point to. Here Señor Granier, with his knowledge of European languages and rare geographical instinct, came to my assistance; he instantly perceived that a place called Umapusa was the right starting-point, and he made every arrangement to that end. On Illimani we had been able to take Indian porters to within a very short distance below our highest camp. We realized that Mount Sorata would not lend itself to so convenient an arrangement, for the mountain has a much wider spread, a large gathering-ground for snow on its upper part, and a more continuous southern slope, so that the glaciers descend in great volume to a lower level than on Illimani, and the highest point that can be reached without entering upon them is more remote from the top. It followed that, as the Umapusa Indians were no more likely than those of Caimbaya to be willing to enter the world of snow, we should be obliged to transport our camp and provisions without their assistance for at least one day, and possibly for more. As this work would have to be done from 17,000 feet upward, where loads in any case must be small, it seemed that repeated journeys would be necessary and the time consumed correspondingly great. Here, however, the preliminary observations we had made from the road came to our help; for we had noticed that the very broken parts of the glacier were the lower parts, and that above these ice-falls there were long slopes of snow, broken here and there, but not for any great distance.

I therefore conceived that we might be able to employ a sledge for dragging our baggage over this part of the ascent. The suggestion fortunately met with Maquignaz's approval, for it did not come upon him as entirely novel. In the previous year, while accompanying the Duke of the Abruzzi to the summit of Mount St. Elias, he and his companions had dragged sledges over ice for six or seven weeks. He was therefore familiar with both the nature of a sledge and the possibilities of using it even on crevassed glaciers, while I, of course, had had plenty of experience with sledges during two summers spent exploring the interior of Spitsbergen. The first thing I had to do, therefore, at La Paz, was to find a carpenter, and make him understand the nature of the machine he was to fashion—no very easy matter; but ultimately the man seemed to get a glimmering idea of what was wanted, and set to work upon it, with the two guides to watch and assist. Progress was unfortunately very slow—first, because everything is done slowly in this country; and, secondly, because a saint's day, that is a holiday, intervened, and the work had to stop while the carpenter enjoyed himself, and for the best part of the following day while he was recovering.

My own time was sufficiently occupied with the necessary packing of collections and repacking of baggage for the new trip, while there were numbers of people to be seen at all hours of the day. One evening I attended a special meeting of the Geographical Society of La Paz, and gave some account of the ascent of Illimani. In the discussion that followed, the question of the derivation of the mountain's name was considered, and the general impression seemed to be that the ancient form of the word was Illi Mamani, which being translated means "bright condor." But Mr. Bandolier told me that, in his opinion, the true derivation is *Hila-uma-ni*, meaning "with much water" (much-water-with). I think it was Señor M. V. Ballivian who told me that the earliest recorded form of the name is *Inti-llimani*, though what that may mean I know not.

CHAPTER XV

THE APPROACH TO MOUNT SORATA

THE sledge and other preparations I have described occupied our time for four days. On the morning of the fifth after our return from Illimani (September 17th), we set forth for Mount Sorata. This time no swift tilbury carried us over the Puna, but a caravan of mules. Very different was the slow plodding with which we rode up the long zigzags to the Alto from the wild excitement of our descent down them on the day of our arrival, for now there was no surprise in store. Having reached the edge of the cliff at the point known as the Alto de Lima,* where an old Spanish tower or pilastron stands, we did not follow the carriage-road, but struck across the high plateau by one of its many paths. From this point, indeed, the radiation of the foot-paths in all directions is very remarkable. They must diverge almost in hundreds from the common centre. Not, of course, that they radiate in hundreds of different directions, but they sunder in groups of parallel tracks, which rapidly multiply as they diverge. It is only wheeled vehicles that make broad roads; South America was innocent of wheels before the coming of the Span-

---

* Another mule-track leads to a point farther south, named the Alto de Potosi. The carriage alto lies about half-way between the two.

iards. The native highway in all parts of South America is the foot-path. Where traffic increases, the number of parallel foot-paths multiplies. It was only when, under Inca government, a wide pavement was laid, as was the case along the main north and south highway, and the old route over the Huallata Pass to Illabaya, whereof traces still exist, that these parallel tracks were supplanted. The Puna, at all events, except for the modern carriage-road, is only traversed by infinite numbers of these foot-paths, along which men, donkeys, and llamas are continuously passing in their ceaseless movement towards La Paz or back to their scattered farms and villages. So featureless is the wide, undulating plain, which, near the Alto, at any rate, is not cultivated at all nor inhabited, that it is easy to mistake the particular track diverging towards the point one wishes to attain. The carriage-road, in order to avoid the deeply excavated stream hollows in the lower slopes —hollows some hundred feet deep and several hundred yards wide—is forced to make a divergence from the direct route. The ordinary donkey-track to Chililaya or to Achacache goes more directly, crossing many of these undulations low down near the flat, but the ancient route, which passes directly through the village of Umapusa on its way to the town of Sorata, goes right over the undulating feet of the mountains, ascending and descending continuously. This route is never followed nowadays except by llama caravans.

We were destined to traverse the Puna, for one reason or another, no less than nine times, and thus came to know it with some intimacy. This time it was practically new to us, for in driving over a country one learns little about it. As the baggage mules and *arriero* lagged behind, we three were alone on the wild expanse. By good luck we took a wrong track, and so found ourselves presently in the carriage-road, to which we thought it wisest afterwards to adhere. Thus we reached the *tambo* of Okomisto, which we should otherwise have missed, where tilburies and post-wagons change horses, and where we found Mr. N. E. Bieber, of the Yani Mine, halting for refreshment on his way to La Paz. I was delighted to discover him, for there were many matters about which he could instruct me better than any one else in the country. He asked where I was going to sleep. I said," At Machaca-Marca," the other principal post-house on the Chililaya road.

" Well," he said, " it's a good thing you met me, for the man would have refused to put you up. Both Machaca-Marca* and Okomisto are merely post stations for the use of passengers by the postal service, and the managers are not allowed by the company to accommodate passing caravans. When I was new to this country I arrived late one night at Machaca-Marca, expecting to stop there, but the manager sent me on, and I had to flounder over the Puna in the dark, hunting about for a *finca* that would take me in. Since then I have made an arrangement with the company, and now I have the right to put up at both places, on condition of my keeping my own store of *cebada* for my mules. I will, therefore, give you a note to the manager, so that you may use my *cebada* and be put up whenever you pass."

* The name means " new building."

I then told him that my next halting-place would be Achacache, and asked information about that, it likewise being situated on the route constantly taken by Bieber between Yani and La Paz. He said there was an inn there kept by a rather suspicious old gentleman, who turned away most people he didn't know, so he gave me a letter to him also, and thus materially assisted me on the way.

If the Puna was monotonous to drive over behind a cantering team of ponies, it was still more monotonous to traverse at the tail of a crawling caravan of mules. Early in the morning and late in the evening, when the sun is below the horizon, the cold, even at this time of year, is liable to be intense, and one suffers from almost frozen feet. In the winter, when the winds blow and the frosts are yet more severe, the dry cold is so trying that even the natives cover up their faces in thick woollen masks, and wrap shawls about their heads and ponchos over their bodies. But as soon as the sun is a little way above the horizon, its direct rays scorch the traveller with their great heat, so that he soon begins to pray for the night, as the lesser evil of the two. For at night, when the stars shine brightly and a great silence descends upon the land, and the Indians, in fear of one another, quit the roads, which are then none too safe, there is a romance about this wide, wild, lonely expanse. By day the burning sunshine so envelopes all the brown, dry, dusty ground that everything in view seems to vanish in brightness; and the eye, unprotected by dark glass, cannot gaze steadily in any direction. However unpleasant to the senses the heat and glaring light may be, this blaze of brilliancy, as foreground to the long snowy wall

that frets the margin of the east, remains as a grand
thing in the memory. But the Puna, in the months
I knew it, is a place of many moods. When the sun
is hottest, little cyclones raise dust-whirlwinds, which
dance along often by scores at a time; now and again
a giant tower of dust, far larger than the ordinary,
reaches from the ground high into the heavens. One
such whirlwind I saw, a black, curving column, which
seemed to descend from a thunder-cloud like the trunk
of some gigantic elephant searching the ground. In
the hot hours mirages flood the plain and make the
Indians' huts dance like boats bobbing on water. It
is a strange sight to see a caravan of donkeys or llamas
emerging from one of these fictitious lakes.

Almost daily, a white cloud-bank gathered behind the
Cordillera to the east. When the sun rose the range was
usually clear; but an hour or two later the crest of the
cloud-bank would be seen over the lower passes, and
the white flood would presently pour round the north
end of Mount Sorata, and then creep along the western
face towards the south, joining other mist cataracts descending from the great gaps in the range, just as the
clouds crept round the south end of Illimani and up the
valley of La Paz. By degrees eruptions of cloud would
rise at different points behind the Cordillera and, bent
over by the wind like some huge breaking wave, would
impend upon the Puna. Detached fragments of these
would drift away westward, with thunder in their bosoms
and trailing skirts of hail or rain beneath them. Travelling on and on, they would meet other clouds formed
upon the western Cordillera, so that, when night came,
lightning flashes often illumined the sky from half

a dozen places at once, and the far-away thunder boomed almost without intermission. But, till the approach of the rainy season, these storms would cease and the clouds fade in the early night, and the bright stars would soon be shining in unveiled splendor from zenith to horizon.

Though, at the time of our visit, the Puna had all the aspect of a desert, large parts of it produce fairly good crops in the rainy season. The lower slopes of the mountains, where they rise from the plain, are covered with tufts of a species of *Deyeuxia*, which is frozen to a golden-brown tint in the winter. Here, too, and lower down are plentifully distributed, like so many mole-hills, domed growths of the resinous balsam-bock named *Yareta* (*Bolax glebaria*), one of the best local forms of fuel, a use likewise served by the hardy *tola* shrub. *Yareta* and *Deyeuxia* are almost the sole products of the first part of the Puna traversed by the tracks proceeding northward from the Alto of La Paz; a mile or two farther on scattered fields are passed, formed by removing immense quantities of water-worn stones from the ground, and piling them up in heaps, the area occupied by the heaps being as great as that of the cultivable ground between them. Westward—that is to say, lower down on the level ground, farther from the foot of the Cordillera—the amount of soil is greater in proportion to the stones, and the fields are larger. Farms become more numerous, and so do villages, and even towns of considerable size, such as Laja or Puca-rani. These fields produce barley (*cebada*), potatoes of different sorts, *Ocas* (*Oxalis tuberosa*) and other tubers, *Quinoa* (*Chenopodium quinoa*), and a few other products. The methods of cultivation are those already described.

More than once, especially in the later weeks of our stay in Bolivia, we rode past a field that was being ploughed. On such occasions, instead of a few plough-men, the whole village was apparently at work. The ploughs used are the roughest wooden forks imagin-able, seldom shod with iron. They are dragged by a yoke of bulls. A great noise arises from the field, for all the folks at work seem to shout at one another and exchange jokes. When they saw me preparing to take a photograph, many of the men posed themselves in positions meant to be funny, and one man rode his plough, balancing himself wonderfully. He came near, to be assured that he was included in my view. Such rare incidents were welcome breaks in the monot-ony of our ride. Of course, we met the usual Indian caravans on the trail, but, save for the slowly changing distant view of the mountains, one mile of Puna is much like another. Except in the vicinity of Lake Titicaca, birds were few. Near swamps we used some-times to see the small gull, named *Gabiotto*, but the commonest birds were the brown *Macata* and the black *Alcamario*, both scavengers. They were not shy, but would let us approach near enough to pot them with our revolvers had we been better shots. Another com-mon bird, especially on the lower slopes of the Cordil-lera, was the *Sintenella*, whose cry was one of the ear-liest sounds heralding the dawn.

By 6 o'clock we reached the post-house of Machaca-Marca, presented our credentials, and were allowed to enter. The place consists of a row of mud cham-

THE OUTSKIRTS OF ACHACACHE

AN INDIAN FUNERAL

bers built round a courtyard, with a couple of large corrals or walled enclosures for mules in the rear. Like Okomisto, it was distinguished from the farms in the neighborhood by the many great stacks of cebada that stood about it, though in 1900 these were absent. The manager was in a very happy state of intoxication, and entirely pleased with himself. "I am drunk to-day," he said—"a little drunk—but I shall be all right to-morrow. Excuse me, excuse me," he said. "You will excuse me—a little drunk—all right to-morrow." He came out and stood beside me on a dust heap by the road, looking out for our baggage mules, which were somewhat behind. Once or twice he fell off the dust heap, but that only added to his happiness. He borrowed my field-glasses, tried to look through them at the wrong end, and returned them to me with the remark that to-morrow he would be better able to use them. Some animals appeared in the distance on the road, and I thought they might be ours.

"No," he said, "that's not Coro's *arriero*; I know him; he's drunk; he's sure to be drunk. Those are Indians—my Indians. All the Indians about here are my Indians. They all work for me—four hundred Indians. Bad fellows! I have this revolver for them, and they know me. If one tries to come it over me— bang! he goes to the pantheon. Very useful, this revolver," he said. "Very useful for the Indians; they know me. I'm drunk to-day, but I'll be all right to-morrow." After which he lapsed into the Aymara tongue, and I could understand him no more.

Making our bed on the table in the room where the post travellers get their mid-day meal, we passed a good enough night, and were on the road again early next morning. For an hour or two we followed the road back towards Chililaya, till we came to a great mud mile-stone, or pilastron, such as in former days they were wont to build for marking the route. These pilastrons are rather confusing, because some merely stand at prominent points, while others are league-posts, marking distances. At this particular pilastron, the Achacache road turned off to the right. This, in fact, was the ancient high-road, for Chililaya is quite a modern port; the old port of Lake Titicaca in Inca days was Achacache, which then stood on the margin of the lake, though it is now cut off from the waters by a mud flat. The main route to the north went from Achacache over the Cordillera to the town of Illabaya, and thence to the gold region east of the Andes. There appears also to have been another route, traces of which are still clearly marked, and are known as the Incas' Way. This led towards the Cordillera at a point south of Mount Sorata, but whether it crossed the range by a snow-pass or whether it merely led to some ancient mining settlement on the mountain slopes I have been unable to discover. In the opposite direction it was said to lead to Tiahuanaco.

In the middle of the morning we reached the large Indian village of Huarina, on the margin of the inner bay of Titicaca, which is called Lake Vinamarca. It is just like some Irish villages, with whitewashed, mud-walled, thatched cabins, and pigs and fowls running about. There were plenty of cattle on the margin of the water, eating weeds that the Indians were dragging out of the lake. Low, rounded hills with bare slopes

ACHACACHE CHURCH

INDIAN CHILDREN

rose on our right hand from the level ground and shut
out the view of the snow-mountains. This line of low
hills is continuous as far as Achacache. We had already passed two corresponding patches of similar
hills between Okomisto and this point. This series of
low hills consists of red sandstones and conglomerates,
ascribed by Forbes to the Permian series. The remainder of our way led beside or among these hills,
with now and again a glimpse of the blue waters of
the great lake.

Reaching the summit of a little rise with a mud pilastron on the top, there suddenly appeared before us
the surprisingly large Indian town of Achacache, with
a bay of Titicaca visible beyond it and a great stretch
of plain around. The main street of the town led
straight down among the houses, towards the great
domed church, with its fantastic towers, occupying
the whole of one side of the large plaza. There were
signs of an abundant Indian population, all apparently poor. On the main street stood two or three
houses of some importance, and a public school, in a
building labelled "Teatro." It was just a mud stage,
roofed over and open to a court-yard. The children,
forty or fifty perhaps in number, were shouting out
their lessons in chorus, in two divisions, the master
on the stage, the pupils in the pit. What surprised
me perhaps more than anything was the exceeding
cleanliness of the streets; no exceptional condition, as I
found during my many visits to the town. All the
streets appeared to be carefully swept every day.

The inn-keeper received us willingly, thanks to
Bieber's letter, and placed at our disposal quite a decent

room, opening on the courtyard, with a smaller room within it, which was actually furnished with a bed. I immediately sallied forth to inspect the plaza while dinner was preparing. It is a big square, surrounded by the church, the sub-prefect's house, one or two low communal buildings, and half a dozen native shops, gay with the bright-colored stuffs which alone take the fancy of the Indians. The colors were surprisingly good and very un-European, yet on inspection it appeared that most of them were cheap goods made in Germany to match samples of the old local products. An Indian woman always wears a short gown of bright-colored, fluffy-textured material; the colors they affect are crimson or orange, and, less frequently, blue or green. The sub-prefect was, unfortunately, absent, so I sought to communicate with the corregidor, a person of somewhat indifferent reputation in this place. He, however, was also away, and his wife was reigning in his stead. The letter from the prefect of La Paz was annexed by her, but nothing further happened; and when I sent to know what arrangements she might be making to supply the guides we wanted to take us next day to Umapusa, the answer was that she was doing nothing. I then sent to get my letter back, but they refused to give that up unless they were paid some money. Accordingly, I went back myself, walked into the room, found the letter, and took it away.

Our dinner was a complicated kind of soup, named *chairo*, served in a massive silver bowl, of simple, undecorated form, evidently very old. It contained fragments of meat and a quantity of potatoes of different sorts, hotly flavored with *picantes*. Bolivia is a great country for potatoes; they are one of the chief articles of food that the Puna produces. Many varieties are cultivated and prepared for food in many ways. I have been told that over a hundred different kinds of potatoes bless Bolivia. Some (called *chuño*) are put out at night to freeze and taken in before the morning sun brings on a thaw; some, on the other hand, are dried in the sun and taken in at night to be sheltered from the frost; some are wetted and frozen, and some are dried and frozen, and there are many other ways of preparing them. In our soup were both black and white sorts, besides tubers which were not potatoes at all.

CHAPTER XVI

OBSTACLES TO ASCENT OF SORATA

O N the morning of September 19th we rode away to find the farm of Umapusa, whence our ascent of Mount Sorata was to commence. Passing through a few by-streets, bordered by huts for the most part in ruins, we climbed over the end of the last of the low line of Permian hills, following a track worn deeply into the rock by centuries of traffic. On the top a wonderful view burst upon us, for at our feet was a very large, flat basin, which in the rainy season becomes an arm of the lake; beyond arose long, gentle slopes, some ten miles of ascent, and then, to crown all, the brilliant mass of our mountain, wreathed in shining clouds. Halting to gaze upon this entrancing vision, I observed an old Indian woman, clothed in rags, who was busy about some religious action. She was arranging loose stones together and apparently muttering prayers. When she had gone, I went to see what she had made, and found a little edifice like a prehistoric dolmen, with three stones set up on edge for walls and a fourth on the top for a roof. Later on, whenever we visited any of the sacred high places of the Indians, we always found them occupied by a multitude of these little models. Sometimes they might be numbered by hundreds, as, for instance, on the top of

Peñas Hill. It seems probable enough that the custom of building these little edifices is a survival from pre-Christian days. On inquiry, however, I was told that the Indians have been taught to call these things "Holy Sepulchres," and to associate them with Christianity.

We descended to the flat, crossed the little Achacache brook, now quite shallow, and, taking a wide circuit to avoid the swamp, gained the foot of the long slope, and so mounted to the *finca* of Umapusa.* It was a short ride, and might easily have been added to the previous day's march, had we known where to look for the place. The major-domo was out, so we had to wait an hour or two. When he came in, he received our letters, promised to give us all assistance, and led us about a mile farther up to a smaller establishment, a mud hut, over whose door was painted in crooked letters the word "Posada." This simple building is, in fact, an inn, situated on the ancient direct llama-track leading from Peñas over the Cordillera to the town of Sorata. From the *finca* to the *posada*, and some distance farther up, the whole slope was covered with the fields and mud huts of a large Indian settlement, while yet higher, bearing somewhat the relation to Umapusa that Caimbaya does to Cotaña, was a village named Fraskiya. The altitude of the *posada* is about 13,000 feet above sea-level; yet even here, and to some distance above Fraskiya, that is to say, well over 14,000 feet, crops are grown—*cebada* near the *finca*, and

* Uma-pusa means, "where water gushes out." The name is appropriate because of the numerous springs of water which rise near it in the damp season.

potatoes higher up. They had not yet begun to break the ground for this year's sowing, but during the course of the following six weeks ploughing and sowing were actively carried on, as I had occasion to observe.

The long day that was still before us was chiefly spent in making arrangements for an early start on the morrow. The manager of the *finca*, Miguel Tarifa, placed his son Cæsar at our disposal to accompany us, and sent up word to Fraskiya that Indians should be enlisted to go along with us next day. The guides employed their time in making collections for me, Maquignaz shooting birds, Pellissier quite as keenly hunting after insects, with satisfactory result. I worked at bird-skinning, and so the day passed. Unfortunately, the weather was none too good, for a strong wind blew, bringing over heavy clouds from the northwest. But the following morning promised better. when we set forth to ride up to Fraskiya. The enormous area and spread of Mount Sorata became apparent the nearer we approached. The summit was now no more than fifteen miles away as the crow flies, and we were directly advancing towards it ; but in so doing we interposed the rounded lower slopes between our sight and all except the tips of the great peaks. Thus we gained no further information of the work that lay before us than what we had acquired from the carriage-road. The slope itself, from the swamp below to the foot of the final rocks above, consisted entirely of alluvial deposits—that is to say, of rounded, water-worn stones and earth. Now and again large bowlders occurred, apparently too heavy to have been transported by water, but they were water-worn. Their presence

MOUNT SORATA

seemed to suggest that they had been carried by ice and afterwards water-worn; in fact, all the material forming the slopes resembled a moraine which had been rearranged by water after the retreat of the ice. This was true not merely of the slope above Umapusa, but of all the corresponding slopes leading up from the Puna to the rocky crest of the Cordillera. Following a little stream gully among the fields, and turning an abrupt corner, we put up four or five wild ducks, which hurried away down to the lake.

Arrived at Fraskiya, we rode into the court-yard of the *finca*, which serves also as burying-ground. To the amusement of the natives, I sat down on the edge of a newly dug grave, with my legs hanging over the side, quite unconscious of what the hole was intended for. All the inhabitants were gathered together, and an immense clatter of tongues arose; but Cæsar proved to be a man of influence, and, after no more than half an hour's delay, five Indians agreed to accompany us. Their names were Ilario Huanca, José and Manuel Mamani, Jeronimo Carbrera, and Manuel Lucan. The best of them all was José, a very wiry old man with a deeply furrowed, humorous countenance and an immense deal to say for himself, not a word of which, unfortunately, could I understand. He was the first to grasp the novel idea that we actually meant to climb the great snow-peak, and he had intelligent suggestions to make as to the best route of approach. Though quite an old man, he was eager to go with us, and was included in the party at his own earnest desire. As far as mules could climb there was no occasion for the porters to carry anything except their own provisions, the chief item of which was a supply of coca leaves for chewing. Cæsar brought dried mutton, of the kind called *chalonas*, a very useful provision for travellers in Bolivia. He also had a store of baked grains of sweet maize, which we found to be a good substitute for bread and easily portable. Bolivian Indians are traditionally supposed to be almost magically supported by coca. You hear stories of the long marches they make without food or rest, under the stimulus of coca. The fact, however, appears to be that the amount of food eaten by a Bolivian Indian in the course of a week is neither more nor less than the amount eaten by natives in other parts of the world. It is only that they have contracted a habit, doubtless by the assistance of coca, of postponing their meals for a very long time and making up afterwards for the fast. They are good, strong men, and excellent marchers, but they are in no wise better or hardier than the coolies whom I employed in various parts of the Kashmir Mountains.

The ascent was continued above the fields up a gently sloping moor, covered with tussocky grass. The view developed behind, over the two branches of the blue lake in the embrace of low golden hills. Clouds were pouring over the Huaillata Pass, which leads to the town of Sorata, and were creeping along the flank of the mountain towards us. A flock of alpacas were grazing at this level of the slope; llamas were met higher up. The alpacas resembled llamas, but their long fleeces were in a very untidy, tattered condition. The llamas were mostly females, for female llamas do not carry loads, but remain in the mountains while the males go off with caravans. The males, after a long journey, require some months of rest in the hills before they undertake another expedition. The first llamas I ever saw impressed me as of ungainly and even uncanny appearance; but it is impossible to become familiar with their splendid, intelligent heads, their beautiful, soft, large eyes, and fine, almost eagle-like expression, the noble outlines of the nostril, and poise of the whole head, without becoming attracted to these animals. On the hill-side they scatter about; but, once on the road, they travel together in a closely packed flock, and are difficult to divert from the direction along which they are travelling. They are timid, and their timidity drives them to huddle together. When annoyed, they spit at the object of their hostility with fatal accuracy and dangerous length of range. But they are perfectly docile in the hands of a driver they know. In size they are about equal to a donkey; their bodies and legs are like those of sheep, but taller; while they have a neck and head roughly resembling a camel's, but more beautiful, and expressive of a totally different kind of character. No man can ever be fond of a camel unless to the manner born; but it would be easy, I imagine, to make a pet of a llama.

After mounting steadily for three hours, it seemed that we were approaching the actual foot of the glacier, till, rounding over a little to the right, we suddenly found ourselves looking down upon a deep valley. It was once filled with a glacier, and is now in part occupied by a lake, held in by an ancient moraine dam, and called the lake of Saint Francis. The sharply outlined lateral moraines of the same departed glacier remain high above its waters on both sides. The valley is cut deeply into the great alluvial slope, and stretches back to the heart of the mountains. We saw its main branch going straight up towards the Cordillera, filled at the head by a considerable glacier, which drains the southeast basin of Mount Sorata. The three glaciers draining the south slope of the mountain, divided from one another below by rocky hills, likewise descend towards this valley and empty their waters into its main stream, and so into the lake of Saint Francis. The nearest to us of these side valleys swept round behind the slope on the crest of which we stood, and altogether cut us off from the great mountain; so that, though we were now at about 17,000 feet, it would be necessary for us to descend into this valley before we could attain the glacier and begin the real ascent. This was a disappointment. Two days' work were required to reattain, on the mountain itself, the altitude to which we had thus ridden on one of its outworks. Obviously, the place for our camp would be in the nearest side valley, at the foot of its glacier. The sooner we got there the better, for heavy clouds had now gathered behind us and were pouring rain upon the slopes up which we had come and upon the village below, though the mountain still continued clear.

Rounding the corner to the left, and losing the view of the lake, there burst upon me as I commenced the descent into the side valley a glorious view of the snowy peaks. At my feet was the valley into which we were to descend. The retreat of the glacier, which formerly filled it and joined the other glaciers I have mentioned, uncovered a series of small lake-basins at different levels. All of these have since been filled up by the mud deposits of the glacier-torrent. They are now represented by level grassy plateaus, fair to look upon. Above the highest of these plateaus rests the present snout of the glacier, which descends in fine ice-falls from the crevassed flank of a snowy peak. For the moment I fancied this to be the highest peak of Mount Sorata. It was, however, only an out-lier, the Hau-kaña peak. The opposite side of the small valley was formed by a rugged range of bare hills, the extremity of a ridge coming from the same peak. Between these rugged hills and the peak there was visible a depression or col, over which, as soon as I had identified the position of Ancohuma, it became obvious that our route to the foot of the highest peak must lie. Thus, it was abundantly clear that our base camp must be planted on the highest dry lake-basin at the foot of the glacier. From thence our next day's route would lie up the moraine and rocky slopes, along the left bank of the Haukaña glacier, to the col, where our second camp must be placed. The remainder of the way would lie up the snow-field beyond the col—that is to say, the snow-field draining directly southward from the high plateau and feeding the glacier which flowed down the next side valley beyond that one into which I was looking. These two glaciers have need to be named for the purposes of my narrative, and I called the nearer one, that by whose moraine we must first ascend, the Haukaña Glacier; and the next one, beyond the col, the Ancohuma Glacier. To the snowy peak straight ahead I gave the name Haukaña Peak.

A good path was unexpectedly revealed by the Indians, leading down to the Haukaña Valley. It soon became obvious that, at some time, not perhaps very recently, there had been much traffic into this remote recess, for a number of tracks zigzagged down or traversed round the slope, all obviously made by men and not merely by grazing animals. Inquiry elicited the information that a gold-mine had been worked by an English company in the immediate neighborhood of the point where I had determined to camp. The name of this mine was Hiska Haukaña, which means "little stroke." A rapid descent landed us on the second and largest of the old lake-basins. It was being grazed by a flock of llamas, who, as I thought, were attended by a Scotchman in a tam-o'-shanter hat; but he turned out to be merely the deceptive shadow of a rock. In such deceptive shadows, mimicking human or fanciful forms, it is probable that the traditions of mountain dragons and other strange beasts have their origin. The old lake-basin was about half a mile long, and afforded admirable grazing-ground for our mules. Some parts of it were swampy. In one corner there still remained a small shallow pool. The multitude of birds that presently revealed themselves in this retired locality was remarkable; it was also one of the most favored places for plant life that we discovered at any high level. A whole flock of green-headed humming-birds fluttered about a bush; two geese and half a dozen wild ducks were feeding on the pool. A pair of gulls took fright when they saw us, and, slowly circling round and round, rose gradually two or three thousand feet into the air, till they surpassed the height of the surrounding hills and could fly straight away to Lake

ROCKTOOTH CAMP (SECOND) ON MOUNT SORATA

Titicaca; but, even at their highest, they were far below
two condors soaring incredibly high aloft. Some snipe
were also put up on the flat, and there were other small
birds, which I was unfortunately prevented from collecting by lack of suitably loaded cartridges. The opposite
slope was formed of débris and broken rocks, among
which great numbers of bizcachas, little rabbit-like
beasts, were skipping about.

From the head of this boggy meadow, a path known
to the Indians still led on, even when the mules could
go no farther, up rocks rounded by the rasping of ice,
to a higher and very small lake-basin where the path
ceased. Close to the abandoned gold-mine we pitched
our main camp in the evening of September 20th. The
position was excellent, for the ground was level, soft,
sheltered, and dry. Near at hand was the foot of the
glacier up which our farther advance must be made.
While the tents were pitching, I went forth and shot
the toughest goose that ever dismayed human teeth.
He took a deal of shooting with the No. 6 shot, which
was the largest I had in my cartridges. Winged at
the first discharge, he waddled off up-hill at a smart pace,
along a llama-track. I puffed and blew, and yet could
not gain on him. A pursuit at 16,000 feet soon ex-
hausts any man. I became almost comatose, but held
on. At last the path ended, and he got among broken
rocks. I still had better ground, and so overtook him.
More dead than alive, I stumbled down-hill with my
burdensome trophy. A couple of bizcachas got up,
and I knocked them over. Next minute I wished I had
not, for gun and game were together so heavy that I
could hardly drag them and myself along. Night came

on, and I was still a long way from camp, toiling hideously. But something moved in the darkness; it turned out
to be the *arriero* looking after the mules. He shouldered
part of my load, and I reached the tents just in time for
supper. The skin of that remorseless goose now rests
in the British Museum. Near the edge of the grazing-
ground the *arriero* showed me his bed, a pile of sheepskins from the pack-saddles, with a heap of harness
close by in a corner of rocks. It looked a chilly place,
though he seemed pleased with it; he exchanged it readily
enough, however, for a small tent which I had brought
for him. He was really a most adaptable fellow, and
would have been content at any time to take up his lodg-
ing between a couple of asses. No persuasion would
separate him from the pack-saddles, on which he always
lay, fearing lest they should be stolen, a fate he appre-
hended for every loose object.

Behind our four tents rose an amphitheatral slope,
strewn with huge rocks fallen from the hill. Dry grass
in tussocks, one to three feet high, grew among the
rocks. The Indians lit this in the darkness. At first
it made a fire, pleasant to warm one's self at; but a rising
wind drove it up the slope. The flames leaped in sheets
from patch to patch, encircling the rocks and spreading
wider and deeper every instant. It was as though all
the gold had come glowing forth from its hiding-places
to mock us. The smoke shone like flame in the general
glare, and eddied round and up till it caught the moonlight, high aloft, and turned to silver. The cirque of
mountains around were illuminated to their highest crest.
Presently the fire disappeared from view behind a bend
in the ground, and only the glare from it could be seen

on slopes and smoke. We might have been on the flank of an erupting volcano. The Indians, flitting about like demons, spreading the fire, added to the weirdness of the scene. It was hard to believe they were men. Not till the conflagration died down did I find it possible to tear myself away from the splendid sight and close out the world behind the thin curtain of my tiny tent.

CHAPTER XVII

FIRST ATTEMPT ON MOUNT SORATA

NEXT morning I sent off the guides and Indians to carry up a relay of baggage and fix on the position for a higher camp. Two of the Indians caused trouble, whether through fear or mere idleness it was impossible to discover. They were with difficulty restrained from throwing down their loads and bolting then and there. They slipped away in the night. So, with only four Indians, we made our final start on the cold, bright morning of September 22d. The way, though steep and fatiguing, was easy from a mountaineering point of view. Sometimes the stones were loose. Now and again we had to turn up the hill-side, by some gully or other favorable gap, to round an obstacle. But advance was regular, and we were soon above the level where the surface of the Haukaña Glacier was covered with stones. We could not take to the ice, for it was too much crevassed. I now noticed what I afterwards had occasion frequently to observe in all the glaciers of Mount Sorata—the curiously dry, stony appearance of the ice, which looked more like granite than compacted snow. This dryness, as already explained, is due to the rapidity of evaporation over high tropical glaciers. With every aspect of insecurity in the form of overhanging *soracs* and incredibly steep ice-slopes, there was yet an unbroken

HAUKAÑA PEAK AND GLACIER

stillness, indicating that falling ice and other violent movements were of rare occurrence. There was no singing of the running waters, no slipping about of stones, no cracking in the substance of the glacier; in fact, no sign or sound of movement, such as the glaciers of the Alps are always emitting. In all the days we spent among the great ice-falls of Mount Sorata I never saw or heard the fall of the least fragment of ice. At times stones fell down the dry débris slopes near us, and then the Indians would cower with terror, saying that the devil was walking across the slope and that the stones were disturbed by the tread of his feet. The guides roared with laughter at this explanation, and their amusement presently affected the Indians, who for the rest of the day ceased to manifest signs of fear.

We thus rose to the point where the edge of the hill-side on our right came down to the level of the ice, and where the glacier surged up against it in splintered and broken masses like the turmoil of a tumbling wave. There was just a crack between the overhanging ice and the rocks, and along this we crept, thus gaining access to the other side of the dividing ridge, and reaching the edge of the Ancohuma Glacier by a short, steep, rock descent. A climb of twenty minutes led to a small tooth of rock, a continuation of the dividing ridge. Here we found a little hollow, where tents could be pitched in excellent shelter. The luggage and the sledge being thus transported to an altitude of nearly 18,000 feet, the work of the Indians was done, and they returned to the base-camp.

No sooner were the tents pitched than the first of a series of snow - showers fell. The temperature kept rising and falling. When the sun shone it was overpoweringly hot; and when a snow-shower passed over, the cold was suddenly intense. Heavy clouds were hanging on the hills. They presently flocked together into a gloomy roof, depressing to the spirits and auguring ill for the morrow. As I sat watching the changes of the scene, I asked myself more than once whether the game was worth the candle, for there was something so cold and unsympathetic about the gloom and the ice and the bare rocks that for a time it weighed like a nightmare upon my spirits. But when the clouds broke a little, revealing the ocherous plain with its ever-varying colors and the constant movement of clouds and cloud shadows upon it, depression passed away, and I lay motionless and happy on the tip of the rock tooth, enjoying the play of nature's mood. There was no sound save the pricking of the snow as it fell on the roof of the tents.

As far as the effects of altitude were concerned, I was comfortable enough; yet it cannot be said that we were in no sense incommoded by it. All three were disproportionately fatigued by the ascent, and were disinclined for any activity. Lying on the ground I counted my breaths—twenty-one and a half to the minute—breaths deep and audible as of a man asleep. The guides were breathing in the same manner. Before half the afternoon was over we were rested, and the men set out, as guides always will in strange places, to hunt for gold. Nor did they have far to go, for all that glittered was gold in their eyes, and they were soon the glad possessors of a number of specimens full of mica spangles. On the rocks round camp was no vegetation. The last plants we had passed were two or

THE COL NEAR ROCKTOOTH CAMP

HAUKAÑA PEAK

three hundred feet below the col. The only specimens of life we beheld were a few tiny midges, which tickled our faces and drowned themselves in the marmalade pot at tea. After sunset, when the tents were closed, we heard the cry of a bird fluttering around.

Little did we suspect, as we lay that night in our warm reindeer-skin sleeping-bags, what was going on below at the base-camp. Thus far our relations with the Indians had been pleasant enough. Though we had heard many stories about their unreliability, and had noticed that all travellers on the Puna went about armed to the teeth, we had seen nothing to suggest any necessity for precautions. This night, however, a party of superstitious natives crept up in the dark, intending to murder us in our sleep. They came from the village of Chiara-huyo, the hostile neighbor of Umapusa. The men believed that we had come to profane the sanctuaries of the mountain gods. If, as they had heard, it was our intention to climb to the summit of Illampu, they had no doubt at all but that we intended to carry away the great cross of gold and bull of gold which tradition asserts to have been planted there. Fortunately for all parties, we were not to be found, so the visit passed off peacefully; for, of course, to come up after us into the snowy regions was an adventure they never dreamed of attempting.

Next morning the weather was bad, a northwesterly gale blowing high aloft and the clouds eddying about on the mountain-side in bewildering fashion. But by noon a temporary clearance took place, so we loaded up the sledge and started out. Before we had gone far the storm settled down again even worse than before.

The four hours that followed were a time of violent and distressing labor both for the guides and me; for the glacier, which below had looked so smooth and gentle, proved to be neither. The slopes from the very start were so steep that it was all we could do to raise the sledge little by little. To begin with, we attached ourselves together by a climbing-rope in the orthodox fashion, so that if one fell into a crevasse the others might be able to pull him out, but the rope incommoded our efforts in dragging the sledge, and was very soon cast off. After trying a variety of adjustments, the guides found it best to walk side by side, each with a drag-rope over his shoulder and their arms linked together like affectionate brothers, while I pushed behind and was ready to stop the sledge from slipping back at our frequent halts.

Curiously enough, none of us this day felt so much oppression from the altitude as we had felt the day before; and the same was the case a fortnight later. when we returned up these slopes. Alike on Illimani, and both times on Sorata, we suffered more in the first struggle up to about 18,000 feet than we suffered from there to 20,000, though above 20,000 the labor became yet more severe. The reason I imagine to have been the same in both cases—namely, that up to 18,000 feet the line of ascent was in an enclosed valley, where the air had the character described by old mountaineers as "stagnant." All too soon there came crevasses involving devious zigzags and painful search for snow bridges. Then followed a snow slope where different tactics were adopted. The whole length of rope in our possession was stretched out, one end at-

DRAGGING SLEDGE UP MOUNT SORATA

tached to the sledge, the other carried up by us to its full stretch. Then, standing together, we hauled the sledge up, and by repetitions of the process attained the next level of crevasses. A more serious impediment had now to be overcome, for these crevasses were of enormous width and stretched from the precipitous face of the Haukaña Peak, on our left, right across to an impassable strip of ice-fall on our right. Fortunately, we always found a snow-bridge of some kind, though in the case of four big crevasses that followed one another in quick succession, the only bridges were flung across from one side to the other as an irregular floor from ten to twenty feet down below the lip of the crevasse. The sledge had thus to be let down to this crazy platform, dragged across the irregular and treacherous surface below, and then hauled up again with incredible toil on the far side. Such work soon tires a man at over 19,000 feet.

The only explanation I can offer for this series of depressed bridges is the following: Assume that at the close of a dry season one of the crevasses is open, and that during the next wet season it is plugged with a wedge-shaped snow-bridge, represented by the shaded area in Fig. 1 on next page. In the following dry season, as the glacier advances over a convex bed of rock, the crevasse will widen, and the wedge-shaped plug may thus descend ten or fifteen feet into the crevasse (Fig. 2). Such, at any rate, was the character of the bridges we had to cross.

Arrived at a point a little short of 20,000 feet, we had done all we could. There, in the midst of the snow-field, under shelter of a blue wall of ice, we set up our

tent and arranged to pass the night. With the petroleum stove snow was melted and boiled, and a light
meal prepared. As night came on the storm continued
to blow, clouds and darkness gathered, and snow began
to fall. But we crept into our sleeping-bags and grew

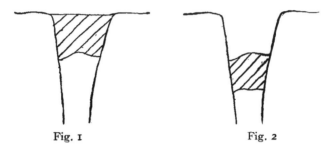

Fig. 1   Fig. 2

warm and oblivious to the bitter cold without. I at
once dropped off to sleep. Not so the others, whose confidence in the firmness of the tent was less well-founded
on experience than mine. The wind rose to a gale, the
tent-ropes sang like harp-strings, the sides of the tent
bulged and strained, and the men thought that they were
every moment going to be blown away. Not till early
in the morning did the force of the tempest somewhat
abate. When day broke we looked forth to find our
shelter almost snowed under. A dense fog hung over us,
and snow was still falling. Now and then the clouds
broke and showed that fresh snow was lying even down
on the Puna. Under such conditions our chances of
making a successful ascent this day were gone, for
the final peak was too steep to be trifled with.

As the morning advanced the weather seemed to be
settling; the sun shone fitfully forth, and presently a
view was obtained of the turquoise expanse of Lake

HOISTING SLEDGE AMONG THE BIG CREVASSES OF MOUNT SORATA

Titicaca beyond the white snow-field and the snow-speckled outer bastion of our mountain. As the sky cleared, the bright, new-fallen snow all round shone brilliantly beneath it. All traces of the discomfort we had suffered the previous evening from the altitude had passed away in the long rest of the night; we were ready and eager to be at work. Though it was too late and the snow was too fresh for our ascent, we still determined to make a reconnaissance. One more big and several smaller crevasses were passed above the camp before we gained the edge of the gently sloping plateau that stretched away at the foot of our peak; the snow upon it was deep and soft and the distance to the foot of the final wall proved to be far greater than we had imagined. Unfortunately, clouds still masked the culminating slope, but they were clouds that formed and faded, bending this way and that and crawling about on the snowy face, so that, as we sat and watched for an hour or two, we obtained a sight of almost all the details, and Maquignaz was hopeful that he had traced a practicable route to the very summit. I did not succeed in so doing, but put trust in his forecast, and entertained the hope of completing the ascent on the following day. While we were sitting on our axe-heads, planted in the snow, a faint mist came over, and immediately we were in a burning, fiery furnace. Instinctively, we covered our faces in our coats and pressed our hands to our eyes. It was a scalding moment. The mist was very transparent, and we could see the hills through it. It passed in a few minutes, and the cool air returned. Having no more observations to make, we ran quickly back to camp.

CHAPTER XVIII

VISIT TO SORATA TOWN

BAD weather now rapidly set in. Clouds regathered, snow began to fall, and wind to blow; so at four in the afternoon, leaving the sledge, the tent, the sleeping-bags, and all the food, we set forth to run down and await better conditions at a more comfortable level. After only twenty minutes of very quick running, we reached the middle camp, from which the ascent had occupied over four hours. Leaving the guides there to pack what was not required, I ran on and entered camp by 6.30 P.M. The Indians rushed up to me, kissed my hands, and hurried off with great willingness to meet the guides and relieve them of their loads. The bad weather had frightened them for our safety, and the *arriero* was loud in explanation of the horrors of the previous night from Indians and snow. "The whole Puna this morning," he said, displaying a very dirty shirt-sleeve, "was as white as this."

Next night the storm was worse than ever. Obviously, the weather was fairly broken. With this quantity of new snow the mountain would not be in condition for an ascent for some days. It was snowing when we awoke on the 25th of September, and stones were falling down the débris slopes in such numbers that many devils would have been required to account for

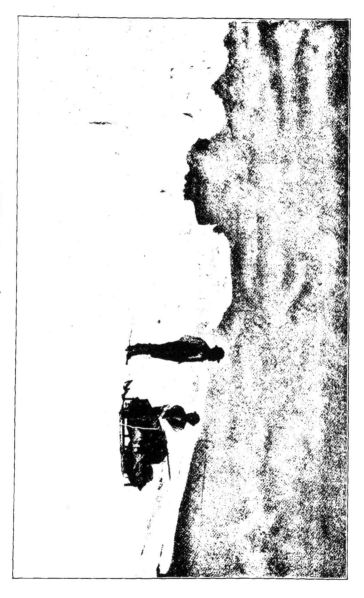

A HALT AMONG THE SÉRACS OF MOUNT SORATA

them. To-day we learned that the *arriero* shared the superstition of the Indians. He declared that on Illimani he had actually seen two devils kicking the stones down, and that they had long horns like a deer; but Maquignaz told him that that was nothing, for up at the top camp he had seen a black devil of extraordinary dimensions, which he proceeded to describe, whereupon the *arriero* said he would like to make haste down to a level inhabited by more respectable persons.

Leaving the camping-ground carpeted with snow, we marched away, preceded by one of the Indians playing on his pipe. We missed the path we came by, and struck another which led us out on to so steep a face of the hill that my stirrup as I rode actually scraped against the rock. Our descent was without incident till we approached the fields of Fraskiya, where a man was ploughing a field with a couple of bulls. At this moment Maquignaz fired at a bird, and so frightened the bulls that they took flight, and scoured the country with the plough flying loose behind them and the ploughman in wild pursuit, to the immense delight of our *arriero*, who shouted at the top of his lungs, "Arunca toro! arunca toro!" At Umapusa the heavy clouds were tearing overhead in the embrace of contending winds, and fog was drifting about on the hill-side. We were informed that morning that at Umapusa itself snow had been lying a span deep, to the astonishment of the inhabitants. Such weather in September is almost unknown on the Puna. What could be the reason? The Indians were in no doubt. It was because the gringos had profaned the abode of the gods on Illampu, and were being driven out by supernatural intervention.

Two youths, dressed in brand-new cowboy attire, wearing leather breeches, fringed all down the sides with little leather ribbons, and bristling with revolvers, cartridge-belts, and rifles, were halting awhile at the *posada*. They greeted me with a welcome bottle of beer. I thought highly of them in consequence, but the *arriero* would have it that they were men of no account. "For," he said, in his proud fashion, "I saw them eat, and they fed like dogs." It was by no means easy to win approval from our muleteer. Notwithstanding his humble station and rough mode of life, he was a man of no little dignity of character and a fine manner. He struck up a warm friendship with polite Louis Pellissier. Though neither of them knew the other's language, they contrived to understand each other remarkably well, but their intercourse was of a very formal kind. "Señor Don Luisi, have the kindness to support this box on your head," was the request I overheard the *arriero* make when he needed assistance in loading a mule. It was only in moments of great intimacy, or on the occasion of a sudden need, that he would call him Luisi without prefix. During the course of the afternoon he described to me the coming of the Indians to their camp, and how they disappeared when they found that we were away. "Cæsar," he said, "was all of a tremble with fright, but not I, for I have been a soldier and know no fear."

The bad weather continuing, I decided to fill the time by crossing the pass north of Mount Sorata and visiting the other side of the range. Accordingly, next day we left our mountaineering kit behind in the *posada* and set forth with our caravan. The road took us close by the village of the hostile Indians, but they were all out working in the fields and did not observe us. At Huarisata, a few miles on, we struck into the main highway from Achacache to the Huallata Pass. From this village to the top the road ascended a valley along the west foot of a series of mounded hills, on whose summits a number of huge ice-borne bowlders were observed. Where the naked rock was uncovered it had evidently been rounded by ice, a proof that the glaciers of Mount Sorata once extended as far as these hills. The road, with its many furrows deeply worn into the hill-side, was apparently an ancient track. Indeed, if one were to seek for the position most probably followed by a prehistoric trade-route across the Andes, it is exactly here that one would naturally expect to find it, for the valleys to the eastward of Mount Sorata, especially the Tipuani Valley, are rich in gold, and have evidently been worked for gold from the most ancient days We know that in the time of the Inca civilization gold-mining was actively carried on. Bearing in mind the former large population of the Titicaca neighborhood, and the ancient tradition which points to the basin of the lake as an important old centre of civilization, it is easy to believe that the Tipuani gravels supplied no small fraction of the gold that made the precious imitation plants of the gardens of the Incas. At that time the important town on the eastward side of the pass was doubtless Illabaya. Sorata town may have been a later foundation.

The road ascends slowly, and is as uninteresting a route as can be imagined, for the low hills to the right shut out all view of the high mountains, while to the left another range of hills hides the waters of the great lake. We did not then know that on the other side of the line of mounded hills there runs a parallel track commanding some of the most magnificent mountain scenery in the world. This day, however, was no day for views; long before we reached the top of the pass, clouds had come down upon us and snow was gently falling. Under such chilly circumstances, it was strange to meet an almost continuous procession of natives coming over from the tropical east, bearing canes in leaf and other arboreal decorations wherewith to embellish the fête that was due in a day or two. By the road-side, sheltering from cold under the lee of little walls of stones, were parties of Indians engaged in making cane pipes for sale. These Indians, I thought, regarded us resentfully; never a salutation came from them nor a glance of human recognition.

Though the attitude of the Indians to the whites differs rather markedly in outward expression in different localities, a deep-rooted hostility appears to exist between the races. Those who know the Indians best love them least. "There is no gratitude in an Indian," they say. "You may love a dog, or even a donkey, but a mule or an Indian, never." In the year 1866 the Indians were attacked and decimated by an epidemic fever, from which the whites were exempt. It is on record that the Indians made persevering efforts on this occasion to infect the superior race. Whenever Indian risings have taken place they have been accompanied by atrocities committed on the whites too appalling to be written down. Not unnaturally their suppression has likewise been sanguinary. After I left Bolivia in 1898 some sporadic Indian risings took place and frightful atrocities were perpetrated, the victims being for the most part half-breeds. Such incidents are, however, relatively rare. As long as the white population stands together they can easily control the Indians. It is only in times of revolution that the lower race gets a chance of revolting. This well recognized fact is the great preventive of serious revolutions in Bolivia.

The highest level of the road passes two or three pools of water, or swamps, representing wet-season ponds, and so leads up to the Huallata Pass (14,110 feet, Pentland). The descent begins with a long circling track that keeps near the top of an unimportant ridge, dividing the basin of Illabaya from that of Sorata town. The sudden change, alike in the character of the sparse vegetation and in the quality of the air, was more convincing proof that we had crossed the watershed than any immediately perceptible downward sloping of the way. But very soon we passed beneath the level of the clouds, and looked along their flat underside as under a ceiling. The picturesque town of Illabaya came in view, and the slopes of the valley, rich in forest, appearing astonishingly fertile to our eyes, so long accustomed to the bareness of deserts. All the way down to Illabaya, and some distance below it, the forms of the rock surfaces showed strongly marked glaciation. Here, in former days, an immense ice-fall must have poured down, while the neighboring valley of Sorata likewise was occupied, at the same time, by a glacier of enormous dimensions.

A romantic feeling always accompanies the descent

from a high mountain region to hot and fertile valleys. It is the charm that every one knows who has exchanged the Alps in a period of storm for the Italian lakes. Through such a transition, though with more marked extension of bareness above and richer fertility below, did we descend this day. Here and there we encountered remnants of the old paved and staircased road of pre-Spanish days. The little Carapata Pass (10,790 feet, Pentland) carried us over the intervening rib and gave access to the Sorata basin. Then there was only a long, zigzag descent down a straight hill-side to the bed of the valley below. We passed houses of more comfortable character than those of the high plateau, and gardens bright with geraniums and all manner of flowers. Thus we came to a pretty old stone bridge spanning the torrent, with a picturesque mill beside it, reminiscent of Italy or Spain. A short, steep ascent on the other side led in half an hour to the beautifully placed town of Sorata, which sits, as it were, at the very hem of the skirt of Illampu, on a jutting point of land close above the junction of two of the principal torrents that drain its glaciers.

Few towns in the world enjoy a more magnificent position. On either side are beautiful slopes, reaching aloft to fine crests of hills; straight in front there stretches away the purple hollow of the deep Mapiri Valley; while behind, the mighty precipices of Mount Sorata fling themselves aloft a sheer 14,000 feet to their crown of ice, and the protruding buttress named Illampu almost seems to overhang. The climate is as near perfection as climate can be, with never any great heat or biting cold, but generally so caressing a mildness in the

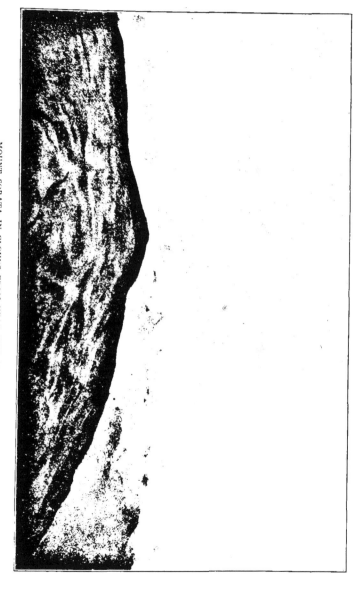

MOUNT SORATA IN CLOUDS FROM NEAR THE HUALLATA PASS

air that the defence of window-glass is dispensed with in many of the houses.* The mountain torrents yield a constant supply of excellent water, which irrigates the fertile soil; gardens produce almost every fruit that is asked of them, and a succession of the brightest flowers. If nature were better seconded by man at this chosen spot, there is hardly a limit to the beautiful results that might be attained. Even as it is, the little town, with its gay square and comfortable houses, is an unusually pleasant place of abode. Such was the opinion of several Europeans who make it their home; for Sorata is an important centre of trade, and is destined one day to become much more important. The tracks leading eastward from it over the next rib that descends from Illampu are the necessary lines of approach both to the gold-bearing valleys and the wonderful india-rubber forests of the Tipuani, Mapiri, and Kaka districts. It was for the purpose of making inquiries into the commercial prospects of this region that I had come to the place.

As if to prove that Sorata was a centre of civilization, I was greeted on my arrival by a newspaper reporter, demanding an interview. Pending the publication of the weekly paper, the reporter's remarks were written out in a clerkly hand and posted up on the saloon wall! He was succeeded by a large and friendly dog, who extended his patronage to me during the time of my stay, and with whom I took many a pleasant stroll. He seemed to be nobody's dog in particular, but enjoyed a large circle of acquaintances, and was familiar with

* Weddell, however, records having found the place cold and damp in the month of August.

the principal men of the town, while ignoring all commoner folk. I spent a pleasant evening in his company, seated in the public garden, by the plashing leaden fountain, decorated with carved swans supporting the basin, and the statue of a local celebrity crowning the whole. Bananas, cabbages, and vines, roses, geraniums, and arum lilies shared the impartial beds, and all manner of wild flowers grew between the cobble-stones of the paths. The whole town is rich in eucalyptus-trees, which distinguish it even when seen from a distance. The Indian streets were choked with pigs, and every other house was a shop for the sale of chicha, bad spirits, and coca, a small centre of nightly intoxication; for, no matter what other trade a man may have, he is sure to add to it the sale of chicha. In the neighborhood of the square were several large European stores, offering chiefly German goods for sale, while the commonest notice stuck up in the windows was " Here we buy india-rubber." A German merchant, Herr Gunther, kindly took me under his wing and made me his guest during the time of my stay. He owns an india-rubber forest in the Mapiri district. I likewise made the acquaintance of most of the representatives in Sorata of the other forest proprietors of Mapiri.

In the billiard-room of the inn that night I met a curious assemblage of persons, including several old inhabitants of the town, and an Irishman, who had spent fourteen years as manager of a rubber forest, and had come over for a week's holiday in this wild centre of civilized dissipation. Many were the stories they told me about the old days, vague traditions even stretching back to the last century, when the great Indian rising took place and Sorata was besieged by thousands of these revolted savages. The small number of Spanish inhabitants defended themselves bravely for a long time against overwhelming numbers, till the Indians, with malicious ingenuity, formed an artificial lake in the slope above the town, gathering into it an immense body of water. Suddenly breaking down the dam, they let the water rush upon the town, carrying down with it a mass of mud and rocks. The mud-avalanche thus formed burst upon the place, breaking through the defences and sweeping away all the houses in its path. The Indians poured in through the breach and massacred every individual in the place, man, woman, and child.

We talked of Illampu and of the chances of ascending it. Thus far clouds had not permitted me to behold it from this point.

"You have come at the wrong time for that," they said. "In the dry weather, in June and July, there is never a cloud upon the mountain, and we see it clear from base to summit, day after day; and a splendid sight it is. At sunset it grows red and shines out against the sky."

"I remember," said one man, "late at night, thirty years ago, long after the sun had set and darkness had come on, Illampu glowed red like fire, and all the people in the town saw it. Such a sight none had ever beheld. In great terror they ran to the church and the bells were rung. They thought the end of the world was come. Presently lightning and storm burst upon us, and the lightning flashed without cessation, so that it was like day, and we could see everything upon all the hills around. That was the most frightful storm that any man remembers. It was a famous event, and the news of it went all over South America, so that you will find accounts of it in the newspapers of the time."

CHAPTER XIX

THE RUBBER INDUSTRY

MY position in Bolivia as a scientific explorer commended to the consideration of the government, placed me in an exceptionally good position for obtaining information about the undeveloped resources of the country and the attitude of the leading men towards foreigners and foreign enterprise. I soon learned that it was the desire of men of all political parties to attract foreign, and particularly English and United States, capital, in order to open up the great mineral and other wealth of the country, which local capital does not avail to exploit. The mines, forests, and communications of Bolivia are mainly undeveloped. Gold, silver, copper, tin, antimony, and other metals exist in profusion in its valleys and mountains. There is a large Indian population existing on the verge of penury, and working for a very low and uncertain daily wage. Security for property is good. Thus, large silver-mines at Huanchaca, Potosi, and Oruro have been worked for many years by English and other companies most profitably, without impediment from the government, which has never manifested any inclination to confiscate by fiscal injustice the results of commercial enterprise.

Some trouble has at times been experienced in respect of the titles to property. This is not owing to the law, but to actual doubts about who the owner of the title may be. Different prospectors, or their heirs, possess, or think themselves to possess, overlapping claims, especially to mining properties in uninhabited regions, and the disputes thence arising lead to interminable lawsuits, which paralyze industry. Thus, in practice, the establishment of a good title may often prove costly. Lands or claims in old occupation, but now unworked, or little worked, are liable to have doubtful titles, which, however, it is no one's interest to dispute till some wealthy individual or corporation buys them from the apparent owner and spends money on their development. But lands such as the rubber forests, to which I shall presently refer at length, which have never passed out of the public domain into private ownership at all till quite recently, and under the provisions of acts of the legislature, are now owned by an indefeasible title which no one attempts to dispute.

It is only since 1878 or thereabouts that the existence of rubber in the eastern forest region has been known. Legislation was passed, in consequence of the discovery, defining the manner in which these lands may be acquired. A small annual rent per *estrada* must be paid to the government, and the lands taken up must be registered, with a map of the area. The annual rent may at any time be commuted at a fixed rate, after which commutation the land becomes the freehold property of the purchaser. If the annual instalments are not paid, the land lapses to the government. Thus the Mollendo rubber forests ought now to be owned on an indefeasible title, and many of them are so owned. The titles of others are defective, either because there has been irregularity in the payment of rent, or from mis-description in the deeds of registration. The map ac-companying the register often includes a very much larger number of *estradas* than the claimant has sched-uled or paid for; and this of necessity, for no one can count or correctly estimate the number of *estradas* in an area which has not been explored in detail. Again, the maps themselves are inaccurately surveyed. Thus a multitude of questions may be made subject of dispute. In other cases, I am told, men have obtained legal posses-sion of a number of *estradas*, patched about, and now claim to own all the land included between those *estradas*. The question of title is, therefore, one that in any par-ticular case needs close investigation on the spot. Up to the present time, however, none of these titles have been contested, and it does not appear to be the interest of any individual to contest them, while the chief in-terest of the government is to induce men of capital to work the forests, introduce immigrants, develop lines of communication, and so increase the general trade and prosperity of the country. It is not likely, there-fore, that the government will attempt to upset titles, even if they are not absolutely satisfactory, provided that the forests in question are properly worked.

The enormous and ever-increasing demand for rubber, made by modern electrical and other industries, renders the development of increased sources of supply a very important matter. From a recently issued United States Consular Report on the Resources and Trade Oppor-tunities of the Amazon Valley, I quote the following im-portant passage:

"I have learned that some accounts which have been

written concerning rubber, although not entirely mis-
leading, have not been quite accurate. The impression
created by the narratives of previous travellers who have
been up the Amazon is that the rubber production is on a
constant and endless increase. It is not generally believed, but it is nevertheless a fact, that the output is
not likely to increase to any marked degree unless a
much larger force of rubber-gatherers is sent into the forests than has been employed during the past year or two.
This is the opinion of the best-informed rubber-plantation
owners. Reports that the supply of rubber-trees is inex-
haustible are largely overdrawn. It is true that there
is no fear of immediate scarcity of rubber, and perhaps
there will not be for the next fifty years. It is believed
in well-informed circles that hereafter there will be a gradual but steady shrinkage in the rubber product unless the
present force of rubber-gatherers is largely increased,
because, in the first place, the trees conveniently located
near the banks of the rivers are naturally the first to be
worked, and in consequence are becoming exhausted
from constant tapping, the milk extracted being weaker
each year; hence the shrinkage in such rubber is very
great. In the second place, the rivers have all been
worked inland for a distance of about three miles from
their banks, and, in order to reach the so-called unex-
plored rubber forests still farther inland, it will require
much more time and necessitate three times as strong
a force. *Owners of rubber farms inform me that
milk drawn from rubber-trees five years ago possessed
twice the strength contained in that extracted from
the same tree to-day.* The islands near Para are all
overworked. Good judges can easily recognize rub-

ber drawn from overworked trees by its peculiar color "

If, therefore, the supply of Para rubber does not show signs of increase, the importance of developing other sources of supply becomes obvious. The following observations upon the forests of so-called Mollendo rubber are the result of my own observations and inquiries, in which I was much helped by Mr. M. Martindale, an English gentleman, whose acquaintance I made in La Paz, and whose long experience of the country was unreservedly placed at my disposal. Unfortunately, he was killed in the forest a year later by the fall of a tree.

In the European market a certain brand of india-rubber is sold under the name of Mollendo rubber. Of course, no rubber-trees grow at or anywhere near the Peruvian port of Mollendo on the Pacific coast. The name applies merely to the rubber which is shipped from that port. All the Mollendo rubber comes from the Peruvian provinces of Carabaya and Sandia, or the Bolivian provinces of Caupolican and Larecaja, the forest-clad valleys of Mapiri, Tipuani, Coroico, Challana, Zongo, etc., which descend northeastward from the Cordillera Real. The rubber is brought over various passes to Lake Titicaca, shipped by steamer to the Peruvian port Puno, and carried down by the Arequipa Railroad to Mollendo. All Mollendo rubber comes from the region above mentioned, and all the rubber produced in that region is exported through Mollendo. The statistics of the rubber exported from Mollendo thus form an impartial record of the production of the Cordillera valleys. The following are the statistics of the Mollendo rubber export for a series of years:

1893–94	37,587 lbs.
1894–95	80,734 lbs.
1895–96	251,341 lbs.
1896–97	292,121 lbs.
1897–98	491,087 lbs.

The statistics of the year 1898–99 have not come to my hands, but the output was very much larger than in the preceding year, and the industry is rapidly developing. The quality of Mollendo rubber, as judged by its price, is nearly equal to that of Para rubber, which is the best in the world. In the year 1898 Para rubber in the English market varied in price per pound from 3s. 5¾d. to 4s. 4½d., while Mollendo rubber varied from 3s. 4d. to 4s. 1½d. These exceptionally high prices, however, have not been maintained.

Considering the importance of india-rubber at the present time, it appears likely that some account of this little-known forest region may be of general interest.

It must be borne in mind that the area under discussion does not include the whole Rio Beni and the region of the plains about it, but only the upper part of that region in and about the foot-hills of the Cordillera. The rubber that comes from the lower Beni is carried away to the eastward, and emerges into the light of commerce as Para rubber. It is only the forests of the lowest eastward Cordillera slopes, and the plain immediately at their foot, that are comprised in the Mollendo district. The rubber-trees there are *Hevea lutea*, a large forest tree, approximately as big as an average English elm. These trees are self-planted. They grow in clumps, or *estradas*, of from 100 to 150 together, and these clumps rise well above the other forest trees, and can be seen from afar, so that the richness of any area can be judged by a general oversight from a commanding position.

In most parts of the world rubber-producing trees grow in a swamp, a condition which renders rubber forests direfully inimical to human habitation. In this respect the Mollendo rubber forest is a fortunate exception, for by all accounts it is not unhealthy; so, at all events, I was informed by an Irishman and a German, both of whom had spent the best part of from ten to twenty years in the forest. Their information was confirmed by many others. There are, of course, unhealthy spots, but the forest is not generally unhealthy. The reason is that the trees do not grow on level swamps, but on the sloping sides of valleys. For moisture they depend upon the almost constant cloud that hangs over them, and is formed by the cold air pouring continually down from the adjacent snowy Cordillera. This cloud is a geographical feature. The upper boundary of the rubber area is a contour line at approximately the 3000-foot level, above which altitude the tree will not yield milk in paying quantities.

The main valleys in the rubber zone are traversed by navigable rivers. The difficulty of transport begins at the upper limit of navigation, whence the rubber has to be carried by toilsome tracks over the high passes of the Cordillera. At present there are no roads and no mule-paths worth mention. There are a few tracks traversable by mules with difficulty. The best are the Mapiri and Tipuani trails, which converge on the town of Sorata, after surmounting passes of 16,000 feet altitude. New and better mule-tracks are now being made. The part of the forest which has thus far been best opened out is the area worked by these trails. Up to the present, therefore, Sorata has been the chief centre of the industry. The Challana and Zongo forests will not be properly worked till better tracks have been made over the two passes north and south of Mount Condoriri and down the respective valleys. Such mule-tracks could be easily made at a relatively small cost. When that preliminary work is done, the production of Mollendo rubber will rapidly increase. A great area in Caupolican is likewise as yet unworked for lack of roads and capital.

At present the main impediment to the development of the industry is not the difficulty of carrying out the rubber, but of carrying in the necessary supplies; for it is important to remember that the forest region is practically uninhabited, and the amount of cultivation is very small. A tropical forest left to itself produces little food for man. At one or two points by the river-banks, where gold-washing is carried on, there are small Indian villages; but the inhabitants are fully occupied, and have no time to spare for collecting rubber. Both labor and food have, therefore, to be imported from the high Bolivian plateau by the same route that the rubber retraces on its way to export. As development goes forward clearances will be made in the forest and the necessary food raised on the spot, as is already being done in the Sandia Company's *go-males*.

We are thus brought to consider the important question of labor. In the department of La Paz there are reckoned to be over 300,000 Indians, most of whom inhabit the high plateau region. These people are agricultural laborers, who work, under a kind of manorial system, for what corresponds to a very low rate of pay—a starvation wage, in fact. They cannot be described as an industrious folk, but they are extravagant, and their extravagance of expenditure on festivals, and especially on festal raiment of a costly and gorgeous character, leads them to temporary emigrations from home, to which also they are frequently driven by dire necessity. They are wont, under such circumstances, to pledge their labor in advance, and their extraordinary honesty makes the avoidance of their pledge an event of extreme rarity. Employers needing labor secure the services of agents, who visit Indian villages, and either directly, or through the corregidors or presidents of the villages, enlist the required workmen. Payment is generally made in advance, for the Indian has to leave money with his family and to provide himself with food for the time of his absence in the forest. He transports the food either on his own back or on that of his donkey, and sometimes he takes his wife and family with him. He contracts either to work for so many days, or to bring out of the forest so many pounds of rubber. The time spent by him on the journey to and fro is not paid for. In the case of a mine or other enterprise that has been running for some time, a certain number of Indians become habituated to working for

it, but they generally do so only for portions of the
year, returning at stated intervals to their homes for
the purpose of pursuing the cultivation of their lands.
All depends upon how the Indians are treated by their
employers. If they are well treated, they will return
and bring others with them, even without payment in
advance, if provisions are supplied to them at the place
of labor. The system is not a very satisfactory one,
and is not capable of indefinite extension; though undoubtedly, if the forests were worked on a large scale,
and the Indians were well treated and punctually paid,
a change in their habits might be brought about. It is
not, however, probable that the forest region could ever
be colonized by plateau Indians, the difference of climate
and level between the two countries being so strongly
marked. Whenever an organized attempt is made to
exploit these splendid forests on a large scale, foreign
labor will have to be imported, and it will be necessary
to seek Chinese coolies in San Francisco, or Italians
from Buenos Ayres, or to fetch Hungarians from Europe
or negroes from the West Indies, as has in fact been
successfully done by the Chicago - Bolivian Rubber
Company in its Huanay forest. Japanese coolies
were also tried but did not give satisfaction. Such
colonists would live in the forest, and would cultivate
the ground as well as work the rubber-trees. Their
labor would be supplemented by that of Indians, but
a steadier industry would be the result.

The extraction of rubber is one of the simplest crafts
in the world, and can be learned quickly by the most
ignorant. The process is as follows: The workman,
starting out very early in the morning (for when the

sun is high the trees cease to bleed), carries with him a number of little tin cups called *tichelas*. Arrived at a tree, he makes one or more small incisions in the bark, and attaches one of the tin cups below each incision, by pressing it into the soft bark. The number of incisions that can be made in a tree at one time is variously stated. A strip of the bark all down the tree, one-third of the circumference in width, must be left unbroken, or the tree will be liable to bleed to death. The cup, of course, collects the drops of sap that bleed from the wound in the bark above it. Ultimately, the wound in the bark is covered by a film of dried sap, which also is afterwards collected. The workman proceeds from tree to tree, attaching his cups, till he has tapped from 75 to 150 trees in his *estrada*, according to his industry and the nature of the ground. After the hour when the sap ceases to run, the man goes round again, carrying a tin vessel with a cover, into which he pours the milk that has run into the *tichelas*. When all the *tichelas* have been emptied, the man returns to his *barraca*. Some collectors tap the trees in the morning and return to collect the milk in the evening, while others tap in the evening and collect in the morning. At the *barraca* the collector lights a fire of palm wood, with which the nut of the Montacu palm is mixed, if it can be obtained. He places a funnel over it to collect the smoke, and then, taking a kind of small wooden paddle (something like a squash-racket bat) in his hand, dips the broad end into the milk, which covers it with a thin layer. He now holds the paddle over the fire in the smoke, turning its faces alternately to the heat. The layer of milk is thus rapidly smoked and coagulated into hard cured rubber. The paddle is then dipped into the milk again, and the process repeated until a large cake has been formed. When the cake has reached a convenient size, it is slit down the sides and stripped from the paddle. The figure-of-eight-shaped lumps thus formed are ready for export. They still contain about 7 per cent. of water, which gradually dries out in the next few months, and for which allowance must be made in weighing. In the Mapiri district it is usual to cure the production of each day separately, so that each collector's work can be controlled. Moreover, rubber so cured can be easily tested for cleanness and purity. Lower down the Amazon the custom is to smoke one day's rubber on top of the previous day's, making large *bolachos*, into which dishonest workmen more easily introduce stones and other adulterations.

The average amount of rubber which one collector produces on one day is very variously stated. On the Lower Amazon, seven pounds daily is the figure quoted; on the Upper Amazon, twenty-one pounds daily. In the Mollendo district the lower of these figures does not appear to be reached under present management. To this cured rubber must be added the scraps and remnants called *sernambi*, which include the cicatrices of the incisions in the bark, the cleanings of the *tichelas*, etc. The amount of *sernambi* is equivalent to about 10 per cent. of the smoked rubber, and its price is from 15 to 20 per cent. less.

The *pica*, or rubber harvest, is collected twice a year in the Mollendo forests, from April to July, and from October to March. It appears that a single tree can only be tapped during three months of one year, and then needs nine months' rest. If thus treated, and if a good broad strip of bark is left untapped from bottom to top, the health of the tree does not seem to be interfered with. For how many years it is possible to go on tapping a single tree, we do not yet know. There is a tree in the *barraca* Christina, in Señor Violand's San Antonio estate, which was stripped of all the bark on one side, and yet has yielded milk from the remaining bark during six *picas* in six successive years; the tree still retains a thoroughly healthy appearance. It is certain that the life of a tree, though annually tapped, is a long one, and exceeds the fifteen years which are required for the growth of a tree from seed, so that the forest may be perennially tapped and will give a fairly constant yield when thoroughly opened up and worked. This, how-ever, implies that the trees are carefully handled; the yield of a mishandled tree falls off. The average yearly output of a full-grown tree is variously stated. Some put it as high as seven pounds; no one puts it at less than three pounds of cured rubber (after 10 per cent. has been deducted for drying).

The cost of production, in Bolivian dollars, of 100 pounds of Mollendo rubber in the Mapiri forest is as follows:

Paid to contractor, per 100 lbs............................	73.00
Loss in weight, 10 per cent...............................	7.30
Freight from the forest to Sorata town....................	5.00
Commissions and road tolls...............................	.60
Cost of administration...................................	10.00
Sacking, packing, commission, and freight to Chililaya, on Lake Titicaca..	2.20
Freight, insurance, and all incidental expenses to London.....	12.00
	110.10

Or, reckoning the Bolivian dollar equal to 18*d.*, the cost of a pound of Mapiri rubber put in London is 19.82*d.*

From the books of two other forest-owners in the same neighborhood I find a slightly higher cost, 20.16*d.* per pound. The present price of this rubber in London is about 4*s.* per pound.

Coming now to a consideration of the possible supply of rubber to be drawn from the Mollendo forests, we enter a region of conjecture, for, of course, the trees have not been counted, nor even the number of *estradas.* A part of one estate has been recently proven to contain 6410 *estradas* (961,500 trees), when, according to the original estimate, the whole estate contained only 500,000 trees. Twenty million trees may be taken as the lowest probable limit of the number of trees, while they may not improbably turn out to reach fifty millions or even more. Now, in the season 1897–8, the amount of Mollendo rubber exported was 491,087 pounds, which, at three pounds per tree, represents the yield of only 163,695 trees, and the same number of days' labor at three pounds per man per day. If one Indian is taken as working for three weeks, it represents the labor of only 7795 Indians out of a population of 300,000 in the Department of La Paz. The possible increase of output is thus clearly enormous. How is it to be brought about?

Without going into financial questions concerned with any possible purchase of the estates and concentration of them under single management, a few essential features of the problem may be pointed out. To begin with, the first necessity is to make good mule-roads over the high passes that lead from the town of Sorata and from the Bolivian plateau to the chief eastern valleys, and down those valleys to the forests. These roads would, of course, be very useful to the gold-miners, coffee-planters, and others whose work leads them to the eastward. They are, therefore, rather the work of the government than of the rubber-forest proprietors; but the government is poor and can only afford to make them by slow degrees. If made at all, in the immediate future, the forest proprietors must make them. The main roads having been made, it is necessary to cut forest-tracks from one *estrada* to another, as only the *estradas* easily accessible have yet been touched. This implies additional labor, wise oversight, and intelligent exploration.

At present all the food consumed by the rubber collectors has to be carried into the forest from Sorata or the plateau—a great waste of labor. It would be perfectly easy to raise any quantity of food in the hot valleys, which are of the richest natural fertility; but such cultivation implies preliminary colonization. As already stated, it would be impossible to colonize these low, hot valleys with Indians from the Tibet-like plateau. Chinese coolies are the class most suited for such work. They could be obtained very easily from San Francisco. A nucleus of such men, who would soon become expert in working the rubber forests, would enable the industry of rubber collection to be far better organized than it is to-day, and opportunities of theft would be reduced. Large areas in these valleys which do not carry rubber are suitable for coffee plantations, and such plantations as do exist produce the finest coffee of South America and some of the finest in the world, so that here,

also, important future developments may be expected.
What is true of coffee is true also of coca, for which a
large local market exists among the Indians of Bolivia.
Such developments of the rubber industry imply not
merely concentration or co-ordination of proprietorship,
but skilled administration and scientific experience,
which could only come in the wake of capital. At
present, everything is done experimentally or by rule of
thumb.

The Bolivian government would certainly favor any
such enterprise, provided that road-making and colonization were an essential feature of it. With their
help the business of recruiting Indian laborers would be
greatly facilitated, for the village corregidors have
much influence over the Indians, and can promote or
hinder their enlistment, or turn them in one direction
or another, very much as they please. Under any cir-
cumstance, however, the future of this region of tropical
valleys descending from the eastern face of the snowy
Cordillera Real of Bolivia is certain to be prosperous,
and its development will soon attract much attention.

CHAPTER XX

THE EASTERN VALLEYS

I HAVE been tempted to write thus at length about the india-rubber forests beyond Sorata because the subject is one of general interest at the present time. It is, however, as portal to a great gold region, not improbably as rich and important as the Rand, that Sorata is destined to attain world-renown sooner or later. From the slopes of Mount Sorata and its neighbors there descend to the north and east four important valleys—the Mapiri, Tipuani, Challana, and Coroico. These four valleys have long been known to be very rich in gold. At the head of the Tipuani Valley is Yani, of which I shall have something to say hereafter. These valleys are all relatively steep. They are traversed by torrents, which rise very rapidly in the rainy season and which carry along immense bowlders. In the rains also great landslips fall down the sides of the valleys. Between the landslips, the floods, and the bowlders, gold-washing on a large scale with the necessary machinery has never been a great success in these valleys. Canals made to carry a head of water to a point above a placer-mine have been made more than once, but nature has destroyed them before they could be used. Bowlders have been blasted and areas of gravel cleared for washing, and then a flood has come and rolled in a new lot of bowlders before the washing could be accomplished. Machinery has been carried over the Cordillera and installed, and then some landslip has buried it or flood overwhelmed it. Add to these difficulties the fact that in a region where gold does in fact exist in great richness, and where it has been known and worked since prehistoric times, there exists no yard of gravel that does not belong to some one. As there does not exist any accurate detailed map, the claims are all ill-defined and frequently overlap. Then many claims have lapsed and new denouncements have been made of the ground. As soon, however, as any one tries to work such a new denouncement, the former owner's representative arises with a law-suit and disputes the new-comer's title. Pending the suit, work has to stop. For these and other reasons it seems improbable that any foreign company is likely in the near future to do much profitable gold-washing on a large scale in any of these four valleys. The gold that is produced from them will continue to be produced by small groups of native workers, operating without machinery in the crudest of old-fashioned methods.

The four valleys mentioned unite near Huanay to form the relatively slow-flowing and navigable Rio Kaka. The gravel and sand-banks that exist along the margin of the Kaka have recently been found to be immensely rich in gold. A company has been formed, which has obtained possession of these banks, and is now introducing machinery to work them. There is no trouble about titles; there are no bowlders and no serious floods. Much gold will probably be derived from these banks during the next few years. The gold in question is a flake gold, and has evidently come from a secondary formation in which it has been submitted to pressure. All the gold-bearing rivers tributary to the Kaka flow across such a formation, slate underlying conglomerate. Both the slate and other conglomerate were picked at by the Spaniards, and many small tunnels may be observed cut into them. The probability seems to be that both the slate and the conglomerate are auriferous, and not unlike the Johannisberg Rand. The application of modern methods of working is about to be applied to these beds, and, if the present showing is confirmed, the whole of the belt of foot-hills formed of them will presently become the scene of a great mining indus-try. When that comes to pass Sorata will wake up as an important transit station. Puerto Ballivian, near Huanay, will be the Bolivian Johannisberg, the Ama-zonian port of the Bolivian Rand.

In this same country, elevated about 2000 feet above the rubber forests, there is a large area of fine grazing land, ranged over by herds of cattle gone wild. These cattle will attract the attention of stock-raisers when the gold rush begins. The surrounding country con-tains any amount of land suitable for the produc-tion of all kinds of food for man and beast. All it requires is population. When the people come, the wealth that they may take out of the ground is almost limitless. There hardly exists in the world an area by nature richer, or more beautiful, or better adapted for colonization by white men than this splendid belt of the northeastern foot-hills of the Cordillera Real.

Having exhausted the time I could afford for Sorata and its neighborhood, we set off to return over the pass to Achacache. The bad weather still continued. As we rose to the col, we entered the cloud, sweeping up, as usual, from the Mapiri Valley and pouring over on to the Puna, a part of that warm drift of damp air from the eastward to which the bad weather owed its origin. All hopes of surveying the north face of the Sorata mountain group being thus postponed, there was nothing to be done but to ride down to the town. Rain-storms pursued us; the energies alike of man and beast were devoted to making headway as fast as possible. The mules, evidently well acquainted with the road, required no urging; as soon as the rugged portion of the track was left behind, and the margin of the plain reached, off they went at a gallop, devouring the way. On arrival at Achacache bad news was encountered; the Indians of Umapusa refused to return to the mountain without some escort that would secure them against the vengeance of their hostile neighbors. It was universally believed that we were responsible for the bad weather, which, coming at this unseasonable time, interfered with farming operations. The sub-prefect was still absent from his post, so that a visit to La Paz could not be avoided. As a matter of fact, the time was not wasted, for the bad weather lasted on until our return, and climbing would have been impossible for that reason alone.

I decided to enlarge my knowledge of the Puna by taking the northern and more direct track, which goes from Achacache through the town of Peñas, a place that derives its name from the crest of peaked rocks intervening between it and the main high-road from Chililaya to La Paz. To the summit of these rocks we afterwards ascended, as will be described in its place.

The track we had to follow led between the hill of Achacache and a neighboring sandstone and conglomerate mound named from Abichaca, a village at its base. This point was decided upon as one of the principal stations for the triangulation which I was to make after the climb of Mount Sorata had been accomplished. Little, however, did we guess what complications this choice was destined to involve. Other sandy and stony hills succeeded on both sides, and for hours we wound about among them, along desert valleys, with seldom any distant outlook towards the Cordillera. The stones, plentifully strewn over these hills and in the valley bottoms, were rounded and obviously water-worn, but the majority of them, I believe, have been weathered out from the conglomerate, and not shaped by recent water action. The summit of Abichaca Hill and of several other similar hills were occupied by small buildings of the type called *chulpas*, most of them being edifices of pre-Spanish erection, built, as the natives say, in "the times of the Gentiles." One summit bore a much larger ruin, whereof a row of piers of considerable size was visible from a great distance. At the foot of the slope there now stands a large church, which has supplanted its loftier predecessor in popular veneration. The policy of the Spaniards appears to have been to consecrate to Christian purposes the sites of ancient superstition.

The corregidor of Peñas sheltered us for an hour or

two in the middle of the day, so that we avoided visiting the inn, of whose existence, indeed, we were ignorant. I afterwards learned that the place has a very bad reputation, for the Peñas Indians are some of the worst on the Puna, and the inn had been the scene of terrible tragedies. It had been noticed that several travellers, known to have passed along this road, were seen no more. Inquiries were instituted, and suspicion fell upon the innkeeper of Peñas, who was observed to be unusually prosperous. The *tambo* was carefully examined. Excavations were made in the floor of one of the rooms, with the result that the bodies of a large number of murdered men were found buried beneath it.

Pushing on, as soon as the mules had been fed, we struck away along the foot of the precipitous face of Peñas Hill, with the long slopes leading up to the clouded Cordillera on our left. Clouds and storm had gathered over the mountains and swept down upon the Puna; black columns of tempest, stretching out from the great mountains, reached over on to the plain, trailing black veils of rain or gray skirts of hail. When Peñas Hill was passed we came out on the open Puna, and found the dust whirlwinds dancing about it in countless multitudes. A violent and wide-spreading storm seemed about to break, but, as no shelter was at hand, there was nothing to be done but push forward on our way. We passed the Tambo de Perez, an inn often mentioned in descriptions of travel in Bolivia, and came to the old *tambo* of Patamanta, just at the foot of the Villaque Hill, which was destined to be our second principal surveying station. The mules were so fatigued that an hour's halt had here to be made. Then forward again in the growing night, along the foot of the hill, and across the wide, almost dry channel of the Vilahaque torrent, where black night overtook us.

Now the thunder - storms, through which we had threaded our way as through the trees of a forest, were raging in every quarter of the heavens. By good fortune, they always passed over the road either before our coming or after our passage. An almost unceasing coruscation of electric fire was playing in the great cloud that covered Illimani. Directly ahead was another storm behind Okomisto. Three more storms flashed their great strokes of light, apparently on the crests of the low hills bounding the Puna to the west. Through a hollow in the overcast sky the moon came out and shone upon the plain. Not a creature was encountered, even after we had joined the carriage-road and were approaching Okomisto; not a light shone in the scattered cottages of the Indians. Between the booming of the thunder absolute silence reigned all around. The tired beasts plodded slowly forward. At last, still far ahead, the lightning showed the peaked outline of the row of stacks that marked the post-house at Okomisto. The cold was bitter, and we were all suffering from an utter numbness, so that from time to time each had to dismount and bring back feeling into his limbs by tramping along the road.

At last the welcome sound of barking dogs showed that the post-house was near; we began to promise ourselves supper and the reward of bottled beer to wash it down. Without the barricaded gate I shouted for admittance, but only the barking dogs replied. We shouted and hammered away for ten minutes, with

sinking hearts, but still there was no voice, nor any
that replied. When at last we were on the margin of
despair, the gate gave way, and we could advance to
the door of the house. But that also was barred, and
the man within refused admittance. He said: "Let me
alone; my children and I are in bed; we cannot take you
in." Presently his heart melted, and he admitted us
to the mud hut where the post-travellers dine. "Here,"
he said, "you may pass the night, if you please." But
the beer was all exhausted, the food all eaten, and the
only condiment of any sort that remained was half a
bottle of that universal commodity of South America,
which no remotest hut seems ever to be without—
Worcestershire sauce. The crazy table still bore the remnants of the last traveller's food, dirty plates, and crum-
bled bread, but there was not so much as a biscuit to be
had. The filthy floor had not been swept since the place
was built, but on it we had to sleep as best we could.
Our host absolutely refused to receive the mules, but
he directed the *arriero* to an Indian's farm, half a mile
away, where they could be fed. Such as the shelter was,
we were glad enough to reach it, for we had ridden more
than fifty miles since morning, and fifty miles at a slow
jog-trot behind baggage-mules continually straying
from the way and having to be brought back is a fatiguing day's work.

Next morning at peep of day we found great areas of
the Puna covered with fresh-fallen snow. Leaving the
baggage-mules to come on at their leisure, we cantered
off, and were in La Paz by nine o'clock. The bad
weather continued during the time of this visit, and
great thunder-storms raged even over La Paz itself,

so that when we returned to Achacache the mountains and the upper slopes of the Puna were all alike whitened with thick, new snow. It was, indeed, as though the elements had combined against the possibility of any high ascents. For years past no such weather was remembered at this time of year.

Early in the morning of the 5th of October we were again at Umapusa, hoping to go up that same day to Hiska Haukaña camp, for means had been taken to quiet the hostile Indians, and the way seemed again open before us. But we had reckoned without knowledge of the Indian calendar, for this day, as well as the morrow and the day after, were fêtes, when every self-respecting Indian at Fraskiya must be properly drunk. The delay proved to be unimportant, for the weather was worse than ever, and snow fell down to our level with little cessation. I filled the time by shooting geese on the swamp below the village and reading a two months' collection of English newspapers backward, which is a remarkably entertaining way to become acquainted with reports of the doings of the world. On the 7th of October the bad weather culminated; snow lay thick down to the margin of Lake Titicaca. Then the sky cleared and the sun shone out on a white earth, in the midst of which glittered the fiery blue surface of the lake. Our projected attack on Mount Sorata was become a forlorn hope.

CHAPTER XXI

CLIMBING ANCOHUMA

O N a brilliantly fine morning we set forward. "In nombre de Dios!" the *arriero* cried, "for we Peruvians pray to God at the beginning of every enterprise, since He has power in all things." Sorry looking, indeed, were the Indians of Fraskiya, who were gathered in a body to meet us in the court-yard of the farm. Most of them had broken heads, for the entire village had concluded its holiday with a free fight, described by the combatants as having been per-fectly splendid. It had left behind it many apparently unhealed quarrels, which Cæsar was called upon to settle. The women were the great talkers; one old and toothless dame waxed eloquent, and harangued him for nearly an hour, while the men stood sadly round and occasionally protested against her words. Ultimately, affairs were settled, and our old porters agreed to come with us, though José for a while hung back. He said that he had pains inside his head, as well as the great visible gash that everybody could see outside it. We told him there was no medicine for a headache like a visit to higher altitudes. His old wife went and fetched him a warm blanket, and he resigned himself to his fate.

The ascent to the camp was diversified by the fall

of a baggage-mule, which unfortunately broke our spirit-bottle into the salt and sugar, but, as a set-off, I presently flushed a small covey of gray partridges. Next morning we climbed early to the higher camp, accompanied by three porters, the weather being still fine. The same little bird that had fluttered around our tents when we were there before was still flying about, uttering a shrill cry; I had no heart to shoot it. The Indians went back, leaving us halted for lunch by our baggage reserve. We then lay for an hour asleep in the hot sunshine. Before sunset we had completed the next stage of the ascent, and were standing beside the tent, sledge, and baggage, which remained as we had left them. The amount of new snow that had fallen could easily be measured by the deep hollow wherein the tent lay, while the sledge was so buried that it had to be dug out. The minimum thermometer inside the tent only registered 12½° Fahr., not a severe amount of cold for a fortnight's stormy weather in early spring at nearly 20,000 feet above the sea.

The tent was soon set in order; the petroleum stove turned the melted snow into soup, coffee, and even punch, with the needful ingredients. In the sleeping-bags we were as warm and comfortable as in beds at home; yet sleep would come to none of us, probably because we had exchanged a moderate for a high elevation so suddenly. When we were here before, all slept well; but we had come up by 2000-feet stages; this time we came up by one 4000-feet stage, and we could not sleep. The secret of how to gain a very high altitude is to ascend by short stages, and to stop a night at each stage. Above 17,000 feet, 2000 feet a day is enough. You can do more, but the loss in rest and re-habilitation outweighs the apparent gain in time. I have slept for four nights at about 20,000 feet, and am satisfied that this is by no means the limit of height where a man can sleep. Probably 23,000 feet is not an impossible camping altitude, if it is reached by stages of 2000 feet or less.

The night was very cold. At one in the morning, when we began preparations for the climb, there were 30° Fahr. of frost. In the polar regions this would be a trifle, but polar explorers work at sea-level, and fill their lungs, each breath, with a supply of oxygen suffi-cient to keep the fires warmly burning within them. If their supply of oxygen were halved, they would find Arctic cold insupportable. At 20,000 feet the air is so thin that the supply of oxygen drawn in at a breath is only about half the sea-level supply.

Before two o'clock in the moonless night, we quitted the tent on our upward way. The glittering canopy of stars was disfigured by patches of drifting cloud of evil augury. A single candle was all the illumination to our dubious way over the hard-frozen snow-slope between two ghostly rows of white mountains. There were many crevasses, and large ones, too; by candle-light they looked gigantic, for we could not see to the other side. All, of course, were profoundly deep, and some were wide open. Others, like those we had dragged the sledge over, were bridged across from ten to twenty feet below the top. Of course, there were plenty of holes and gaps in these bridges. To lean over the edge of a great crevasse and peer down to see whether there were a bridge below or not was a weird experience. Sometimes we were not sure, and had to let a man down to ascertain. The sides were roughly vertical and difficult to scramble down in day-time, when one could see to cut steps and hand-holds; by night the difficulties were much increased. We had to peer about to find the solid parts of the snow-bridges and to avoid the holes going through into the bowels of the glacier. To clamber up the far side of the crevasse afforded another troublesome problem. Notwithstanding these petty miseries, the climb in the night up the glacier was delightfully romantic. The darkness, the uncertain flicker of our fire-fly candle, the utter silence, the angry clouds, the starry heaven, and the vaguely felt, rather than seen, expanse of snow and surrounding peaks in the bonds of a frost like the grip of a demon's hand, combined to produce on all of us an immense impression. None but necessary words were spoken. The silence was too awful to be lightly disrupted. We advanced as rapidly as the altitude permitted, though our powers were thus submitted to a severe and painful strain, for the cold was now much more intense than at camp, and was doubtless many degrees below zero. Our breathing was hard and loud; our hearts beat audibly; we were working up to the verge of our possible strength, all three being in the finest state of physical condition.

Half-way up the long last slope of the glacier, the basin-like slope that seems from below to be a plateau, we beheld the waning crescent of the moon just above the edge of the eastern crest. For a moment of indescribable beauty it hid behind a stately pyramid that looks down on hot Tipuani, and the deep, damp valleys, whose streams roll over ungathered gold, and whose banks bear countless rubber-trees of the finest quality in the world. But the moon was not to help us; in a few minutes it had passed behind thick clouds and all its light was blotted out.

Thus about 4 A.M., in absolute night, we approached the base of Ancohuma's final peak. We had arrived too soon, for, in the enveloping night even the main features of the great face of snow, that rose above us with an appalling and unanticipated steepness, could not be distinguished. It was too cold for halt or hesitation. All we could do was to make for the foot of what, if our memory of the previous inspection were correct, should be a long, unbroken strip of snow leading far up. In what difficulties it might involve us above we had no notion at all. During the last hour the condition of the snow had altered for the worse. Near camp it had been hard as rock. Higher up came a softer substance. Here at the foot of the peak it was like flour, each granule of ice so hard frozen that it "disdained its brother." We recalled the upper levels of Illimani with regret. The storms of the last fortnight had left traces not quickly to be obliterated. Quantities of new snow had fallen, and, as mischanced, the form of Ancohuma had caused it to drift round and accumulate with special thickness exactly on the slope we were about to climb. Perhaps that slope owes its existence to the fact that it is habitually renewed and increased by an eddied snow-drift.

The moment we started up the slope we realized that the work we had done was child's play to what was to come. No amount of treading would make the snow bind. It poured over the feet and about the legs like sand. How it maintained its position at all on the steep incline was a mystery. A small provocation would evidently start the whole mass sliding in a mighty avalanche. To avoid this danger it was essential to mount in a directly upward line. Any incline to right or left would have drawn a furrow across the slope and thus almost inevitably have started an avalanche. Straight up, therefore, we went, no easing zigzags possible. We sank in at first to the knee, presently to the waist. People often talk vaguely of walking through snow waist-deep. Of course, it is impossible to advance at all if you sink in up to the waist, for, thus buried, the leg could not be withdrawn and advanced for a step. The deepest snow you can walk through on a level place or gentle slope is half-thigh deep. Beyond that you must roll, as we discovered in Spitsbergen. When I say we sank in as far as the waist, I am referring to conditions on a steep slope, where the broken edge of the snow in front of each man came level with his waist or even his chest; behind him, of course, the step was open. To take another step the snow in front had to be beaten down, and then trodden and trodden and trodden again before it was firm enough to bear. When the next man came to it, it was all smothered in white powder and had to be beaten and trodden afresh. The increasing elevation, the steadily worsening snow, and steepening slope made the toil ever greater. As we were working up to the margin of our strength, the pace consequently diminished. We breathed violently and sometimes in furious paroxysms. Already, on the snow-field below, the guides had beaten their feet with ice-axes to maintain circulation. Now the beating was

almost continuous. Both complained that they were
losing sensation in the extremities. I shouted up to
Maquignaz that Pellissier said his feet were being frost-
bitten. "Let him beat them, then," was the answer.
"But he is beating them, and it's no good." "Then
he must beat them harder; there is no other way."
Both guides were frost-bitten on that dreadful slope.
I only escaped, thanks to my footgear. My feet were
not warm, of course, but they were never quite misera-
bly cold.

As we rose the dawn broke, not rose-red nor fiery,
as in the Alps, but pale and thin. Yet when it comes,
in these equatorial latitudes, it comes quickly. The
light of it lay upon the level bed of clouds, floating over
all the eastern region; but the sun itself we did not see,
for the mountain we were on hid it from us, and the cold
continued. Indeed, we thought the cold became more
intense. Daylight brought knowledge. We saw what
was above us, and the sight gave little satisfaction.
There was not a diminution, but an increase, of difficulties and dangers ahead. Huge masses of ice overhung
in cliffs one hundred feet high. Vast crevasses split the
face across. Everywhere the deep, soft, floury snow
mantled the slopes, up which the route, if any were possible, must lie. On the other hand, the summit was
now not far off. We had climbed more than half the
height of the final peak. No more than six hundred
feet remained to mount. So we pushed on, slanting
now a very little to the right, of necessity, though any
departure whatever from the straight-up track was
fraught with some danger. We came at last to the edge
of a great crevasse, perhaps fifty feet wide, that split

ANGOHIMA FROM THE UPPER SNOW-FIELD

the whole slope across. It would have been possible to cross this, but we didn't try, for the slope beyond it, leading straight to the top, in, perhaps, three hundred feet, was obviously unsafe in present conditions. It was a little steeper than the slope we had come up, and it was covered with the same powdery snow; but, whereas thus far we had been able to climb straight up, it would now be necessary to take a diagonal course, for the summit was above on our left hand. If we had fallen from any point on the hither side of the great crevasse, we should have come to rest somewhere on the level snow-field below. Even if involved in an avalanche, we might have extricated ourselves safely, as I have more than once done in similar circumstances. But in the traverse above, on the far side of the crevasse, we should have had it below us to tumble into, for the first part of the way, and, farther on, an ice cliff of one hundred feet to fall over. Moreover, the probabilities were that we should start an avalanche, and, if we did, it was certain we should all be killed. To have accepted the risk would have been the act of a fool.

A fortnight or three weeks earlier, before the series of storms which piled on the new snow, we should not have had too serious difficulty or danger to contend against. There would have been much step-cutting, such as we had had on Illimani, but undoubtedly we should have accomplished it successfully. Now the fates were emphatically against us. With bitter regret I gave the word to return. Before actually starting down it was necessary to set up and read the barometer—not an aneroid, but a mercurial barometer of the Boylean-Mariotti pattern. To fiddle with the little adjustments of an instrument under such circumstances of cold is misery. Hands must be withdrawn from gloves; the body must be kept still, and, at the moment of adjustment, the breath must be held, an act of torture when the lungs are thirsting for oxygen, which continuous breathing only gathers in quite insufficient quantity. Constant practice, however, invests the reading of instruments, for the scientific traveller, with the character of a duty. The whole energy of the mind is concentrated on the effort to obtain an accurate observation. All else is for the moment forgotten. The instrument was set up, hanging vertically from a tripod of ice-axes. I grovelled in the soft snow to bring my eye level with the top of the mercury. The vernier was screwed down, and the reading taken. The whole operation was then repeated, and the second reading agreed absolutely with the first. The mercury stood at 12.42 inches. This reading, compared with an almost simultaneous reading at La Paz, gave 24,255 feet for our altitude above sea-level at that moment. Add 250 feet for the remainder of the peak; the summit should thus be at 24,500 feet above sea-level. This agrees well enough with the altitude, 24,812 feet, of the Bolivian government survey. I was not, however, satisfied with this result, but later on devoted a fortnight to a careful triangulation with a 6-inch theodolite, as will presently be described. From the mean of eleven different measurements, the height of Ancohuma* came out

* The best measurements of Ancohuma known to me are: Pentland, 21,286 feet; Minchin, 21,470 feet; Conway, 21,710 feet; mean, 21,490 feet. Other measurements are: Pentland, 25,250 feet; Bolivian government survey, 24,812 feet; Raimondi, 23,620 feet (probably meant for Illampu).

21,700 feet. My corresponding figures for Illampu are 21,520 feet.

Before turning to descend I took a glance, but only a glance, at the view. There was not light enough to photograph it. Standing, as I did, backed against the steep slope, within a corner of the face, the outlook was over less than half the horizon. On either hand there stretched out from the peak the ridges, or rather snowy ranges, that border the deep plateau by which we had ascended. Both were almost wholly white. That on the right was a knife-edged ice *arête* dipping gradually to a snowy col overlooking the valley of Sorata. This col might be easily reached, but the *arête* thence to the summit of the peak is as long and narrow as that of the Lyskamm. It would be dangerous to ascend, because it is so exposed to wind, and if a strong wind (such as almost daily blows there) were to assail a party on that *arête* they would certainly be blown off. Beyond the snowy col came a domed peak, and then the Haukaña peak. We could see both over the col and the ice *arête*, but only clouds were visible beyond. The series of peaks on the other side were less remarkable for form. In the distance we saw the wide area of the Puna and a large portion of Lake Titicaca, with the Western Cordillera beyond, but there was no overpowering effect of distance observable. Clouds hid the view along the main Cordillera to the north.

The ascent of the slope we were on had taken three hours; the descent was the work of a few minutes. The whole day was still before us, and I was not without hope of even yet gaining the summit by way of the peak's south ridge. To the foot of this we, therefore,

turned with renewed expectation. But success was not
to be won that way either. For some distance the ridge
was practicable, but it only gave access to the foot of
the same slope which had turned us back, and did not
conduct to the summit. One might have turned from
it either to the right or to the left at the point where it
was cut away, but in either case a slope of the same impossible character (under these present conditions) had to
be mounted. Again, therefore, we were driven to descend,
with regrets which time has done nothing to alleviate.

As our climb recedes into the past, the memory of
its dangers grows less, while the desire for complete
success abides unchanged. I ask myself whether that
slope might not have been crossed; whether a better
man would not have risked it and won. There come
hours when I stand condemned at the bar of my own
judgment. But in saner moments another conclusion
obtains the mastery, and I decide that, at the supreme
instant, I did right, not merely not to risk my own
life for what is, after all, a passing triumph, but not to
risk the lives of my two admirable guides. The tangible
results of a journey of exploration are not the mere
attainment of particular points, but the accumulated
group of observations and collections, whereby the sum
of human knowledge is, however little, increased. In
turning my back on the peak, I knew that I did so for
the last time. Maquignaz might come to it again
with another employer, but I should not return; for that
year it was certain the mountain would not come again
into climbable condition before the beginning of the
rainy season (November to March), while future years
would bring me other duties. I leave, therefore, not the

highest point, but one of the finest and most historic peaks of the Andes untrodden. We overcame all its permanent difficulties and found the right way up, but a temporary impediment stopped us from actually standing on the top. Whoever comes after us to reap the reward of complete success must follow in our foot-steps, and will think of us kindly, I doubt not, when he stands on the proud eminence, with Lake Titicaca abroad at his feet. Him, whoever he may be, I con-gratulate upon the good-luck denied to us.

The plod back to camp down the plateau was a depressing effort. I was surprised to find what a dis-tance we had come. Had I been in a happier mood, it is probable that the white scenery would have pro-duced a different effect upon me; as things were, the unpeopled solitude struck me as strangely mournful. At camp we soon packed up our things and trundled the sledge down in fine style. When the big crevasses had been crossed, we simply let the sledge go of itself down the snow-slopes. Arrived at the middle camp, Ma-quignaz went on at once to call the Indians up, while Pellissier and I repacked the goods into loads before leisurely following. We met the men about half-way, and were pleased by the heartiness of their greeting. They rushed up to kiss my hands, and begged me to drink from their dirty spirit-bottles. An hour after I arrived in camp the first of them appeared on the hill-side, almost running down, with two loads on his back, and singing at the top of his voice. When all had arrived I paid them off and thanked them for their services. Some thereupon hastened away to their homes; others stayed to accompany us down next day.

CHAPTER XXII

SURVEYING UNDER DIFFICULTIES

ON the 11th of October we descended with all baggage from Hiska Haukaña to Achacache, leaving behind on the top meadow one of the mules who had died from some internal complaint. He was only ill for an hour or two, but by some curious intelligence the condors discovered it. When we departed half a dozen of them were already circling overhead, and no doubt descended for their feast as soon as our backs were turned. Bad weather had again come on; there was thunder in the bosom of Mount Sorata as we descended the Umapusa slopes. At Umapusa, Maquignaz borrowed my gun and struck straight across the great swamp round the edge of which the mule-track passes. He shot a goose, and then made his way by the devious track, avoiding pools and quagmires, and ultimately issuing through a little village to the solid ground again. In the village he was attacked by furious dogs, and was driven to shoot one in self-defence, whereupon the Indians issued forth in great rage and threatened him with knives and stones. It was only by levelling his gun at them that he succeeded in getting away.

The time was now come for commencing the triangulation of the Cordillera. By measuring the apparent

size of, or, in mathematical language, the angle sub-
tended by, a rod of known length, held perpendicular to
the line of sight, the distance of the centre of the rod
from the observer can be easily deduced. Armed with
a suitable rod, say ten feet long, and with an instrument
for measuring the angle it subtends—in other words, a
theodolite — you can measure any reasonable length
by putting yourself at one end of it and setting up the
rod at the other. Having determined this distance,
if you go to the point where the rod was and send it on
farther, and if you keep on repeating the process, you
can measure your way across a continent. Moreover,
the theodolite enables you to determine also the distance,
height, and position of any points that can be seen
from any two of the stations where it is set up. In this
way you can make a map of the country through which
you travel. It is called making a "bar-subtense survey." The idea is simple enough, but it is one of those
apparently obvious notions which a genius is required
to originate. The practical originator of the method
was the late Colonel Tanner, of the Indian Survey,
a splendid surveyor, an admirable artist, and a first-
rate man in numerous respects.

To walk through a country, performing the simple
operation thus roughly described, would seem to be
an unprovocative operation enough; but, as a matter
of experience, I am enabled to state that, in those parts
of the high plateau of Bolivia which are inhabited and
cultivated by Indians, it is as perilous an occupation
as the most adventurous man need desire, unless the
surveyor and his assistants are accompanied by a military force. The theodolite I employed was a six-inch

instrument by Carey, kindly lent to me by Mr. E. A. Fitzgerald. It was, in fact, one of the instruments used by him in his survey of Aconcagua. The rod scarcely requires description. At each end it carried a square board, with a black cross painted on a white ground. From the centre of one cross to the centre of the other was exactly ten feet. Half-way between the two was attached a sight, by directing which on to the theodolite the rod could be placed at right angles to the line of collimation. A level was used for making the rod horizontal. The rod was generally supported on a pair of ice-axes driven into the ground.

Calling each distance thus measured a range, it was further necessary to measure the angle made by each range with the next. Thus, at each station quitted by the theodolite a man had to be left behind, with a flag, to mark the exact position that had been occupied by the instrument. Another man had to go ahead with the rod, and the observer had to accompany the theodolite. Hence our party of three was always split up, each of us being sundered from the other by the length of a range, a distance of perhaps half a mile. The *arriero* accompanied the observer with a baggage mule for carrying the theodolite. With less than four persons it was impossible to undertake work of this kind. In order to carry the levels from a known altitude we had to make our first station on the margin of Lake Titicaca, whose height above sea-level has been taken very accurately by the Mollendo railway surveyors.

One fine morning we rode away from Achacache, over the wide pampa to the edge of the lake, coming ultimately into a hybrid region where the land is encroaching upon the water, and where banks jut out into the lake and lagoons penetrate the land. Here the multitude of birds was greater than I found anywhere else in Bolivia. Ducks were feeding along the margin of the water, and there were herons and coots and a great variety of small birds whose names I did not know and which we could not shoot with a theodolite, the only weapon we were carrying. The whole range of the Cordillera was magnificently clear, and the peaks shone forth in their new white raiment as though clothed in silver. A couple of bulls seemed inclined to dispute with us the site of our first station, but were presently persuaded to evacuate it. For two or three hours the work went forward easily enough, but then we touched cultivated land and the first signs of trouble arose. One or two Indians came from their huts to watch us, and concluded that we were up to no good. They saw the strange instrument, the waving of flags, and galloping to and fro. One of them, more intelligent than the rest, concluded that we were making preparations for either a road or a railway, innovations equally distasteful to him. He said that we were going to interfere with his lands, and no protests of ours availed to quiet his fears. "We want no roads," he said, "and we want no railways; we want nothing but to be let alone as we are."

The next station was close to a little hamlet where the dogs were turned out on us and much abuse was shouted forth by the inhabitants. But after that we could follow the road, and so approached Achacache without further trouble. The golden evening drew on, and the sun sank into the lake. A great shadow swept across the plain and up the foothills, making them purple and the snow pink, with shadows of a vivid green such as I never saw before. It was a swiftly transient effect, followed by no afterglow. In a few moments the pallid night swallowed all. This was the first finely colored sunset I had seen in Bolivia, for in these mountains the sun rises and sets with more rapidity and far less splendor of tint than one is accustomed to in the Alps. Once or twice from La Paz I saw Illimani shining pink at the moment of the sun's departure, but there again the effect came and went in a few moments.

Next day our work was continued, the weather being still perfectly clear. We advanced along the Umapusa track and so reached the base of Abichaca Hill, which, as I before said, was chosen for one of our principal points of observation. Maquignaz went to the top and set up the rod; I was at the station below; Pellissier held the flag at the preceding station. I noticed that Maquignaz was presently joined by two or three Indians, but thought little of it, for the hill was, of course, uncultivated. Where I stood I was surrounded by protesting Indians from the very village in which Maquignaz had unfortunately been obliged to shoot a dog. My work finished, I rode on to the foot of the hill and slowly scrambled up it, first by a path; afterwards, dismounting, I had to drag the mule almost straight up the steep final slope of loose stones. The top was a small plateau with a *chulpa* at one corner and several ruined walls about. A little way down on one side was a great hole, dug some years before by a party of native

CHULPA ON ABICHACA HILL.

gold prospectors. As soon as I arrived Maquignaz started away to make another station. While he was on the road I had time to examine my surroundings.

About a dozen Indians were already collected on the summit; they watched my proceedings with scowling interest. The *chulpa* proved to be a little building about six feet square with a thatched roof supported by walls on three sides and by a round arched doorway on the fourth which faced the east. There was a step or altar within along the west side. On this, and in two niches in the side walls, were collected a few saucers of common pottery containing one or two pieces of incense or a little grain, and there were bunches of dried pinks and a few other simple offerings. The round arched door suffices to prove that this particular *chulpa* has been built, or, at all events, rebuilt, since "the times of the Gentiles." No doubt it occupies the position of a prehistoric building. There is no sign of Christianity about it, though probably enough the Indians would now consider it a chapel.

During my examination of the *chulpa*, more Indians had gathered on the top of the hill. As soon as I began to set up the theodolite, they rushed with one accord to the corner of the *chulpa* and shouted down excitedly to the village of Abichaca, five or six hundred feet below. I commenced my observations and paid no attention to these men, signalling to Pellissier to come and join me as soon as I was able to release him. Presently a great number of Indians arrived on the top, led by an old fellow with as evil a face as ever I saw. He walked truculently up to me and seized my hand in anything but a friendly manner, while holding his other hand behind his back under his *poncho*, evidently grasping a weapon. He could talk a little Spanish, and demanded what I was doing on their hill. I did my best to palaver with him while continuing my work, for the mountain range was tantalizingly clear, and who could say when it would be so again? The old fellow shrank with horror from my instrument, and evidently thought there was something uncanny about the whole performance, for the theodolite was just then pointed at their sacred Illampu, and they probably conceived that I was in some way engaged in drawing magic from the mountain. Once again they cried aloud with united shouts, and more Indians came rushing up in response, converging from all sides. Then the whole of them collected in a walled enclosure near the top, where a noisy debate was carried on.

The *arriero* signified to me that it would be better to pack up the theodolite at once, unless I was willing it should be destroyed. We accordingly packed it, and were loading the mule when the whole crowd of Indians, now some two hundred or more in number, rushed forth and surrounded us, yelling, "Gringo! Gringo!" I felt like a single llama spitting at a pack of curs. They seized the *arriero's* and the baggage mule, and tried to seize mine, but I retained possession of it. The upper part of the hill being too steep for riding, I led my beast down the slope of loose stones which, fortunately, as it turned out, were sharp-edged and not of the rounded pebble character so common on these smaller hills. By luck rather than design I diverged gradually away from the little track that comes up from the village, while the naked-footed Indians were obliged to keep on it. Thus

I became separated from them by a few yards. Perceiving this and realizing the cause, I chose the nastiest way I could find, but the stubborn mule refused to follow. The Indians now began to throw stones at me, luckily only hitting the mule, and so urging him forward. Thus I was enabled to descend at a good pace and to reach the somewhat gentler slopes, while the crowd were still forced to stick to the path. When they observed that I was escaping, half a dozen of the better-class villagers, who wore leather sandals, ran after me and snatched at the mule, but I drew my revolver and frightened them off. They called out, "To the *finca*! to the *finca*!" To gain time I re-echoed their words and made signs asking which was the way. Having thus reached the path below at a ridable place, I jumped on to the beast, and ostentatiously rode towards the *finca*, gradually increasing the pace to a quiet trot as the path improved, and keeping my guards a little way behind.

I noticed that the *arriero* was not being troubled by the crowd, who regarded him as one of themselves, and, content with holding the mules, allowed him to go where he pleased. With only myself, therefore, to shift for, and being now down close to the village, where the fields were fairly flat, I suddenly switched my mule off the path, clapped spurs to him, and made the best of my way towards the well-known track leading from Umapusa to Achacache. This necessitated my passing through the end of the village among a number of huts. Out of every hut came one or more natives, who set their dogs upon me, heaved stones at me, and sometimes rushed at the mule to try and collar it; but I kept them off also with my revolver, taking care, of course, not to hit any one, for that would have made matters infinitely worse and would have put an end to the possibility of completing my survey. Once out on the open plain, I galloped off, still hotly pursued by fleet-footed Indians, who never dropped far behind, and only gave up the chase when I entered the edge of Achacache, a place whose inhabitants, if not hostile to those of Abichaca, would certainly not make common cause with them.

Meanwhile Maquignaz and Pellissier were being independently pursued by other groups of Indians. Maquignaz, indeed, was driven away before he had even set up the rod. He arrived at Achacache by a circuitous route. Pellissier was headed off in another direction, and reached the inn a very short time after I did. My escape was a lucky one; for the population of this part of the Puna was thoroughly enraged with me, believing that I had violated their sacred places and that I had brought on the bad weather of the preceding weeks. When the Indians do run amuck with a gringo they are not content merely with murdering him: they torture him first with great ingenuity. Finding that we had escaped into Achacache, the rioters of Abichaca began to think of the consequences that might follow. Being also very frightened at the theodolite, on which they dared not lay a finger, they called for the *arriero* and begged him to remove it; thus about sunset he also arrived at the inn with mules and the instrument uninjured.

The worst part of the business was that my work on Abichaca Hill was not finished, and that it was necessary for me to return there and spend at least two more hours on the top. I therefore called on the sub-prefect, who had now returned to his post, and applied for his assistance. He was willing to do all he could, but he said that there were no police nearer than La Paz, and no soldiers, and that it was only by moral suasion that the Indians could be controlled. He said they were frightened, and that if some man in whom they had confidence would explain the matter to them and would accompany me up the hill, all would go well. The manager of the *finca*, who lived in Achacache, came to apologize and promised to ride out to the place next day and lecture the villagers. I was advised to wait a day or two before attempting to repeat my visit to the troublesome neighborhood, the reputation of Abichaca, as I now learned, being durably bad.

We filled up the intervening time by carrying a plane-table survey up to the Huallata Pass, but ill-luck again pursued us. The north face of Mount Sorata was covered with clouds on this occasion also, so that I could not obtain a near view of it. Endeavoring to solve the somewhat tangled topography of the Huallata region of rounded hills and labyrinthine dells, all deeply scraped by ancient glaciers, I gained the neighboring pass to the east and discovered that this is the true geographical saddle at the head of the Mapiri Valley. The direct track for llama-caravans from Sorata town crosses the watershed here and descends to the village of Umapusa, whence it skirts the lower slopes of the Cordillera to La Paz, without touching Achacache or Peñas, or any of the places we knew. From this eastern Huallata Pass the view of Mount Sorata, whereof

I only saw glimpses, must be splendid. I do not believe
that it would be possible to find in the world any grand-
er near view of a great mountain. On our return we
joined the main track at a point where the decaying
carcass of a donkey disfigured the way-side. This was
the donkey that Bieber had found turned out to die,
and in the last stages of suffering. He drew his revolver
and mercifully shot it, whereupon the entire population
of a neighboring hamlet rushed forth upon him and made
him pay fifteen dollars for killing their beast.

In response to an invitation from the sub-prefect,
I went one morning to his house and met an assemblage
of notabilities. All were armed to the teeth with rifles
and Mauser pistols or revolvers. There was the owner
of Abichaca in attendance; there was also his son, and
the manager of the *finca*, and there were some other
persons believed to have influence with the Indians.
Every one was well mounted, so that our cavalcade
made some show as it filed out of the town. An Indian
funeral was encountered coming in from the country,
for every native prefers to be buried in the great cemetery rather than on the unconsecrated hill-side, if he
can afford it. The body, wrapped in a *poncho*, was carried on a stretcher, and the funeral party were running
along at a spanking pace. That same afternoon we
met them again scattered along the track, at intervals of
a hundred yards or so, where they had fallen on their
way home in a state of the most complete intoxication
it is possible to conceive.

One of my companions related to me how, a year or
two before, at the end of June or beginning of July,
he had crossed the Cordillera by the third main de-

pression south of Mount Sorata. He said that the snow-field above the glacier was as hard as rock, so that he could ride over it without dismounting, and that the weather was perfect. In his opinion, June and July would be the best months for mountain climbing, unless the cold should prove to be too great; but he said that at that time of year, even on the Puna, the cold was of the most bitter kind. The sub-prefect told me that he had seen me and my guide near the top of Ancohuma. He said he watched us for a long time, but that we did not move, and he pointed out to me the place where we had been. On looking through a telescope, I saw three rocks emerging through the snow at the point in question.

Word had been sent ahead that the Indians were to collect at the *finca* to meet their proprietor, who, after all, did not come with us, but sent his son in his place. I was informed that he did not dare venture among his people. The plan was that all the Indians were to be gathered into the court-yard of the *finca*, where the sub-prefect was to address them while I climbed the hill. Once in the court-yard the doors were to be locked on them, and they were to be detained until my work was done. Unfortunately, the event did not turn out so simply, for the Indians refused to come together, and only a few (and those the least truculent) entered the court-yard at all. The others scattered themselves about in small groups in the fields, and would not come even when men went to fetch them.

Without wasting a moment, I rode straight up the hill in company with the major-domo and followed by two natives. The major-domo, riding an active pony, of which he was very proud, rushed at the steep upper slope without dismounting; but he paid for his temerity by a bad fall, the pony rolled over him, cutting open his head, and, as afterwards appeared, dislocating his wrist. He said it was a matter of no account, and walked on to the top, where he sat down and discoursed with the Indians in Aymara, describing to them, as well as he could, the nature of the work in which I was engaged. It soon became evident that all the Indians were coming up, as they had done before, so I went ahead with my work as quickly as possible, in the midst of a very troublesome crowd. To avoid leaving a man behind with the flag, I built a cairn of stones before descending. By this time the patience of the Indians was exhausted, and once more they began to throw stones and shout "Gringo! Gringo!" But nothing serious happened, and we were able to ride away without molestation. Before we had reached the next station, however, we saw all the Indians return to the top of the hill and throw down our stone-man, a serious matter for us.

Fortunately the next station was planted in the midst of an uncultivated area where no one came to trouble us, so we spent a couple of hours there, lunching and resting; by that time the hill was deserted. I sent Maquignaz and Pellissier to ride back together as quickly as possible to the bottom of the hill on the side remote from the village, where one of them was to hold the mules while the other ran up with a flag and held it for a moment at the spot on which the cairn had been built. I was to wave a flag to him as soon as the observation had been made, and he was then to run down and escape. Unfortunately, they forgot to carry away

EARTH PYRAMIDS ON THE WAY TO THE ALTO DE ANIMAS

the field-glasses, so that, having arrived at the top of the hill and planted the flag, Maquignaz could not see my signal. He stood waiting and waiting and peering about, twenty-five minutes longer than was necessary. By that time all the Indians had gathered once again, and the whole country-side was loud with the cries of men. Perceiving that it was necessary to retreat, Maquignaz made the best of his way down and just reached the mules in time; but he said that they had difficulty in evading pursuit, for the enemy was arranged in groups all round the hill. There was also a man on the top, who, indeed, had been there at the moment of their arrival, and whose business it was to shout down the direction which they were taking, so that those below might concentrate towards the point whither they were descending. Watching them with a field-glass, I saw that they got away in safety, and then I rode off and returned to Achacache by another route.

Having thus passed what we believed to be the great obstruction of Abichaca Hill, we hoped that it would be possible to continue our work without further interference on the plain by following along the Peñas road. Next day we returned to our last station by a very devious route from Achacache, keeping at first on the other side of a low line of hills and crossing a pass right on to the station. In this way we thought we should arrive without the Abichaca people knowing anything about it. But we had no sooner reached the pass than cries were heard, which were taken up and repeated farther and farther off and in all directions, so that it became evident that we were awaited,

and that preparations had been made and men stationed
on the lookout in all the villages around. Neverthe-
less we set to work. Maquignaz went away with his rod,
I set up the theodolite, and the observations began.
But I had no sooner limbered up to move on than I saw
Maquignaz riding away with the rod on his shoulder.
I joined him quickly and asked why he was thus hasty.
He replied: "Well, come back and see for yourself."
So we rode back to the top of the little knoll where he
had been standing, and there met half a dozen enraged
Indians, and saw, two or three fields off, another twenty
or thirty converging upon them, and half a mile away
yet others, while through the glass we could see, from
every village, people streaming forth and all gathering
towards the same centre.

Under such conditions it was impossible for three
men, all necessarily separated from one another by
long distances and unable to offer mutual support,
to continue the bar-subtense survey. There was only
one thing to be done: to change our method of operations and to substitute a triangulation for the bar-
subtense method, treating the total distance thus far
measured from the margin of Lake Titicaca as the base
for the triangulation. It involved making two more
principal stations on the summits of the Peñas and
Villaque hills, each of which bore to the neighboring
village or town the same relation that the hill of our
troubles bore to the village of Abichaca. We realized
at once that unless protection could be obtained it would
not be possible to spend a long time on such sacred
high places. The sub-prefect strongly advised us to
go back to La Paz and obtain the help of a small body

MR. N. E. BIEBER AT THE TOP OF THE ALTO DE ANIMAS

of *gendarmerie*. Without them, he said, we could not work at leisure, and we might find it necessary to pay several hurried visits to each station before our observations could be completed. In his opinion, we should save time by settling the matter once for all on a sound basis.

Till the small hours of the morning Achacache was noisy with the beating of drums and the cries of festivity, for there was a great fête in the town, and a fête among the Indians is another name for a drinking-bout. At three o'clock, when we started for La Paz, the orgies were still in progress; but the only persons in the street were lying about overcome with alcohol, so that our departure attracted no attention. It was a warm night, and lightning flashed behind the Cordillera like the sword of a god glittering on the battlements of the world. Otherwise the darkness was profound, and even the road was scarcely visible beneath our feet. Before dawn came frost, and the earth was whitened as with salt on the level plain. When the asses began to bray, and the *sintinellas* to utter their plover-like cry, we knew that the dawn was at hand. Light, creeping over the sky, manifested Indians evidently posted for observation on the hill-tops commanding a view of the line we should have followed in our farther survey, while two or three men dogged our steps, running when we trotted and always keeping close behind. It was not till we had passed Huarina and joined the carriage-road to La Paz that they dropped behind and left us to proceed unobserved.

Once again, therefore, we had to traverse the weary Puna, whose monotony began to oppress us. Machaca-marca was gained before noon, and a long halt made there to bait the mules, while a violent thunder-storm burst over the place. In the afternoon we started on again, and, if our animals had been better beasts, we should have ridden through to La Paz, but on arrival at Okomisto they broke down and another night had to be passed on the floor of that wretched hostelry in similar circumstances to those described before. We reached La Paz early next morning, and made application for the assistance of a small body of *gendarmerie*. The application was readily granted by the authorities, but they said it would be some days before the men would be at liberty. So, to fill up the interval, I arranged to accompany Bieber on a visit to the newly opened gold-mine of Cusanaco.

CHAPTER XXIII

THE GOLD-MINE OF CUSANACO

BIEBER and I, without the guides, or any other companions except a baggage mule, rode out together one bright morning by the route that goes down the valley, the same that leads to Illimani. I could not fail to observe, on passing Obrajes, how rapidly vegetation had advanced since I was there before. Every bush was in flower in the gardens, and the profusion of roses was a joy to behold. Each cactus plant bore a delicate waxen blossom, and all the trees were decked in young green leaves. Just below Obrajes came the opening of the Calacoto Valley, up which we turned. Narrow below, and spreading back fanlike to a *cirque* of mountains once very much loftier than they are now, it offers some of the strangest scenery that can be imagined. The valley, or rather the *cirque*, is cut into the thick alluvium, whose excavated walls and towers stand round it as high hills, and divide from one another the several deep-cut gorges, which might be likened in arrangement to the ribs of a fan. Extremely well-developed earth-pyramids are found in clusters in several directions. The gorges are utterly desert, like the *nalas* of Western Tibet. But on the slopes between them, and below, near the mouth of the valley, there are large and fertile *fincas*, depending chiefly upon artificial irrigation.

With little delay we pushed forward in an easterly direction, mounting to one of the two principal depressions along the left watershed of the basin. The depression we arrived at is called the Alto de Animas. Over it passes the mule-track to Palca, another important mining centre, and then on, still easterly, to the Pacuani Pass (15,226 feet, Pentland), which crosses the Cordillera between Illimani and Mururata and is one of the main ways from La Paz to the fertile province of Las Yungas. I always intended to devote a week to visiting Yungas, which can be reached by a yet directer route going northeastward from La Paz over an easy col. Leaving La Paz in the morning on a good mule, you can sleep the same night far down the other side of the Cordillera in orange gardens and the luxury of semi-tropical vegetation, while another day will take you to the plantations where coca is grown and the best coffee in South America, and, indeed, some of the best in the world. Yungas can likewise be reached more laboriously by descending directly down the La Paz Valley and traversing by its gorge the deep gap in the Cordillera.

Arrived on the Alto de Animas, an indescribable view of Illimani burst upon our gaze, practically the same view that one beholds from La Paz, except that the mountain is nearer and more imposing, rising as it does above the intricate multitude of ribs and green hills that cluster at its foot. A little lake, almost on the crest of the pass, mirrored the peak in its calm waters, while the sharp earth-pyramids close at hand contrasted well with the suave forms of the wide Palca basin that spread before us. If we had crossed the

GORGE IN THE PALCA VALLEY

neighboring pass to the south, it would have taken us into a remote valley belonging to the village of Collana, a remarkable Indian community, which manages rigidly to exclude all white people from dwelling among them. If a white man comes that way (as in the rainy season is not uncommon, seeing that the La Paz Valley road is then impassable, and this hill route is the only one that can be taken by travellers who have to go in that direction), the villagers will put him up for the night in the rest-house and will sell him necessary food, but the next day he must go on. No exception is made, even in the case of a government official. As the villagers are always well behaved, the government wisely respects their prejudices and leaves them alone. They collect the taxes themselves and pay them with due regularity. They seem to live the life of ancient days almost unchanged.

Either pass would have led to the mines, which lie far down in the main gorge that collects the drainage from Mururata and the northwest side of Illimani and empties it out into the La Paz River at Esquino de Pongo, near Taguapalca. Riding along a good path among cultivated fields, we presently bent away to our right from the Palca road, and descended into the bowels of a deep gorge. Its walls, cut out of thick sandstone and conglomerate deposits, for some distance were vertical, and there was one splendid tower of rock standing out in the very midst of the gorge like a great monument. From this point we had to follow the very bed of the now almost dry torrent. There was no path; the mules had to pick their difficult way among great bowlders and most irregular ground. When it was explained to me that every piece of machinery for the mine, and all the large pipes required for it, had to be transported on the backs of mules by this route, I easily understood how much expense, and, still more, how much organizing energy, were necessary to open up profitable mining in such a country. All along the bed of this valley, and more especially after the junction has been reached with the main stream from the glaciers of Mururata, gold is found in the gravel, and the natives have been accustomed for centuries to wash it out in an inefficient manner. The main deposit is found against the bed-rock under the gravel, and more elaborate means than they possess are necessary before that can be worked in any quantity. We passed one small mining station, worked on behalf of a La Paz gentleman by a few laborers. I was informed that the area of valley claimed by him is undoubtedly rich in gold.

Below this point the gorge again narrows to a width of a few yards and is encumbered by enormous bowlders, cast about in utter confusion, over which the mules have to scramble as best they may. One or two of the larger masses, which quite barred the route, have been blasted; but, even so, the passage of this and similar narrow places remains a slow and difficult process. Before the blasting, the only way of arriving at a lower point in the valley was by mounting the hill-side on the left to a considerable height, traversing a giddy path along it for some miles, and then descending steep zigzags, which I afterwards saw. Bieber related to me how, the last time he came that way on a visit to the Cusanaco Mine, he brought a friend and some newly purchased mules, which were the pride of his heart.

MINERS' HUTS AT CUSANACO

Reaching the corner where the descending zigzags commenced, he dismounted from his own mule. At that moment the narrow path gave way under the leading baggage-mule; he slithered down a few feet of slope and then fell in two or three bounds to the bottom of the gorge below, where he was utterly smashed up. The second mule blindly followed and was overtaken by a similar fate. The third likewise began to slip down, but caught in some extraordinary fashion on a shrub growing out of the slope, and Bieber was able to rescue him and drag him back on to the path. The skeletons of the unfortunate beasts were still, at the time of my visit, lying on the spot to which they fell.

The narrows were succeeded by an open basin, and that by more narrows and another basin, and so on, each of the basins being occupied by the flood-bed of the torrent, and of course littered all over with bowlders, large and small, which are compacted together below the surface with other bowlders and smaller gravel and sand. It is these basins that were about to be worked by the company whose installation we were going to visit. The first sign that we were approaching the end of our march was the appearance of a big, newly made canal-bed, carried away from the bottom of the stream along the hill-side on our right. It was about fifteen feet wide and very carefully levelled. Being itself almost horizontal, and the valley steadily and sometimes steeply inclined, the canal soon diverged from the torrent-bed, and thus, at the end of about a mile, was some 500 feet above the level of the bottom of the valley. Thus, in the rainy season, a great head of water would be obtained, for it is only in the rainy season that there is water enough to reach the canal at all. When we were there, the torrent was quite small and could easily be forded at any point; but when the rains come down, the stream rises in the narrow gorges to a great height and overflows all the basins. Then, of course, the canal would be filled, and the head of water become a powerful source of energy. The canal was still in process of being made, though it was approaching completion. It was an astonishing sight to behold in so wild and remote a solitude the signs of such elaborate human contrivance, evidently the work of a large body of organized men. Its after history was less noble than its promise. When the rains came the hill-side began to move, and fell in great land-slips on the canal, obliterating most of it in a very short time. Such are some of the disappointments of gold-miners in these difficult and remote countries.

As yet there were no men in sight, but, on rounding a corner, the little habitations of the mine came in view on the hill-side above. Turning another corner, we emerged upon the basin which was to be the scene of the first great gold-washing. Hundreds of Indians were at work, most of them busily engaged either in drilling the bowlders for blasting or in removing the shattered fragments of the previous day's explosions. The broken rocks had been carefully and elaborately built together down the middle of the basin into a long wall, about as wide as a road, which I was told was not planted merely on the surface of the alluvial débris, but had been built down in an excavation to bed-rock below. The object of this wall was so to divide the basin that, when the rainy season came and the flood descended, the whole of it might be diverted to one side of the wall, leaving the gravel on the other side dry and able to be washed through the sluices. Every bowlder, therefore, and rock too big to be passed through the sluices had to be removed, not merely from the surface of the side first to be worked, but right down to bedrock—an immense labor. This work, and the building of the wall, were likewise approaching completion. At the moment of our arrival the ground may be said to have been almost prepared for the commencement of operations. There still remained the machinery to be installed. That had arrived in La Paz, but had not yet been brought up. An important part of it consisted of a great pipe, into which the water in the canal was to be turned, as I shall presently describe in connection with another mine.

We were kindly received by the director of the works, Professor A. A. Hard, of the United States. He took us to his cottage on a shelf of the hill, half-way between the canal above and the gravel-basin below. It looked none too secure in position, and I was not surprised to hear that, a short time before, a great bowlder, rushing down the hill, had crashed into it on one side and out the other, carrying clean away the bedroom walls, roof, furniture, and everything. Fortunately no one was within at the time. In the rainy season, when the hill-side is on the move and mud-avalanches are not rarities, I should imagine that a hut thus situated would be far from a restful place of abode. The professor was one of the quietest-mannered men you can imagine. Nothing seemed to disturb his perfect equanimity. His benevolent face looked forth beneath its covering of white hair with equal composure upon whatever might happen. He had come a year or two before merely to give an opinion upon the prospects of the deposit, having then been, as he imagined, about to start for Java; but he had stayed on from month to month in response to the urgent requests of his employers, with few comforts beyond the commodities of his portmanteau; but he took things as they came, with no trace of irritation. He knew neither Spanish nor, of course, the Indian dialects, and he made no attempt to learn any of them, for, he said, "I just speak to them all in English, slowly, quietly, and distinctly, and they understand." He said: "When I take you down among the men, you will see they all know enough English for our purposes; I find they rather prefer to be spoken to by me like that than to be worried in their own tongue by other people."

His experience with Indians, the majority of whom came from the neighborhood of the exclusive Collana village above described, was very interesting. He said that if well treated, and prevented from obtaining intoxicating drinks, they were easy to live with. But he said, "If I find a bottle of spirits in the possession of any of them, it is immediately confiscated and broken over the hill-side." He found them honest, and, to my surprise, described them as good-tempered; and I am bound to say that when I accompanied him among the workmen and saw the smiles with which they greeted him, I felt that he had justified his claim on their behalf. He said that the trouble with Indians was that they had been so often swindled by white men; but that when they found that they got their money in return for their

ALTO DE ANIMAS

THE PALCA VALLEY ROAD

work, and their prejudices were not interfered with and they were kindly treated, they were very easily managed, like children. Their delight in explosions, he said, was very great. Every evening the last thing done was to fire all the cartridges that had been placed in position during the afternoon; this was a great event, and was looked forward to not only by the workmen, but by all their wives in the village of little arbors that had sprung up around the workings. I perfectly sympathized with this attitude of mind, and thoroughly enjoyed the blast myself when it took place; but the way the stones shot up into the air, one of them flying even over our heads, though we stood at a great distance, was somewhat terrifying.

A delightful evening was spent with our hospitable entertainers. On such occasions, when men meet from various parts of the world in the rough accommodation of a camp, knowing that on the morrow they will probably separate forever, there springs up without delay an easy kindliness of mutual relation that closely resembles established friendship. Adventures are related, and an almost intimate exchange of personal experiences takes place. We talked of Indians and of sport, of the gold deposits of Bolivia, of our various difficulties, our various failures and successes. I examined the professor on the immediate geography of the neighborhood, which he had to some extent explored, and I induced him to describe to me the condition of affairs in the rainy season, which appears to resemble in all material respects the monsoon in India. To give an idea of the force of the torrent when in high flood, he showed me enormous bowlders, which I should never have imagined that water could possibly move, and related how one of them had been brought down a distance of about fifty yards in a single night. He described the thunderous rumbling of these great rocks as they pounded against one another and rolled on and on in the cataract.

Next day we returned by the way we had come, accompanied for a mile or two by the professor. Near the *finca* of Calacoto my good friend Don Federico Granier rode up, horse and man larger than one often sees in Bolivia, and took us into the beautiful garden of the *finca*, where we sat for a while in the summer-house and refreshed ourselves with wine and fruit before riding back together to La Paz. Alas! when I revisited Bolivia in 1900 and asked after him, I learned that he too had joined the majority.

CHAPTER XXIV

THE YANI MINE

THE Yani Mine, of which my friend Mr. Bieber was managing director, was the only other Bolivian gold-mine I had an opportunity of describing. Bieber was a young Englishman, of a type resembling that of our subalterns on the Indian frontier, rather than the ordinary man of business. He was full of life, energy, sport, and delight in adventure. His superabundant activity led him to master the practical part of whatever work came under his hand. If he had a few months' holiday, he would rush off to some big Argentine ranch, learn the craft of the *gaucho*, and return with new skill in the managing of mules and horses, the loading of caravans, and the driving of them in difficult places. He was devoted to his mule-train and equipments, which, in fact, were the best I saw in Bolivia. The mules had been carefully selected during a period of two or three years. Their saddles, instead of being the clumsy and heavy native articles, were of the light and well-designed Californian pattern. Bieber could load, shoe, doctor, and drive his animals. The saddle was his true home; he was forever dashing from La Paz to Yani, from Yani to Chililaya. Even when business did not propel him, he found pleasure in opportunities of further exertion. He was the reorganizer of the races at La Paz—

a man never at rest, the very life of the whole country-side.

He had had previous experience in gold-mining in the Araca Valley, and I dare say elsewhere, but the Yani Mine was his creation, and his whole existence was bound up in its success. It is situated in a high valley on the northern spur of Illampu, just at the head of the famous Tipuani River. Here there was reported to be—and careful experiments confirmed the report—a bank of auriferous gravel some hundred feet or more thick, deposited along the side of the Challapampa stream, a tributary of the Tipuani. To wash the gold out of the gravel-bank water is needed, and this the river only supplies during the rainy season, November or December to April or May. In other months work has to stop. At Yani, as at Cusanaco, a canal was cut from a certain point in the stream and carried for a mile or so, nearly level along one side of the valley, till the end of it came to be 400 to 500 feet above the valley bottom. Here the canal water was to be turned into a great iron pipe that goes straight down-hill. The pipe is four feet in diameter at the upper end, and narrows down below to eighteen inches.

At the bottom is a kind of fire-hose nozzle arrangement, called a giant, through which the water, now under enormous pressure, is issued and directed in a stream, which may be as much as eight inches in diameter. This huge water-jet will leap like a fountain 400 feet into the air, with a force measured by 2260 horse-power. The use of this mighty agent is to cut down the gravel-bank; the jet is directed by a skilful Californian piper against the foot of the bank, where it hollows out a cave and undercuts the hill-side. The moment at last comes when the superincumbent gravel, almost as hard as conglomerate, gives way, and 10,000 tons of the mountain fall in a man-made avalanche. Skill is required so to direct the undercutting that this huge mass may fall exactly in the right place, where it can be dealt with easily afterwards; for the whole of it must be washed down a trough into and through the sluices, which catch the heavy particles of gold and allow the lighter rocks, pebbles, and sand to be swept away by the rush of water over the dump at the end of the sluice, and down into the natural torrent.

The gold found is for the most part relatively large and angular, showing that it has not been carried far from its ancient mother-lode or much rubbed by movement. The lower parts of the bank are, of course, richer than the upper, for gold tends to sink as a balloon to rise, but all levels of the bank were believed to contain some gold, and all have to be washed through the six-foot sluice. Some of the abundant water-power is employed to produce electric light, whereby work can be continued night and day during the rainy months. It will thus be seen that 1400 feet of heavy iron piping, the great giants, a quantity of lumber for sluices, the dynamos, water-wheel, and other electric-light plant, had to be installed before work could begin. All this machinery had to be fetched from San Francisco, landed in the open roadstead of Mollendo, where the surf always furiously rages, hauled by train over a pass as high as the summit of Mont Blanc, transshipped across Lake Titicaca, and carried on the backs of mules to the mine.

Compared with the last stage all else was child's play.

The "road" from Chililaya to the mine was a thing that home-dwelling folk will find a difficulty in imagining. It is nowhere a made road, but only a worn-down track, littered over with loose round stones of all sizes, from that of a bale of cotton to a pebble. It rises gently enough from the lake to the Huallata Pass (14,110 feet), then it plunges down in a few miles, as already described, to the little town of Sorata, at about 8000 feet. That is the first day's journey. From Sorata the track rises again to a pass about 16,000 feet high, and only gets there by coasting frightful precipices and climbing hideous staircases, which most men would not care to pass on foot. It reminded me of Kipling's lines on the troubles of Tommy Atkins with mountain-guns:

"There's a wheel on the Horns o' the mornin', an' a wheel on
    the edge o' the Pit,
  An' a drop into nothin' beneath you as straight as a beggar can
    spit :
  With the sweat runnin' out o' your shirt-sleeves, an' the sun off
    the snow in your face,
  An' 'arf o' the men on the drag-ropes to hold the old gun in 'er
    place."

After a descent of 1000 feet comes yet another pass of over 16,000 feet, whence in two leagues you go down to the mine, whose altitude above sea-level is about 11,000 feet. To transport some hundreds of loads of costly machinery over such a route was, indeed, a difficult enterprise. It was carried out under the personal supervision of my friend in a most sporting fashion. One or more of the loads could not be made to weigh less than 600 pounds.* The average load

* The regulation load for an Indian-government-service mule is 100 pounds.

was nearly 300 pounds. Time and again the heavy loads had to be dismounted to relieve a fatigued mule. In bad places a gang of men had to carry the larger pieces. When night came on, all had to sleep where they happened to be. In case of a fall, mule and burden would have gone perhaps 2000 feet, bounding over a precipice, before aught would have stopped them. Such a fate would have ended the utility of a big piece of cast-iron, and the installation of the mine would have been delayed perhaps over a whole rainy season. The fact that no such accident happened on so appalling a track speaks volumes for the energy of Bieber, who, I am told, was ever in the thick of the struggle, loading and leading the mules himself in the worst places, and always directing his huge caravan of beasts and men. He would have been a most useful transport-officer on an Afghan frontier campaign. When, after repeated journeys, all the plant had been brought to the mine, the big pipe had to be riveted together and put in place; the mile of canal had to be dug out; the sluices had to be set up. They dug the first sod of the canal in August. The machinery began to arrive in September. By January they were washing gold. The following dry season—that during which I was in Bolivia—was devoted to the installation of the electric light. As soon as the rains should really break, gold-washing was to be seriously begun.

It must be remembered that all this work was accomplished by native Indian labor, under the direction of only five white men, none of whom knew the Aymara tongue. My only experience of Indians has not been pleasant, but it was my ill fortune to be engaged on work which violated their prejudices and excited their suspicions. Mining and transport they understand, and the manager of Yani told me that he had found them good men to work with. The fact that they are distrustful of white employers is a patent criticism of the way they have been treated in the past. From a man they do not know they insist on payment in advance, partly as a guarantee, partly also because they have to buy their own food and take it up to the mine with them, besides providing for the needs of their wives and families in their absence. These men have to be enlisted from their villages, and most of them come from the Puna, for the population in the eastern valleys is very small, there being little or no food produced in the forest region, fertile though it would be if any attempt were made to cultivate it. Some trouble is experienced in enlisting the men, as the employer is liable to be dependent upon the village corregidors, who are not always willing to put themselves out for his convenience. Recruiting agents are also employed, sometimes with good enough results. In his first year Bieber had to employ such agents, who went to Indian villages and paid out no less than 10,000 Bolivian dollars in advance to native laborers. At the end of the season only forty-two of these dollars were not worked off, and even for them security was given—a remarkable proof of the honesty of these peculiar people. They work hard for rather more than ten hours a day, for pay varying, in accordance with their skill, from about eight pence to about two shillings per day. The men come in gangs of a dozen or so, and usually remain at work for fourteen or twenty-one days; then they go, and a new gang must be arranged for to take their places. This year, however, men had undertaken to come and work for the whole season without asking for their pay in advance. Such is the result of a single season's good treatment.

The great trouble with the Indians is the intolerable number of holidays and fêtes they are accustomed to observe. In an agricultural community the mischief is not important, but in the case of a mine, in which much capital has been sunk, and where climate prevents work during eight months of the year, every hour of the remaining four months is, of course, important. What the future of the Yani Mine may be I have no means of knowing, nor can I state whether it is really rich in gold. My interest in it was quickened, not by its position as a commercial venture, but by the energy with which it was worked, and the opportunity it gave to a young fellow-countryman to display, on the margins of South American civilization, the self-same qualities which have made the British Empire. It was with great sorrow, therefore, that shortly after my return to England I received the news of the sudden death at Yani of Mr. N. E. Bieber. A big land-slip came and ruined much of his work, and the shock was the cause of his death.

S

CHAPTER XXV

ASCENT OF PEÑAS HILL

IN response to my application to the authorities, and after no undue delay, an officer of the *gendarmerie*, with a dozen men, whom he described as "the force," marched away from La Paz to reach Machaca-marca in two days. We followed and caught them up at the post-house. All the men were apparently half-breeds or *cholos*, bright, merry fellows, with much vivacity and physically strong, though short. In many respects they reminded me of Ghurkas. Their officer was a decent fellow and had the fear of the prefect before his eyes, though there is no doubt that under any circumstances he would have done his duty well; but the history of my previous misadventure with his comrade, who got drunk on the way to Illimani, having been related to him, he felt that the credit of his branch of the Bolivian forces was at stake.

On the following morning we rode away over the Puna towards the foot of the Vilahaque Hill. There was no track in the direction we took, so we had to strike across the newly ploughed fields. For the men marching on foot with heavy packs on their backs the way was fatiguing enough, I have no doubt. But they covered the ground as fast as we did, keeping up a sort of trot and continually shouting as they went.

"THE FORCE"

THE CUSANACO GOLD-MINE

For footgear they wore leather sandals, to all intents and purposes the same as the *chapplis* worn by the natives of Kashmir. I observed that the Indians held the men in much respect and ran away in all directions when they saw them coming; but such Indians as they did come close to they hailed with jests and laughter, and the whole atmosphere that surrounded them was an atmosphere of merriment and good-fellowship.

We had started at an early hour, and the fields were practically abandoned. About seven o'clock the agricultural laborers came forth and began their work. Evidently they are a lazy lot of men, for they do not begin to work before from seven till nine in the morning, and you see them all leaving off about five in the afternoon. My Alpine guides had much to say about the backward character of the system of agriculture. "If this was our country," they said, "it would look very different; but these people don't know how to work, and, for that matter, judging by all these ruined farm-houses that we see, the country appears to be going backward rather than forward." The large number of fields lying fallow added, of course, to the abandoned appearance of a great part of the land. Occasionally one came across a group of fields far better cultivated than the rest, and well manured. Much land is wasted by the broad piles of stones collected upon it; they were quite unnecessarily expansive, and Pellissier said that in his country, instead of piling the stones on the surface of the ground, they would dig a deep trench and bury them. In some parts almost a quarter of the cultivable area seemed to be wasted on stone - heaps. What I think struck my guides more than anything else was the appalling waste on the part of nature in putting so fine a range of mountains as this snowy Cordillera in such an out-of-the-way country. "If we could have these mountains, or even one of them," they said, "in the Val Tournanche, it would be a fortune to our village; but here, what good are they to anybody?"

Thus about nine o'clock in the morning we reached the foot of the broad Vilahaque Hill, which stretches in a northwest-southeast direction, parallel to the Cordillera and cut off by valleys on its east side from the slopes that rise to the great range. In the middle of its Puna face there is a great bay reaching into the hill; at the mouth of this bay is the *finca* of Santa Ana. The Indians of the *finca* received us with unusual respect and hurried away to fetch the major-domo, who, in a broad and general fashion, placed the whole country-side at our disposition. Had we not been accompanied by "the force," things would not have gone so smoothly, for the Indians of Santa Ana have a bad reputation. It was here that Mr. Bandolier, when he was excavating for the remains of prehistoric Bolivia, suffered so many tribulations at the hands of the natives, and ultimately had to be protected by *gendarmes* before he could finish his work.

After a brief meal we rode on up the corrie to ascend the highest point of the hill behind, the soldiers following a short time afterwards and covering our rear, but not coming to the top. A rough track circled round more or less in the direction we wanted to go, traversing some smooth surfaces of red sandstone and beds of conglomerate, the same formation we had struck at Abichaca and were presently to find forming the mass of the Peñas Hill. Higher up came a regular alp. Thus, by steepening slopes, we gained the final ridge, where a number of teeth of red rock and curiously weathered lumps of conglomerate stuck out like the edge of a saw. Keeping along beneath these and then mounting a final rounded divide, we attained the summit. We arrived not a moment too soon, for a snow-storm was gathering and presently burst upon us. These snow-storms are in the nature of showers, and pass away almost as rapidly as they form. When the storm had gone by, and the main range cleared once more, we were surprised to find how much snow had fallen along its track in a brief time.

A couple of natives joined us on the top, and we saw a good many more collected down below watching us, but frightened from approaching owing to the presence of "the force." There was a ruined *chulpa* where we set up the theodolite, and evidently this also was a more or less sacred place. Miniature pots, a tiny flag, a small wooden cross, a new spindle, and a saucer with bits of charcoal and incense in it were lying about. After completing the observations on the highest point, I built a stone-man. Then we visited an outlying point, with a jutting rock on its summit, whose position I carefully fixed. The object of so doing was to have a point to fall back upon in case my stone-man on the higher point should be thrown down by the natives, as that on Abichaca had been. It was well that I took this precaution, for, after we had quitted the neighborhood, the village Indians came up and removed every trace of the stone-man.

Descending rapidly by the way we had come, we

joined the troops and rode back to the *finca*. In discussion with the officer, I learned that in his opinion
the uncertainty of the weather at this time was due to
the moon. He said that if the moon was unfavorable
you always had bad weather on the Puna, three days
before and three days after its change. This was the
view of almost every man in Bolivia with whom I spoke;
for them the moon was the great agent in making good
or bad weather, though none of them agreed as to when
the bad weather came—whether it was, as the officer
said, on either side of the change, or whether it followed
or preceded the change; as Sir Thomas Roe observed
in India, "the moone is a great ladie of weather in
these parts and requires much obseruation." The ex-
traordinarily universal belief in the effect of changes of
the moon upon weather is one of the most remarkable
of modern superstitious survivals.

Leaving the *gendarmes* to spend the night at the
finca, we returned to our baggage at Machaca-marca,
it being arranged that the men should march across
on the following day to the Pariri *finca* at the foot
of the Peñas Hill, where we were to join them in the
evening. The night spent at Machaca-marca was
far from a restful one. The manager of the place had
gone away, and there were only *cholos* in charge of
it. Having already spent several nights in this post-
house, its ways were well known to us. The room in
which we were wont to sleep was the chamber where
luncheon is served for travellers passing between
Chililaya and La Paz. There was an inner room, which
could only be reached by passing through ours, and
this inner room used to be occupied by the women ser-

vants of the place. This night, however, a couple of men were in occupation, and they evidently had something on their minds. No sooner had we retired to rest than one of them came out, fidgeted about, and retreated. Presently he came out again, locked the outer door leading from our room into the court-yard, and was on the point of going off with the key. We fortunately observed the action and deprived him of the key, though not in the least understanding what his idea was. During the next couple of hours he kept coming out, borrowing the key, unlocking the door and going away for a few minutes, after which he would return and make another attempt to carry off the object of his desires. Baffled in this plan he remained quiet for a time.

I went to sleep, and so missed some of these manœuvres, but the guides, convinced that something was wrong, remained awake and kept a light burning. About midnight they roused me, and we heard just outside the place a few notes blown softly on an Indian pipe. Then several men, coming from a village on the Puna, crept up to the window of the next room and held a whispered conversation with the man within it. It now became evident that his plan had been to give them the key of the outer door, so that they might obtain an entry to our room, when we were asleep, and steal some of our goods. Not having the key, they, nevertheless, crept round to the door, and we heard them fumbling at it. Coming quietly up on our side we unlocked it and ran forth, each armed with a revolver, whereupon the Indians took to flight as fast as their legs could carry them, some scouring away over the plain, others hiding among the hay-stacks. We routed them out from their concealments and drove them off. Later on, I believe, one of the guides heard them return, but they gave us no more trouble.

Riding away, with all our baggage, at an early hour on the following morning, we struck over the fields in the direction of the mountains, and so crossed the road which the *gendarmes* would have to follow. An hour later they came in sight, and we went on together to the Pariri *finca*, a rather large establishment, with a mud-built church of the usual pretentious and not ineffective architecture of old Bolivia. Near to it was the house of the proprietor, consisting of a plain outer court, with a cloistered court farther in, and a corral behind for cattle. The middle court was surrounded by rooms, which were placed at our disposal. The cloister consisted of a raised tiled pavement, carrying octagonal columns made of mud, with tile capitals supporting depressed arches. The rooms were in a state of bad repair, as is usual in all these *fincas*. They had tiled floors, and paper falling from the walls, the ceilings likewise falling in. There were no windows; all the light came in at the doors.

Ample time remained to have ascended Peñas Hill and completed our work this day, but the weather was atrocious; a gale of wind blew, and snow-storms swept down from the Cordillera one after another. The delay was annoying both to us and to "the force," for they were anxious to get away to another duty that awaited them. It appears that an Indian village on the Puna, not far from the town of Pucarani, was in a state of anarchy. It was divided into two parties, quarrelling with one another; and there had been fights of a murderous kind. The corregidor was powerless, and had been forced to send to La Paz for assistance. I asked the officer what he would have to do. He said that such Indian troubles were always arising. As a rule it sufficed to call the people together, and discuss the matter with them; after a long palaver, they generally settled down peacefully enough. "But," he said, "sometimes they resist, and then, of course, it comes to shooting." I could see that the job was distasteful to him, and that he was anxious to acquit himself well in the matter. When I met him afterwards, in La Paz, he told me how the thing had gone. He said that the village was assembled, and that he harangued them, and the corregidor harangued them, and that they had a great deal to say for themselves on both sides, but that ultimately they forgave one another and promised to live thenceforward "like brothers," whereupon he took his departure with joy and gladness. The Indians of Bolivia are a noteworthy proof of how much can be accomplished by management, and how seldom actual force is essential to the maintenance of peace.

The only hope of completing my observations in the unsettled weather that now obtained was to gain the summit of Peñas Hill at a very early hour in the morning. Accordingly, we started forth in the night and wound our way upward, first over fields, and then across a slope difficult for mules. If we had known better, we should have gone straight to the crest of the ridge and followed that along the well-made path by which we descended. As it was, we had to find

a way across a series of difficult gulleys. Dawn showed
the plain buried beneath a sheet of white fog, but, as
the sun rose, Illimani stood clearly up against a lemon
sky. The rest of the Cordillera was hidden from view
by the mass of the hill we were climbing. After scrambling along with much difficulty, and being compelled
to lose half the height we had gained, an excellent
path was struck, and proved to be the direct track over
the hill from Peñas to the Puna. Following this, we
reached the final ridge, and were astonished at what
we there discovered.

Instead of being a mere abandoned hill-top, such
as hill-tops generally are, with hardly a trace of man,
it bore signs of much human activity. There were
tracks in all directions, bordered by countless numbers
of the little model dolmens I have previously referred
to, and by some few of a considerable size, two feet
high or thereabouts. These paths converged from
all directions on a large chapel, now disroofed. The
altar was placed against a wall of native rock, in which,
about thirty feet above the floor, was a natural hollow
or small cave. The mouth of this cave was decorated
with a withered wreath, and there was an artificial
star within it. On the floor of the chapel were some
seven-branched candlesticks, and numbers of withered
flowers and small offerings. Before entering the enclosure the soldiers took their hats off, evidently regarding it as a sacred place. Numbers of small birds
were flying about. There were also two or three huts
close by, well roofed and securely locked up. Evidently this is a place of pilgrimage, sought not merely
from Peñas town, but from all the country round,

RUINED CHAPEL ON THE TOP OF PEÑAS HILL

and there can be no doubt that the Christian chapel on the top occupied the site of some religious edifice of "the times of the Gentiles."

It is not so much the situation of the hill that attracted superstitious attention to it, but the strangely shaped rocks (Peñas means peaks), weathered masses of conglomerate, which stand out along the crest of the ridge and seem to cluster themselves together where the chapel is built. In fact, the chapel may best be described as surrounded by these strangely shaped masses. Some of them are mere cubical lumps, others are like balloons on a narrow stem, others again mimic the shape of birds and beasts. On beholding them I was reminded of the holy rocks of Alvernia, with their huge clefts and openings (fabled to have been miraculously split up at the hour of Christ's crucifixion), at which St. Francis of Assisi wondered, and where he saw the vision of the seraph and received the *stigmata*. At the moment of arrival on the top there was no time for examining this curious high place, for clouds were gathering behind the Cordillera, and a series of observations had to be made with all possible speed. By good fortune the angles of the last endangered peak had been observed just a moment before the cloud came down upon it and finally blotted out the whole range.

The descent was made by a pilgrimage-track along the crest of the ridge, in and out among the conglomerate teeth and over a succession of hill-tops. From the last an easy slope led down to the *finca*. Pellissier, who did not make the ascent with us on account of illness, felt himself a little better and was eager to hasten to La Paz and see a doctor; so, at noon, after a hasty lunch, the baggage was packed on the mules and we prepared to set forth. The soldiers were drawn up to bid us good-bye. They said: "We are good soldiers, aren't we? Tell us what you think of us." I told them my opinion in the clinking silver tongue which all the world understands. As we set forth on our diverging ways, I heard the officer say to one of the men: "Well, we've got through that job all right. I hope we shall get as well through the next."

There was now before us the tedious Puna once more to be crossed. We made a great vow that we would reach La Paz that night by the Patamanta road. Hurrying on we passed again through the fields of the Santa Ana *finca*, which were being ploughed by bulls gayly decorated with flags and ribbons. As night approached we were abreast of the little Cucuta *tambo*, where the *arriero* stopped with the tired baggage-mules. But we rode on in the moonlight over the rolling desert ground, by a path that rose and fell, crossing a series of transverse undulating hills and valleys. Four leagues before the Alto a polite Bolivian was overtaken, driving three laden mules; he joined himself to us, and we went on together in silence. The undulations became deeper than before, and we gradually stretched out into a long line about shouting distance from one another. Each crest, as it loomed ahead, seemed as though it were the last. I kept imagining that I distinguished the tower which marks the point where the road dips down over the Alto; but each feigned pilastron, as it was approached, proved only to be some small rock or heap of stones. Thunder-storms were flashing in several remote quarters of the horizon, but between

SHRINE ON PEÑAS HILL

HUT NEAR THE TOP OF PEÑAS HILL

them was a sky utterly serene. When the last daylight had faded away the cold became intense, and the contrast of temperature after the broiling afternoon was keenly felt. My legs ached from the long jog-trot ride; my feet fairly froze; the hours passed painfully and slowly.

At last a final roll of the land displayed the Alto close ahead. It is a known robbers' rendezvous. Our Bolivian companion was a quarter of a mile behind. He had been joined by an Indian on foot, but the Indian had now dropped back. As I approached the pillar, where the road enters a short, deep cutting, worn by ages of travellers, I perceived a compact body of approaching Indians. Generally the Indians you pass on the road are bearing burdens or driving donkeys. To see a dozen in company, unemployed and apparently roving about, each armed with a stick, is an unusual thing. The guides coming up, we rode through them, while they halted and watched us in an unfriendly manner. I thought no more about them, and on reaching the edge of the cliff dismounted to promote circulation by walking. Down the zigzag we went as fast as we could, for a thunder-storm was now coming nearer, and my one desire was to gain the inn before rain burst upon us. We just succeeded. Early next morning the *arriero* arrived with our baggage and the news that he had seen the body of a murdered Indian at the Alto; that the police had gone up in pursuit of the criminals, and that the murderers were the group of men we had encountered, a gang who prey upon such solitary and defenceless travellers as they may chance to meet. An hour or two later a mule was led through the town, with the body of the murdered man lying across its back, a shocking sight. He proved to be a native of that same village of Abichaca whose Indians had given me so much trouble.

The remainder of my survey could be completed from the edge of the Puna in the neighborhood of La Paz, so that it was only necessary for us to ride out in the morning and back in the afternoon. In this fashion we worked all along the Alto around the margin of the Achocalla Valley. One of these days was the eve of All Saints' Day, pre-eminent among the ever-recurring fêtes of Bolivia, for it is observed almost universally. For three days work ceases, not only in the country, but in La Paz also. As we stood at the edge of the Alto it was a wonderful sight to see the multitude of Indians, in their bright-colored *ponchos*, streaming out of the town, climbing the steep face of the Alto like so many bright-colored beetles, and then threading their way over the Puna in all directions towards their scattered villages. Each man was driving his donkey or carrying his burden, and all alike had been attending the market at La Paz and buying supplies for the fête. The market, of course, had been unusually animated during the preceding days. It was always a wonderful sight, especially on Sundays, the blaze of moving color being its main characteristic.

On one of the fête days in La Paz the Alameda was given up in the afternoon to a promenade of *cholas*, the women turning out in their brilliantly new attire, their short skirts made of bright plush or other heavy-textured material, with a great quantity of lace petticoat displayed beneath it. They are ugly women almost without exception, and their costumes by no means add to their attractiveness, but the mass of color thus brought together in the bright sunshine and among the trees was undoubtedly striking and even beautiful. A herd of children were rushing up and down with loud shouts, dragging a stuffed lion around the place. The usual peaceful inhabitants of the Alameda, a tame emu and vicuña, were much disturbed by the noise and the coming and going of people. In the middle of the promenade is a small pond about fifteen yards long, whereon are kept some ducks from Lake Titicaca; they share the pool with a rather large, flat-bottomed boat, which on this fête day was in continual occupation. Though there was not room enough to row it, it was pushed about from one bank to the other, apparently to the great satisfaction of the occupants.

On the third day of the fête every one goes out to the cemetery, carrying wreaths to deposit on the tombs. The better class of ladies all wrap themselves up in their black manteaux, but the *cholas* could not have too many opportunities of displaying their new bright-colored dresses. These cemetery visits are the occasion, later on in the day, of much intoxication among the lower orders. Indeed, there is hardly any ceremony, either civil or religious, which the common people do not make an opportunity of drinking; and whenever they drink they drink too much. It is this habit, no doubt, that accounts for the multitude of small liquor-shops where *chicha* and the cheap native spirits are retailed.

Chicha, which may be described as a kind of beer, made in many varieties out of maize and other substances, is not a bad drink. In some parts of the country it is very much better made than in others; a true Bolivian will tell in a moment in what manner any *chicha* offered to him may be made. *Chicha* does not last very long, and has to be drunk within a few days of the brewing. It is a drink that comes down from prehistoric days, and is still made in the manner in which it was made in the time of the Incas. Civilization, however, has not failed to introduce beer into this remote centre. Not so long ago all the beer there was had to be imported at great cost from far away. Now, however, there are two, if not three, breweries in La Paz, which brew an excellent German beer and are driving a great trade. In fact, it is impossible for them to supply the actual demand. Many and many a time we hurried forward on the Puna to one of the post-houses, hoping to slake our thirst with a draught of good La Paz beer, only to find that the stock was exhausted, and that, though reinforcement had been sent for perhaps a week or two before, the brewery had not yet been able to supply it.

On one of the mornings I spent in the town—a Sunday morning, I think it was—word went round that an Indian murderer was going to be executed on the open drill-ground in front of the prison. The crime of which the man had been convicted was no less than compassing the death of his wife and family of children. Not apparently having the courage to kill them himself, he hired a couple of bravos to do the work. All three had been arrested and found guilty. This day the principal was to pay the penalty with his life. The whole city turned out on the great square, near the prison, to see the execution. Military bands playing sad music concentrated on the square, and a considerable body of troops were drawn up to keep order, after they had been employed skirmishing about the town to collect together a number of Indians to witness the execution. The Indians were driven on to the parade and drawn up immediately in front of the place of execution, where they sat down on the ground, with the soldiers surrounding them outside and the general public farther out.

It was a bright morning with a clear sky, and the brilliancy of the sun shining on this field of ponchoed natives made them look from the far distance like a bed of flowers. Punctually at the hour appointed the prison doors opened and the three men were brought out and placed some distance from one another in a row, the principal malefactor, the only one who was to be executed, being in the centre. He marched forth, utterly unconcerned, and took his place without the smallest sign of fear; but the other two, whose hour had not yet come, were almost in a state of collapse from terror. There was something in the brave bearing of the murderer that won for him the respect of the crowd. He was allowed to stand forth and make a speech, in which I am told he expressed himself quite satisfied with what he had done. "The woman," he said, "merited the death brought upon her, and so did the children." He in nowise regretted the action he had taken. When he had finished he took his place on a sort of little stool with a post for a back, while great cries and shrieks arose from the assembled Indians. The firing party did their work without delay, and the culprit was killed instantaneously, among the lamentations of the people of his race. The body was left for many hours where it fell, and the Indians were encouraged to go forward and inspect it, the object of the whole ghastly performance being to strike terror into them.   Thereupon the other two men were removed back into the prison, one of them to be brought forth and shot a month later I was told, the other, a young man, to spend his life in penal servitude.   According to a report which reached me, whether well grounded or not I cannot say, there were at that time within the prison walls over two hundred convicted Indian murderers, but capital punishment is seldom enforced except in the case of parricides and murderers of a particularly atrocious kind.

CHAPTER XXVI

TIN - MINES OF HUAINA POTOSI

BEFORE starting to visit the volcanic ranges to the west and south, I made yet one more expedition to the Puna and towards the Cordillera, my object being to inspect a great vein of tin which had recently begun to be worked. It is situated on the very flanks of that fine Mount Cacaaca* whose glorious pyramid had so often attracted our gaze while traversing the plateau or standing on the summits of the Puna hills. Bolivia is one of the few countries in the world that are rich in tin. No tin-mines are known to exist in the Western or Coast Cordillera, and I believe no tin has been discovered either in Peru or Chile. It is only along the flank of the Cordillera Real and its prolongation to the south that tin-mines have been opened. Stream tin has been found by gold prospectors in one or two of the eastern valleys, Tipuani for instance; but known veins are all along the western side of the range, near the junction of the Silurian formation with the intruded igneous rocks. Some of the best tin lodes are said to occur in the porphyry

---

* The name Caca-aca means "by broken rocks." The altitude of this peak, according to my measurement, is 20,560 feet. Other measurements are : Minchin, 20,170 feet ; Reck, 20,292 feet ; Pentland, 20,650 feet ; Pinis, 19,961 feet ; mean, 20,250 feet.

or altered andesite, but in a few places lodes run through slate and trachyte. According to Mr. C. C. Pasley,* the veins in the porphyry are generally the richest and of better quality, the other being mixed with antimony, iron, and copper pyrites, zinc blende, and sometimes with bismuth and wolfram. The tin usually contains traces of silver, and the lodes frequently have a capping of iron. The chief tin-producing districts are four: Oruro in the centre, La Paz in the north, Chorolque in the south, and Potosi farther to the eastward. The most important of these districts is Oruro. Tin is also found in the Quimsa Cruz Mountain.

My visit to the mines was made in company with my friend Mr. M. Martindale, an English engineer who had lived for many years in South America, and was familiar with the mines of many of its countries. Leaving La Paz early one morning, we rode straight up the main valley, instead of turning sharply to the left and climbing to the Alto of Lima, as I had always hitherto done on my Puna expeditions. We noticed that the La Paz River was much fuller of water than it had been, for the frequent snow-storms upon the mountains and the thunder-storms lower down, forerunners of the rainy season, were beginning to produce an effect. There were blossoming apple-trees in the cottage gardens, and many cactuses bearing bright flowers by the side of the mule-path. In fact, the spring, which we had found two months before at Cotaña, had now climbed even beyond La Paz. In two or three hours we had passed round the bend of the valley, and lost sight of

* "The Tin-Mines of Bolivia," a paper read before the Institution of Mining and Metallurgy, December 21, 1898.

THE NEIGHBORHOOD OF MOUNT CACA-ACA

the town and almost all traces of habitation. A steep rise, which took us near two or three pools of water, finally landed us on the Puna, perhaps five miles to the north of the point where we usually struck it. Our position might be better described as on the lowest slopes of the Cordillera rather than on the Puna at all, though the slopes here sink down to the plain with so gradual a slope that the transition from slope to plain can scarcely be marked.

Thus far the weather had been cloudy, and the view restricted, but now the sun burst forth and the sky was blue among dissolving clouds. The distant plain was smoking with dust whirlpools like the smoke of bonfires. We soon came on the traces of old moraines. Continuing our northward way, over a rounded hog's-back, and circling somewhat about the end of a great outlier of the main Cordillera, we entered a surprisingly large valley that penetrates to the crest of the Cordillera and gives access to an important mule-pass leading over to Zongo. Mount Cacaaca, glorious with its wide-spreading base and bladed icy tower, was revealed in all its splendor standing north of the pass, while to our right hand were cliffs and ridges of purple rock forming part of the next snow-mountain to the south. Following the left bank of the valley and gradually descending towards the stream and lake at the head of it, we came presently on the buildings and workings of the Milluni Mine, situated 15,100 feet above sea-level.

At present the mine is only being worked on a small scale, and the buildings are of a simple character. The engineer's house had been placed at our disposal by Señor Farfan, the owner, who lived in La Paz; but, agreeable as it was to have a roof over our heads when the bleak night came on, we could have wished that the room had been less draughty, or the gale of wind that arose at sunset less severe. The people told us that such a gale springs up daily, and is one of the chief annoyances to their life in this dreary solitude. Clouds were trying to pour over the pass from Zongo, but they faded away on the col. For a brief moment the sunset coloring played upon Mount Cacaaca so that it shone like a spear-tip newly withdrawn from the furnace, but the ice-slopes grew steel-gray as the pallid night came swiftly on.

Some hours of the next morning were devoted to an inspection of the mine, which is tentatively worked at several different levels by tunnels running into the mountain. I am informed that, since my visit in 1898, great developments have been accomplished, and that I should hardly recognize the works in their present condition. The property has passed into the hands of a wealthy French syndicate. Standing at the foot of one of the tunnels and gazing abroad over the valley, it was plain to see how great a glacial extension there had formerly been in this place. Now the actual crest of the range can be reached at the col without touching glaciers at all; only a few snow-beds have to be crossed. Of course, Cacaaca, and the peak opposite to it, are draped with beautiful glaciers, but the ice does not descend to the bottom of the principal valley. Once it filled that valley and stretched down towards the Puna, a distance of several miles. On its retreat it left exposed a series

of lake basins, since filled up, with the exception of the two highest. The tin lode, averaging about five yards in thickness, comes to the surface, and can be traced right up the hill-side, running approximately in a northwest-southeast direction, and at a very high angle of dip. It almost looks as though some mighty power, wielding a gigantic sword, had cloven the hill and filled the gap it left with this great lode. There are also several other parallel lodes. The ore is in some places very rich indeed, while in other places the tin contains a large admixture of antimony.

Later on in the day we rode off to cross the main southwestward buttress ridge of Mount Cacaaca by a pass 17,100 feet in height. Descending to the bottom of Milluni Valley, and traversing a wide swamp, we gained the foot of the opposite slope, and mounted it by a faintly marked track, which leads over shales and grits to a desolate rounded region of débris, among which the pass is situated. The ridge rising thence towards Mount Cacaaca, soon becomes sharp and bold in form, breaking into needles of rock and ice *arêtes* of exceeding narrowness. It leads to a minor summit, beyond which comes a deep-lying saddle of ice, and then a long and most difficult *arête*, with a precipice on either hand rising to the summit of the peak. By this route it was plain that no ascent could be made, nor, I think, will the mountain be climbed from the east or directly from the Zongo Pass. On all sides that I saw, Mount Cacaaca presents quite unusual difficulties to a climber, but I am told that on the other side of the range there is a slope by which the mountain might be attacked with some chance of success.

When standing on the col, and facing towards the snowy peak, there was behind us a radiating group of rounded hills spreading widely and sloping steadily towards the Puna. To this mass properly belongs the name Huaina Potosi, by which Cacaaca is now popularly known. Silver having been found hereabouts, hope arose in the minds of the finders that great wealth would ensue. They therefore named the hill (but not the snowy peak) after the famous Potosi, calling it Huaina, which means "younger." As far as silver is concerned, the hill has not justified its name.

Instead of descending at once to the valley, I wandered round along the crest of the hill outwards to a stone man, which commanded a very magnificent view alike over the plain and towards the mountain. Hence one could look into the next deep valley that leads to the southwestern foot of Cacaaca, where a beautiful glacier, broken into blue ice-falls and backed by splendid ice-slopes and precipices, empties its waters into an emerald green tarn. And now we could see, nearer at hand than I had yet beheld them, the continuation of the main ridge to the north, where the mountains are for a certain distance more splintered and needle-like than at any other part of the Cordillera. The fine peak, named Condoriri (19,950 feet, according to my measurement), marks the neighborhood of another important pass that likewise leads to Zongo. From this peak several lofty and broken buttress ranges stretching towards the Puna hid the further view along the range in the direction of Mount Sorata. Farther around came the distant Lake Titicaca glittering in the sunshine, and then the broad plateau, always impressive as a contrast with the rugged peaks. On the very crest of the Huaina Potosi Hill was a huge block of granite, which must have been brought there by ice from Mount Cacaaca, a great part of whose mass consists of granite. At that time the deep valley which now lies between the point where the bowlder stands and the mountain itself must have been entirely filled with ice, an accumulation which would have involved a flow of many miles in length before it could have melted away, for the bowlder stands at least 17,500 feet above the sea, while the intervening valley bottom is less than 15,000 feet. There are plenty of similar bowlders to be found on the southwestern slope of Huaina Potosi, but lower down most of them are water-worn; those that have maintained themselves on the crest or upper part of the slope alone retain the sharpness of their original angles.

The tin-mine is situated on the northern slope of the hill, while the Ingenio, where the ores are sorted and some of them reduced, was planted close to the glacier-lake, which supplied the water-power for the work. The valley from this point down to the Puna is of very gentle slope, so that carts can be drawn right up to the workings. The lode is the same as that of the Milluni Mine, continued in this direction, and is from two to ten metres wide, and very rich in tin. There is almost an exhaustless quantity of it, so that when the machinery, which we were informed was on its way, is installed, no doubt very good results will be yielded.* The same engineer manages both this and the Milluni

* I hear that this was accomplished in 1900, and that work on a large scale has begun.

Mine. He rides over the intervening 17,000-foot pass twice a week or oftener, and thinks nothing of it. He had been down to La Paz, and now arrived in company with a Belgian friend, so that we formed a pleasant party in a far more comfortable house than that we had occupied the previous night. Its situation at the foot of the splendid cliffs of Cacaaca, and near the lake in whose waters that mountain is reflected, is one of the most wildly beautiful that we saw in Bolivia.

We sat on late after the evening meal, talking of the mine and its prospects, of the mineral wealth of this side of the Cordillera all along, of the need for prospecting, and the comparatively little good work of that kind that had been done. The mules in the court-yard, just outside the door, were champing their fodder with great content; they seemed more inclined to eat than to sleep. Maquignaz, speaking from experience, asserted that properly fed mules never sleep for more than two minutes at a time. In his own farm at home, he said, the mule-stable was in close proximity to his bed. Wake at what hour of the night he might, he never failed to hear his mules feeding; they might stop for a minute or two, but that was all; yet when the morning came they were ready for a long day's work.

"How much food do you give them?" I asked.

"The rule with us," he said, "is to give them all they can eat. They work at it from the moment they come into the stable in the evening till the moment they start again the following morning. So it goes on day after day and week after week, with only Sundays off."

Next morning we were taken to see the shed where the big machinery was to be installed when it came. At present they had only a thirty horse-power water-wheel, worked by the overflow of the glacier-lake, and much of the ore was pounded up by human labor. In this case the ore, broken small by hammering, was spread out on a flat stone, and a big rounded bowlder was rocked about upon it by means of a staging fastened across the top of the bowlder, on which a man stood, with legs well apart, throwing his weight alternately on one foot and the other. This, no doubt, is the ancient native method of working. The ores are of various degrees of richness, and the work-people (mostly women) who break them into small fragments attain great skill in sorting them into different heaps, according to their fineness. Ores of low grade are pounded up, rolled, and washed on the spot, while the richer ores are packed in bags and conveyed to the coast for reduction. The engineer said that the Indians are skilful in all mining operations, and can easily be taught new processes. From the most ancient times mining traditions have been handed down among them, so that they approach all mining processes with a ready intelligence. The work-people we saw engaged came from the neighboring Puna. Some merely stay for two or three weeks, then return to their agricultural pursuits; others remain for months, and even years, in continual employment, making good wages.

CHAPTER XXVII

LAST RIDE OVER THE PUNA

ABOUT the hour when we were ready to start away, half a dozen vicuñas appeared, grazing high up on the almost open hill-side opposite to us—a slope of the strangely regular sugar-loaf outlier of Cacaaca, whose symmetrical, rounded top forms so remarkable a contrast with the bladed peak of its great neighbor. Having no rifle with me, I was unable to attempt a stalk, but our Belgian fellow-guest went off in great haste, and began running up the hill. He soon found that at this elevation such activity could not long be maintained; his trot became a walk, and his walk a slow crawl, before any considerable fraction of the distance had been covered. Without taking advantage of the inequalities of the ground, he made straight for the vicuñas, whose attention he soon attracted, whereupon they turned and fled. This was the only group of vicuñas I ever saw near the snow-line in the Cordillera. On the Puna, and especially the southern part of it, in the direction of Sicasica, we encountered several close to the high-road. There they allowed us to approach within a distance of three or four hundred yards, while they hardly took any notice of a carriage or wagon passing along the road.

Our day's march led straight down the valley along

the left bank of the stream. The direct trail to La Paz lies right over the Huaina Potosi Hill; by it we sent away the muleteer with the baggage. My object this day was to investigate the group of valleys which descend from between Cacaaca and Condoriri, converging one upon another, and finally issuing on to the plain near the back of the Vilahaque Hill. The existence of these valleys, and of others like them all along the range, is scarcely suspected by the traveller who has never been among them. The Cordillera, seen from the Puna, appears to slope gradually down from the foot of the snow to the plain by a series of undulating inclines, seamed here and there by valleys of inconsiderable dimensions, eroded by mountain torrents.

It is only on a closer inspection that the magnitude of these eroded valleys and the intricacy of their upper extensions are discovered. They have a tendency to throw off, just below the snow-level, lateral valleys parallel with the main ridge. Such was the Haukaña Valley on Mount Sorata; such also is this valley at the back of Huaina Potosi. We were desirous, moreover, of finding out the direction of another important pass, which crosses the range south of Condoriri. I even hoped to identify the position of a considerable lake, marked on a rough published map that professes to indicate a possible line for a road leading from Peñas by a pass over the Cordillera to Challana. I was, however, unable to see this lake; but there is little doubt that it is a much smaller sheet of water than the road-plan made it appear. The road, however, is doubtless well designed, and should be made at an early date. No important physical obstacles have to be overcome. The Challana Valley is by nature very rich, and would well repay settlement and development, but the local Indians are troublesome. The road passing through it would be the easiest and most direct route from the Bolivian plateau to Puerto Ballivian, at the junction of the Huanay and Coroico rivers, the Rio Huanay being the stream that unites the waters of the Mapiri, Tipuani, and Challana valleys. The distance by this road from La Paz to Puerto Ballivian would be three hundred and twenty-two kilometres. The united river below Puerto Ballivian is named the Rio Kaka. This, when united to the Rio de La Paz, becomes the Rio Beni.

Riding along the easy floor of the wide and almost level valley below the mine, we followed the trail marked out for the cart-track, and thus presently reached another important side valley, likewise filled at its head with one of the glaciers of the Cacaaca massif. A couple of high lakes below the glacier occupy hollows in the rock, once covered by ice, and form a beautifully picturesque foreground for the mountains behind. We presently approached yet a third side valley, at whose mouth are situated the ruins of a once important Spanish silver-mining establishment. Its corrals are still found useful for the caravans of beasts of burden that come up to the Huaina Potosi Mine. Formerly the three side valleys — that, namely, in which the mine is now placed; the second, which has lakes in it; and the third, opening on the mine ruins —discharged themselves directly and independently down the main slope of the Cordillera to the plain. But the two former have been beheaded, and their waters turned into the third by means of this side valley, down which we had come, for it has eaten its way back across them one after the other. The traces of their older beds may still be observed on the lower main slopes.

Thus far Condoriri had been a fine sight, with its splendid precipices and bold summits. Indeed, seen close at hand, it fully rivals Cacaaca in beauty, though not quite equalling it in altitude. The southern face is in part too precipitous for snow to rest upon, so that the glaciers below are not now of great dimensions. Formerly, however, they reached far down towards the plain. The ice-worn valley, with its glacier-lake, once the bed of this great ice-river, joins, below the Indian village of Tuni, that down which we descended. At present these valleys are sparsely peopled; once they must have supported a larger population, for many ruined huts and signs of abandoned cultivation lie scattered about. Below Tuni the snow-mountains are gradually hidden from view by their own shoulders, and the deep valley becomes barren and desolate past description. It winds gently down between bare slopes, with a stony and sometimes boggy floor, including a wide stream-bed, which in the rainy season is filled from side to side by a torrent, but was now a mere waste of water-worn stones. For eight or ten miles we rode down this depressing hollow, with the clouds gathering heavier and heavier overhead, till rain pattered about us.

I insisted upon continuing the direct descent, being

determined to discover which of the streams, known
to us on the Puna, was the one that derived itself from
this source. In the rainy season it might, no doubt,
be easy enough to identify from the Puna the places
where the various streams, whose beds are crossed by
the highway, issue from the mountains; but when, as
during the time of my visit, these streams are almost
without exception dried up, it is impossible to trace
their beds far back. Even from commanding positions
like the summit of Peñas and Vilahaque hills, it is difficult to be certain of the course followed by the streams
down the plain. Coming at last to where the valley
opened, the mystery was solved, and the Rio Sehuenca,
whose bed crosses the road just west of Machaca-
marca, proved to be the one derived from this valley.
This river empties into Lake Titicaca near Aigachi.
A remarkable feature now revealed to us was the
great artificial and ancient canal, which here taps
the stream and carries off almost the whole of the
dry season supply of water. This beautifully engineered canal sweeps around the slope of the hill and
irrigates the fields between Vilahaque and Machaca-
marca, an admirable piece of native work.

Satisfied thus as to the main object of the day's
march, we mounted the great brown moorland close
by, following a track till we lost it among the grass
tussocks of the hill. A snow-storm now burst upon
us, and blotted out all distant view, so that for a time
we wandered rather vaguely, not quite knowing the
direction which should be taken. In the interval
of a brief clearance the plane-table was set up and
the correct bearing of the Alto de Lima observed, so

that thenceforward we were able to steer by compass in whatever fogs or storms might overtake us. A wide prospect of apparently featureless slope stretched ahead, and it seemed as though the route should prac tically be level. But appearances were deceptive; the slope, far from being continuous, was seamed by an almost countless number of ravines, separated from one another by round-topped ridges, between every pair of which was a deep and often, in its lower part, very steep-sided gully. From gully to ridge the ascent might be two hundred to three hundred feet. The moment you reached the top of a ridge you commenced the descent into a new gully, the distance from crest to crest being anything from a quarter of a mile to nearly a mile. This undulating character of the country is not visible to a person gazing across the undulations in the direction of his way; he may see signs of a depression ahead of him, but there appears to be nothing beyond but an unbroken slope. This deceptive appearance is so constant that, even after a dozen such ribs and valleys have been laboriously crossed, it still seems as though the next rib should be the last. Of course, such ascents and descents, continually repeated, are both fatiguing and monotonous, and the fourteen or fifteen miles of this kind of ground over which we had to travel before reaching the Alto were wearisome alike to man and beast. Once or twice we came upon secluded villages hidden in these valley bottoms, but they were small and wretched centres of population. Below, to our right, a wide, inhabited area of the Puna was always visible; it was only when we approached the Alto that the cultivated land was

U   305

left behind, and the last open mile or two traversed
almost on the level of the high-road. Shortly before
sunset we dipped over the edge of the Alto and left
the Puna for the last time. We had traversed it in
one direction or another no fewer than nine times,
and were heartily sick of its dreary, bare expanse.

Of course, there was much more work that I might
have undertaken in the northern part of the Cordillera had weather permitted, but clear days, and even
clear mornings, were now so few, and the storms of
rain and snow, blotting out all views, were of such
every-day occurrence, that any hope I might have
entertained of being able profitably to explore the high
valleys intervening between Mount Sorata and Condoriri had to be abandoned. A couple of months
might well have been spent penetrating their fastnesses and visiting the different passes by which
access may be obtained to the other side of the range;
but in the rainy season that kind of work cannot be
pursued, and the fact that the rainy season was approaching could no longer be doubted. In the previous year the rains had held off till the month of
January, and all of November had been fine; but the
penalty was now being paid by the unusually early
on-coming of the rains this year, to my no small misfortune. I still hoped to devote a few days to the examination of the volcanic mountains (whereof Sajama
is the highest) on my southward way, but I found
it impossible to hire mules for the expedition, for the
people in La Paz were just then in a state of no little
excitement, and the first signs were perceptible of a

political movement, which presently culminated in a small revolution.

According to the then existing constitution of Bolivia, one after another of the principal towns had the right to take its turn as the capital. Sucre, Cochabamba, La Paz, and, I believe, Oruro, have all been the capital at one time or another. La Paz, as by far the largest town and greatest commercial centre in the country, not unnaturally felt that its business received less attention from a legislature residing in Sucre, which was at that time the capital, than it would receive if the legislature were at La Paz itself. It must be remembered that Bolivia is by no means a homogeneous country; it is formed by the union of provinces differing from one another to the most marked extent. Some consist chiefly of tropical forests; others of almost Arctic table-lands. Some are agricultural; the wealth of others is entirely mineral. Some contain lands as rich as any in the world; others are mere deserts. It follows that the interests of such different localities are widely divergent from one another, and the problem of harmonizing those differences is by no means easy. Again, there are few lands in which the problems of locomotion are harder of solution, for, under present circumstances, railways cannot be carried to some of the richest areas of the country, owing to great natural obstacles. Other parts might easily enough be supplied with railways but for the not unnatural jealousy of richer places which cannot be so supplied. It follows that to pass legislation in Bolivia for the development of any isolated part of the country is difficult, and the influence of the place where the legislature meets is necessarily an important factor.

La Paz for several years had been deprived (and in the opinion of its citizens unjustly deprived) of its right to receive the government and legislature. Its inhabitants now began to clamor for their city to take its turn as capital. Unfortunately, La Paz is difficult of access, and lies quite out of the way of all the southern and southeastern part of Bolivia. The representatives of the parts of the country which are not in easy communication with La Paz formed the majority in the legislature. After a period of temporizing, they finally passed a measure by which it was decreed that for the future Sucre, and Sucre only, should be Bolivia's capital. Now Sucre is a place of very little importance in itself, and would have no claim to be capital were it not for the big government buildings that have been raised there, and the fact that a number of influential persons have built themselves houses and settled down there. Sucre is not a centre of agriculture, manufacture, or commerce. The diplomatic representatives of foreign countries make La Paz their home, and only pay Sucre occasional visits. Not unnaturally, therefore, the people of La Paz felt that by this measure their interests were seriously compromised. Enthusiastic meetings were held during the last days of my stay in the town, and it became evident that resistance would be made.

A provisional government was formed in La Paz and a proclamation issued to the effect that, if Sucre was to be the capital of Bolivia, the constitution should be altered to a federal form, so that the Department of La Paz should become a self-governing state in a Bolivian union. Ultimately, the matter was referred to the arbitrament of war. Government troops from Sucre and the south generally occupied Oruro, while the people of La Paz marshalled their forces for their own defence. The attempt to besiege La Paz and reduce it failed. At last a battle decided the issue and La Paz won the day. It is now the capital, while the former President, Alonzo, had to give place to General Pando, the commander of the northern forces. His position having been legalized by an overwhelming popular vote, he was duly installed President, and has proved himself to be one of the most capable and energetic Presidents the country ever possessed.

As far as fighting was concerned, little blood was shed; but during the disturbances the Indians tended to lapse into an anarchical state, though the mischief did not go far. One or two local Indian risings, I believe, took place. In Zongo, for instance, the *gomales* were raided by Indian workmen, who plundered them of whatever was of value, besides putting some people to death. At Corocoro also, the great copper-mining centre, there was an Indian rising, and the white manager of one of the mines fled with his wife and daughter. Some blundering official, through whose district they were passing, turned them back because they had no passport!—the result being that they were overtaken by an Indian mob. It is asserted that their lives were not in danger, but at all events the man thought they were, and, mind-

ful of the past history of Indian uprisings, he shot
his wife and daughter and took his own life. But
these were sporadic cases of lawlessness. Order was
quickly restored. The fact that no general rising took
place serves to prove how well, on the whole, the Indians are restrained by the small white population of
Bolivia, whom they outnumber by at least fifteen to
one.

At such a time it was not, of course, easy to organize
a mountaineering expedition to Sajama. I was re-
luctantly obliged to abandon the project and to content myself with journeying down to the coast by the
ordinary high-road to Oruro, and the railway thence
to Antofagasta. The baggage was packed and delivered over to the carriers, and the last morning of
my sojourn in La Paz arrived. It was a brilliant
day, and I was early afoot, when the Bolivian ladies,
in their black manteaux, were just returning from
mass. In the shade, under the blank pink wall over
against the church, sat a long row of women behind their
baskets of flowers—roses, pinks, verbenas, and many
garden blossoms unknown to me. The street was
flooded with sunshine, and the dark shadows hid themselves under the wide eaves. The Alto wall around
the town, and Illimani in the far distance, were check-
ered with blue shadows. White towers of cloud were
mounting behind the Cordillera into the blue sky.
Doctor Bridgeman, the able and kindly United States
Minister, was awaiting me at the door of the Legation,
with a big horse ready saddled for my use. We rode
away, noisily caracoling down the cobbled streets,
through the Alameda, and so out along the road bor-

dered by suburban gardens, all a mass of blossom, fragrantly scenting the air. The hedges of rose and cactus followed, and the place where water drips over and covers a cliff with moss and little starlike white flowers. Once again I entered Obrajes, that charming country resort of the gentry of La Paz. We visited an old lady of courtliest manners, who took us into her garden, showed us all its rich promises of fruit, and would have burdened us down with nosegays of flowers had there been any means of carrying them off. Before the heat of the day we trotted back to La Paz to breakfast at the United States Legation. The rest of the day was devoted to paying bills and calls, and making the last arrangements for departure. The usual thunder-storm and downpour of rain came in the afternoon, and not until late at night did the stars look forth.

CHAPTER XXVIII

LA PAZ TO ORURO

THE heavy rains of November 12th were succeeded by a brilliant morning of hot sunshine, cool air, and dust for once well laid. At an early hour the guides and I sallied forth from our hotel, accompanied by a party of our best friends, and proceeded to the post-station, where the public coach that was to carry us and two or three other passengers to Oruro was drawn up, with the baggage-wagon behind it. Both had a ramshackle appearance. The baggage-wagon seemed, and was, too light for the unusually heavy load that my luggage amounted to. At seven o'clock, after many delays, all was ready. The horses were cast off; the driver stamped and whistled; we waved farewell to our acquaintances, and, for the fourteenth time, began traversing the zigzags that lead up to the Alto. As we rose, the surrounding mountains disentangled themselves from their lower slopes and mounted into the air. Illimani, with a school of white clouds floating around it, was almost like a thing transparent, seen through some of the self-same veil of azure firmament that hides the night of space behind the fiction of sky, which to-day was pervaded by a fiery light unusually fierce. Cacaaca, in another quarter of the horizon, shone sharp and solid in its mantle of new-fallen snow.

which trailed all around it far down on to the plain. The little fields of the suburbs were all fresh with young green shoots, and Indians were piping among them. Driving with great energy, and helped by an extra team of mules hitched on in front, we made quick ascent, topping the Alto in an hour and a half, and gaining there our last glimpse of the hospitable town we had left.

We galloped off at a splendid pace across the plain, and saw its wide undulations stretching away in many directions, white with snow, the pink hills lifting themselves beyond it to the west in hot sunshine. For several miles our jehu drove with a fury that expressed itself in the agitation of his voice and of all his limbs at once. He carried under his seat a large collection of rocks, which he violently and skilfully threw, one by one, at the leaders, hitting them where he pleased, and sometimes making an intentional cannon off a wheeler on to a leader, or off one leader on to the other. He also carried an extra trace-bar, fitted with loose rings at the ends and middle. With it he jabbed the wheelers in the rear, making a great clatter with the rings, or sometimes merely knocked the thing against the foot-board to make the rings rattle, an indication of readiness to act which his team was quick to understand. Thus stamping his feet, yelling, throwing stones, rattling his bar, or taking a turn at the whip, he stimulated the team to great exertion, and covered the ground at a wild speed, and this, notwithstanding the roughness of the road, the short, steep ascents and descents, the stones that lay about, and the consequent leaping and jolting of the vehicle, which made the passengers hang on to their seats like grim death and rattled the teeth in their heads. Such hysterical vigor could not be prolonged all day. We soon found that it alternated with periods in which our driver blissfully slept on his box, sitting upon the reins, while his mules or ponies crawled along at a snail's pace. The duration of periods of activity and repose seemed, however, to be well calculated, for, except in case of an accident, we never failed to arrive at the different post-stages very nearly at the prearranged time.

For some miles the way was well known to us, and the scenery remained of the kind characteristic of the Puna, save that the Cordillera was more and more hidden from view by intervening low hills. We could see the clouds piling themselves up behind it and gradually nodding over, but Illimani remained clear and grew to be almost insignificant beneath the mighty mountain of white cloud that was elevated behind it. The power of the sun soon made itself felt, and the light dust began to fly, so that we breathed it in and had our clothes saturated by it. Mirages, like broad Titicaca itself, inundated the plain, and the western hills rose out of them like islands, pink in sunshine, purple in shadow. Vicuñas were not infrequently seen in different directions, and once a splendid condor rose from the road just in front of the horses and soared magnificently aloft.

Every two or three hours there was a halt to change teams, and the humors of the different beasts formed the chief interest of the way. They were generally wild at starting, calling forth the reserve power of

BETWEEN LA PAZ AND ORURO

our driver, really a splendid whip. The way he dealt with a couple of rearing leaders, who turned round and looked him in the face, was a sight to see; he appeared to assail them simultaneously with his whip while jabbing at the wheelers and enveloping the whole team in a shower of stones. Gradually the wide plain we were traversing narrowed to a mere valley as we passed, at no great distance, a small square-topped hill with a broad ramp artificially contrived for its ascent. It had the appearance of some staged Mexican temple in ruins, and was doubtless another of the sacred high places of prehistoric Bolivia. The population now became sparse, the villages few and far between; it was seldom that we encountered any one upon the road. At mid-day, under the glaring vertical sun, drowsiness invaded us all, and we slept till suddenly awakened by the approach of the mail-cart coming in the opposite direction from Oruro, the first civilized vehicle we had encountered. Both drivers stopped and gazed in silence at one another for some time, as though pleased to meet, but having nothing whatever to say. At last one inquired: "What news?"

"Nothing," replied the other.

"What did he say?" asked the first, continuing, doubtless, a conversation a fortnight old.

"Nothing," was the answer.

"Good," said the first, and they drove on.

This was the longest conversation I heard our driver take part in during the three days we were together.

The land about us was generally stony and uncultivated, but once or twice we passed through green, sweet-smelling areas where dwarf junipers were growing. Sometimes we encountered caravans of llamas travelling their slow way along the road, or again we met them scattered abroad over the country, picking up the nourishment they require from dried plants, of whose existence the eye scarcely made one aware, while their drivers were resting near the piled-up loads.

A mile or two before reaching the village of Ayoayo the road began to be bordered at regular and frequent intervals by tall mud-built piers of the time of the Spaniards, each simple in form, but by their mere multitude and regularity of alignment producing quite a noble effect. They are the remnants of the long series which, I am told, in ancient days marked out all the route from Lima to the famous mines of Potosi. As we approached the village where we were to spend the night, heavy clouds gathered overhead and began to drop rain. There was every sign of an approaching thunder-storm, but no considerable amount of rain fell. At sunset a stream of glowing color poured forth through an opening in the heavens, framed by the leaden earth below, the leaden clouds above, and by pillars of thunder-storm on either hand—a window to the west bordered and barred with gold. The mellow light, caught by the mud walls of the fields and houses of the village, transfigured them into the likeness of palaces built of precious stones.

The general round of a day's experiences in travelling over the high Bolivian plateau at this time of year closely resembled the experiences of a traveller in the desert mountain region within Kashmir. The

early morning was always so brightly cold that one's
feet became numb, and the whole body suffered great
discomfort from chill. Only by beating the arms
against the chest and stamping could a little sensation be maintained in hands and feet. Sunrise brought
a blissful hour of thaw, in which sensation returned
to the body, while the radiant heat of the sun was
tempered by cool air. All too quickly this pleasant
time passed, as the sun rose, raging, into the heavens,
flooded the wide, bare landscape with its glare of light,
too brilliant for the eye to rest upon, and poured its
torment of heat on the suffering wayfarer. The
power of observation was quickly burned up, and the
traveller settled down to a dreamy condition of suffering, in which the hours dragged themselves slowly
along and the hoped-for evening loitered. Late in
the afternoon, perhaps, clouds which had long been
gathering around the horizon rose high enough aloft
to hide the sun, and a great relief and joy was immediately felt. The evening hour, whether cloudy or
not, brought a delicious return of comfort; the mind
resumed its control, observation awakened, the landscape regained its beauty and grew even yet more
beautiful, until the sun set in momentary glory and
the night came on. Even then the cold hesitated to
return, for the hot earth kept it at bay for hours after
the stars had come out in all their splendor and the
evening clouds had faded away.

The second morning of our drive was cold and gray,
till the sun rose colorless in the midst of a white mist.
The road lay along a well-marked river valley, with
pilastrons beside it at frequent intervals. The most

interesting sight was an abandoned prehistoric village of little rectangular mud huts roofed with mud, every hut standing separate from its neighbor, most of them arranged in a row in echelon, each so situated that the side in the midst of which the door was cut faced the east. The ancient inhabitants were buried beneath the floors of these houses. The hideous pile of human remains recently excavated, which lay about the huts, witnessed the activity of the Bandoliers. A little way farther on came the village festively named Patac-Amaya (Hundred Corpses), the site, I suppose, of some ancient battle. Here occurred a change in domestic architecture, the usual Indian house now apparently consisting of a round building and an oblong one in connection. Such round houses I had not before seen in Bolivia.

As we halted to change horses, Mr. Bandolier and his wife, who were on the lookout for us, walked up, to my great delight. The top of Illimani was still in sight in one direction, and Sajama would have been visible in the other if the weather had been clear; so, at all events, they told me. I still had hopes of being able to make up a caravan at Oruro to visit Sajama and ascend the mountain from the tin-foundry Changamoco. Mr. Bandelier promised to come with me. He gave an account of his excavations, which had been productive of very interesting results, enabling him to reconstruct much of the ancient village-life of the people in this neighborhood. A mile or two farther on a wheel of the coach went wrong as we were passing a rather large farm. The driver appealed to the farmer for assistance, and the curious process of adjustment was begun. A rough kind of screw-jack was produced. Lifting the axle off the ground, the wheel was taken off and the hub packed with a lot of old sacking, richly greased and wedged in with a number of bits of wood. Unsatisfactory though the mending seemed, it apparently sufficed, for after half an hour's halt we were able to proceed, though only at a snail's pace. The team was a wretched one. Every mule had a sore back and shoulder, nor could the driver, even by cruelly searching out the sores with his whip, provoke the miserable beasts out of a walk.

The scenery remained ever the same. On the left was the long line of hills which had begun in the neighborhood of La Paz, there forming the right bank of the valley of the La Paz River and the eastern margin of the Puna. On the right, isolated hills emerged from the plain, which was covered here and there with patches of the green juniper, called *guarda roseo*. There was hardly a house, or even a ruin or abandoned field. A long, gentle ascent led over a wide col to the town of Sicasica, whence a broad sort of basin came into view, with the next post-station, Aroma, visible at the far side of it, and the long dip and rise of the road clearly traceable between. With a new team we made fine progress, and were just approaching Aroma when news was brought, by a horseman galloping after us, that the baggage-wagon had utterly broken down a mile or two back, the wheel being smashed past hope of repair. No such thing as a cart was to be had nearer than Oruro in one direction, and La Paz in the other, the place where the accident occurred being practically half-way between the two. It was decided, therefore, to telegraph from Sicasica to La Paz for another wagon to be sent, involving a delay of two days. The wagon ultimately arrived, after the loss of one more day, loaded up the baggage, and brought it on another quarter of the journey. Then another smash, and consequent further delay, occurred. This time they rode into Oruro for assistance, brought out yet a third wagon, and with that delivered our goods safely, but nearly a week late, at the railway station. This loss of a week finally knocked on the head any possibility there might have been of my visiting Mount Sajama. Fortunately, I had a few packages in our own vehicle, and so was not entirely deprived of comforts in the interval, as were most of my fellow-travellers.

In the hot afternoon we ascended and descended some valleys, trending in the same direction as the road, and crossed two low passes. I slept most of the time, holding on to the seat, till soft, hazy clouds covered the sun at 4 P.M., and a cool breeze sprang up. In less than an hour Carocollo was reached, and the day's journey ended. Carocollo is rather a large Indian village or town, occupying the site of an ancient settlement. On the hill, without the present boundaries of the place, there lie ruins of mud huts like broken towers. I spent some time examining them. They were not square on plan, as from the distance they appeared, but oblong and very narrow inside, the walls being thick, and the roofs formed by a false arch held in place by the immense amount of material piled up. The doors were small and low, pointed at the top, with false arches. It was necessary

A BAGGAGE WAGON

to go down on one's knees to crawl in. There were no windows, and the chambers were more like graves than places for dwelling. Here also, with but few exceptions, the doors opened towards the east, and the houses were so planted that one should not interfere with the eastward view from the door of another. In Mr. Bandolier's opinion, this eastward position does not necessarily imply any sun-worship, and may have no religious significance, but merely be due to the desire of the people for warmth, the low sun striking in from the east, bringing the morning warmth most quickly into these cold shelters. I was interested by his statement, but unconvinced.

Beyond Carocollo we entered an immense flat, with hills on the left, and others far away to the right. Straight in front was a separate group, seen end on, at the farther extremity of which, we were informed, was the town of Oruro, nine leagues away. For traversing these nine leagues a single team of mules was alone supplied, there being no post-house between Carocollo and Oruro. In three leagues came green, mossy, boggy ground, whitened with a saline deposit as with hoar frost. The road was heavy even now; in the rainy season all this flat is a great swamp, over which the coaches have to be dragged hub-deep in slime. They are often stuck, and even broken up, at that time; so that it is no matter for wonder if Bolivians prefer to stay at home during the rainy months and do their travelling in the dry time of year. The endless row of pilastrons stretching across this great flat, league after league, was really an imposing sight, while the road, wandering about to right and left to avoid old ruts or specially noxious swamps, was of very mediæval appearance. Our team was soon tired, and seldom quickened its pace beyond a walk. Once or twice halts were made of half an hour's duration to rest the beasts. Thus, in the cold morning some of us preferred walking, and gained a considerable advance upon the coach. Our Colombian fellow-traveller was farthest ahead. I caught up with him resting under the shadow of one of the pilastrons, when the heat began to prevail. He called to know if I had any food. I said "No." "Yesterday," he said, "breakfast little, bad, and dear; dinner little, bad, and dear; this morning no breakfast. I am hungry!" I fully sympathized with him, so we sat down and hungered together.

I found by experiment that the distance between two pilastrons was one hundred and forty paces. When the coach caught us up, I climbed on board, and asked the driver how many pilastrons go to a league. "*Segun*," he replied, "according to circumstances." Every one presently went to sleep, nor did I wake till the Oruro Hill was at hand. Along its foot are the clearly marked traces of a former lake that once submerged it to a depth of two hundred feet or more. The whole of the plain that here surrounded us is the bed of an ancient lake, whose margin can still be traced afar. Mr. Minchin reckons that this inland sea, now shrunk to the dimensions of Lake Poopo, was formerly twenty thousand square miles in area. Whether its waters were anywhere continuous with those of the expanded Lake Titicaca, I do not know, but such was probably the case.

The fact that we were approaching Oruro was manifested by the signs of mining activity on the slopes of the hill to our right. At last, from the summit of a gentle slope, the town came into view; not a Spanish-looking town like La Paz or Arequipa, but rather an exaggerated Indian village of mud huts, crowded together along cobbled road-ways. Only when the heart of the town was reached did we come to streets of civilized houses and to municipal buildings of some dignity. It was a pleasure to find a reasonably good hotel, and a still greater delight to be presently received into the comfortable house of Mr. Penny, proprietor of the famous San José silver-mine. His home is the centre for all English visitors, and I was made free of it with the kindest hospitality. There I had the good fortune to meet Mr. Minchin, whose knowledge of Bolivia is second to no man's. During many years he surveyed important areas of the country for the Bolivian government, and he has been connected with most of the important mining centres.

CHAPTER XXIX

ORURO TO THE PACIFIC

OWING to our baggage troubles, I was delayed several days in Oruro, where the guides had the misfortune to fall foul of the local police. What they did that offended against the laws they hardly seemed to understand. At all events, one of them was "run in," and the other went along with him. Arrived at the police station, a *gendarme* told him that he must pay five dollars He refused. "Then," said the *gendarme*, "you must stay in prison." Both guides protested loudly, and demanded that I should be sent for. This was refused.

"Ultimately," as Pellissier related, "I began to think that in this country people generally asked more than they intended to get, and that by bargaining you could beat down the price of anything you wanted to buy, so I thought I would try and bargain with them. I said, 'I have not got five dollars, but I have got fifty cents, and that I will give you.' They said no—four dollars would do. So then I appealed to my comrade, who said he had ten cents more, so we offered sixty cents." The police then lowered their price, and ultimately terms were arranged on a compromise of eighty cents. The relation of this story to my friends brought out many more about the Oruro police, who do not seem to enjoy a very favorable reputation among the foreign inhabitants of the town. I suppose their main business is to keep order among the Indians, and I judge by appearances that they do that work well enough. It is more than possible that between a set of ill-paid, uneducated men, endowed with the power of police, and a party of foreign mining engineers, accustomed to the habits of European countries, relations may sometimes be strained. The substantial fact, however, must be borne in mind that in this remote country order is preserved among an overwhelming body of semi-savage Indians, so that important commercial enterprises can be carried on and substantial profits made.

In La Paz and its neighborhood I had only met three Englishmen or Americans, the foreign colony there being almost entirely composed of Germans engaged in retail trade; but at Oruro there were over forty English, all managing mines or machinery. Speaking generally, this was characteristic of South America: where work was to be done involving the management of men in any numbers, or of machinery, there was generally an English-speaking person in control; whereas, where it was a question of selling cheap goods to suit the local taste and requirements, such trade was in the hands of Germans. Germany has learned what England has not, the importance and profitableness of exporting her shopkeepers. In the great tide of English emigration, the shopkeeping element has taken but a small part.

One day my kind hosts drove me out to visit the mine. The well-appointed laudau and pair, with a stylish coachman on the box, was rather a strange sight in a street of Indian mud huts and on the desert outside the town. The hill, in which the San José and other mines are situated, lies immediately behind the town, and is visible from all parts of it. It has been known for its rich silver deposits since the days of the Spaniards, and the gash made by the old Spanish workings is a prominent feature on the hill-side. At one time its wealth was believed to be exhausted, but large veins of ore of great richness were afterwards discovered, and it will be many years before they are worked out. The hill is now tunnelled with many galleries, while there is a shaft a thousand feet deep descending into the very bowels of the earth. The trouble here, as in so many other Bolivian mines, is to keep the deep level workings free of water, for the water that rushes in is strongly impregnated with chemicals which eat up iron and render ordinary pumping operations impossible. The water has to be hoisted out of the mine by an endless chain of great leather buckets, which alone can resist the chemical action. For this and other purposes considerable steam-power is required. Whatever coal is used has to be brought up by the narrow-gauge railway from sea-level to this high altitude, a distance of nine hundred and twenty-four kilometres. By the time it arrives, it is a very costly fuel. The only fuels produced by the Bolivian plateau are the resinous balsam bark, called *yareta*, the *tola* shrub, and the droppings of llamas. A large trade is done in the last mentioned, which up till recently was the commonest fuel at Oruro, though coal, I believe, is now beginning to displace it.

Not without astonishment, when I entered the pre-cincts of the San José Mine, did I observe the elaborate and excellent machinery in operation, every piece of which, brought at great expense to the town, had after-wards to be dragged up the hill through several hun-dred feet of altitude by human labor. The adventures of a large boiler in this last part of its transit were described to me as most exciting, but Indians have the capacity of working well together in large bodies, pulling at word of command; and it is found possible to convey a machine of almost any weight to whatever position may be needed by the labor of men and mules. On a square space outside the entrance to the principal gallery a great multitude of Indian women were gath-ered, breaking up and sorting the ore, putting the rich pieces in one heap, the second quality in another, the third in another, and so on. The best ores are sent to Europe for reduction; the worst are treated in the neighborhood. Much tin is found with the silver, besides some copper and antimony, while there are, unfortunately, many patches of pyrites. The whole hill is permeated with metallic veins. In the im-mediate neighborhood of the mine are numbers of small houses for the laborers, of whom an average of eight hundred are kept at work. Some of these people stay for life; some only come between the sowing and reap-ing of the harvest or for the dead season.

The view from this point looking abroad on the Pampa to the hills, over which runs the road to Cocha-bamba and the fertile regions of the east, was wide, barren, and rather monotonous; but there were pointed out to me in all directions the sites of mines or of mineral deposits of known wealth—difficulties of working, lack of water, or impediments to easy access, and consequent costliness of fuel, alone preventing, under present conditions of restricted capital, the whole area from being the scene of a great activity. The range of hills running northward from this point towards La Paz is rich in minerals. About Sicasica several mines are worked in a tentative fashion, and there are large known deposits both of silver and tin. In order to exploit them properly, the railway would have to be extended from Oruro, a matter of little difficulty; for it would be possible to lay down a line almost exactly along the route followed by the road, whose gradients are usually quite gentle. Only one or two cuttings of moderate size would be required, and no tunnels whatever. The same railway might easily be prolonged to the great copper-mining centre of Corocoro, and thence to the edge of the La Paz Valley. Such a railway, of course, would not pay, unless it were made in connection with some large mining concessions; but railway and mines together would undoubtedly produce a large profit, if the requisite capital were brought together and directed honestly and skilfully. From the mine we drove across the Pampa to the pumping-station which supplies Oruro with water. The furnaces of the big engine were being fed with llama droppings, and, as usual, I found an intelligent Scotch engineer in charge.

Throughout these days at Oruro my poor guides were terribly bored. They lay on their beds most of the time, yearning for the guides' room of a Swiss hotel and utterly unable to take any interest in their surroundings. They did not even care to walk up to the mine, though I procured for them an order to view it and the kind promise of the foreman to show them over. This lack of interest in anything outside their profession is a normal characteristic of Alpine guides. The only one I ever came across who was always on the alert for new impressions and information of all sorts was my excellent companion in the Himalaya, Zurbriggen. Wherever he went he always wanted to know everything there was to be known, and the amount of miscellaneous information he used to pick up in a day's journey was quite remarkable. His note-book was his constant companion; its pages were filled with sketches and statistics of all sorts. Thus time never hung heavily on his hands; he was as happy in a new town as in a new range of snow mountains. Travelling guides of that calibre will, I suppose, always be few, but ultimately the future of mountain exploration will largely depend upon them. Maquignaz was as good a guide in the mountains as one could wish to have, and a most cheerful and merry companion in rough places, but in towns he became perfectly miserable, and all my efforts to interest him met with poor success.

With the assistance of Mrs. Penny, I was at last successful in procuring a suit of Indian clothes. The difficulty in getting them was that they are not sold ready made, but are usually stitched together for a man by the women of his household. One of Mrs. Penny's native servants, however, knew of a local tailor, and went to order the things. He came back to inquire when the person for whom they were in-

tended would go to be measured; he was sent back to
say that they were wanted to fit no particular person,
an answer which completely staggered him.

"But how can I make the clothes for nobody in
particular?" he said.

"They are for a gentleman who wants to take them
to Europe," was the answer.

"Then, I suppose, I must make them to fit him."

"No, that is not necessary; he does not want to
wear them."

"Then who is going to wear them? Is he big or
little?"

It took two or three visits before the man could be
made to understand the situation, and, when the clothes
were finished, the tailor was still protesting that if they
didn't fit it was not his fault.

Mr. Minchin gave me a boxful of beautiful specimens of the ores in the neighboring hills, and also
presented me with a valuable series of tracings of his
surveys in the parts of Bolivia I had traversed. Thus
enriched, and with my baggage at last safely delivered,
I was ready to depart from Bolivia.

From Oruro to the port of Antofagasta, the journey
is made by a narrow-gauge railroad. There are three
trains each way every week, and each of them takes
three days to accomplish the distance. But the one
that starts on Saturday halts for Sunday at Uyuni,
while none of them move during the night. There
was a great assemblage of passengers and their
friends at the railway station, and the tame vicuña
of the town came down, as its habit is, to see the train

off. This vicuña lives a rather worried life, for the dogs of the town constantly chase it about, and it has to fly for protection to its scattered human friends. But at the railway station it received much attention, and went about apparently taking notice of who was going away, and levying contributions from such persons as had food in their pockets. It happened that the prefect and his staff were going to a place about fifty miles off. I was invited to share their carriage. The railway manager, Herr Kempf, was of the party, so I had the great advantage of conversing with him for two or three hours as we went along.

There was no change in the character of the scenery, which still resembled in all essentials that of the Puna. Oruro is 12,200 feet above sea-level, approximately the altitude of Lake Titicaca, and we were destined to spend the best part of three more days in these high desert regions. On one side of the line is the continuation of the Cordillera; on the other, island hills emerge from the alluvium, with the old water-line of the lake traceable on their flanks. The talk in the train was all about the mineral deposits in the surrounding country. Here, they said, tin was to be found; there, copper; there, silver. Great wealth was promised to the man who properly developed each of these mines. As we advanced southward the sun rose higher in the heavens, and the day became hot. Once more mirages invaded the plain, and the hills rose out of them like islands, while the little mounds resembled rowing-boats, and sometimes the tussocks of grass close at hand were mistaken for the sails of ships in the distance.

During several hours of the morning we must have been in full view of Lake Poopo, for which I was constantly on the lookout, yet never once was I certainly sure of beholding it, and my note-book bears evidence of a strange perplexity. "Lake Poopo (?) in sight, with hills on the far side of it prettily colored." Again, "Fascinating view; dead flat desert, with meagre *yareta* mounds and wire-grass, dotted with llamas; shepherds' huts floating in mirage. Farther on, whether mirage or lake I know not; then pearly hills and soft blue sky. But one should see such a view as this from a camel's back; a train is an anomaly here. After all, I conclude there is no lake in sight. It is all mirage. . . . No, it is not mirage, it is Lake Poopo, with mirage along its meagre shore." This deceptive landscape lasted two or three hours, till the mirages faded away and the clear desert emerged once more — the beautiful, shining desert, with its bright sand, gay or sad according to your humor, the purple-pink hills beyond, the clear sky, and the great sense of space, which even the hills neither limit nor destroy, except when they come close and show the barrenness of their unfurnished sides.

We sometimes came near enough to the foot of the hills to see their naked rocks undercut by the long-ago dried-up waves of the inland sea. Then we entered a more broken-up region, in which were winding canyons, gay with all the tints of Colorado—strange shapes of red earth, with mounds cut into queer forms; red hills, horizontally stratified with interposed slabs of harder rock, denuded into terraces and seamed up and down by a multitude of parallel gullies. Swinging round a corner, we burst suddenly upon the view of a wide, dry river-bed, snow white, with the salt deposit cutting across and strongly contrasting with a series of steep-tilted slates, green, red, blue, purple in color, and distant blue hills peeping over behind them. All trace of human beings had now vanished; there were not even the footprints of man, but only the tracks of wild vicuñas visible in sandy places. Presently, as the sun was sinking, the desert widened out once more, smoking with blown dust in the far distance, where, out of it, as from a cloud, low blue hills undulated against a lemon sky. It seemed as though we must be on the very margin of the world, the limit of human habitation, when suddenly the train rattled into the big railway station of Uyuni (12,010 feet), an important centre of mineral traffic.

Having deposited the guides at a good French hotel near the station, I proceeded to try and make arrangements for visiting the Pulacayo silver-mine, to which a branch road goes up from Uyuni. I was amply supplied with efficient letters of introduction, and was at once put in communication with the mine by telephone, but was rather puzzled to find that a visit would not prove welcome to the people in authority. The mystery was afterwards satisfactorily explained. The mine, till a few years ago, was one of the richest silver-mines in the world—so rich, in fact, that the amount of traffic it was capable of supplying enabled the railway to be built from the sea up to Uyuni. Later on the line was carried to Oruro to tap the mines there, as no doubt in future it will be carried to Sicasica for a similar reason. Unfortunately for the shareholders of Pulacayo and of the neighboring reduction-works at Huanchaca, which depend upon Pulacayo, the day came when the mine was inundated with a great in-flush of water, submerging five million dollars' worth of silver ore at that moment in sight. The mine being situated in a hill, and the bottom of it above the level of the plain, this would not have mattered if in the days of its prosperity some of its abundant profits had been invested in boring a big drainage tunnel from the bottom of the mine out to the open plain. As it was, the inundation was fatal, and mining oper-ations were thenceforward much restricted. My pe-culiar misfortune was to arrive just when, through the breaking down of some machinery, the water made sudden headway and invaded the levels that were still being worked, thereby threatening the very ex-istence of the industry. Not unnaturally, the moment was regarded as inauspicious for a visit from a traveller well known in the country to be taking notes. I am, therefore, unable to describe one of the largest and most elaborately organized of the mining enterprises of Bolivia. Since 1898 the company has entered upon a new period of great prosperity, fresh lodes of valu-able ores having been discovered above the water-level.

The whole of the following day (being Sunday) was a time of very pleasant repose. Late in the after-noon I wandered forth from the little town on to the great desert that surrounds it, a desert almost incredi-bly flat and uncompromisingly barren, covered over large areas, at or close to the surface, with a cake of rocklike solidity, beneath which was sand. Numerous skeletons of mules were lying about near the tracks radiating from the town. The gaunt bones, sticking up through thin layers of mirage, looked like the ribs of wrecked ships. The same atmospheric agency distorted an approaching caravan of llamas into the semblance of a forest. At sunset the desert became black beneath a motionless canopy of high mist, barred with blue. The remote hills, no longer vague in the trembling heat, stood forth as clear-cut purple islands against the light green western sky. There was no flying dust nor flurrying wind, but all was calm, silent, and reposeful.

In the clear, cool morning of the following day the journey was resumed, still over the flat desert, whose surface is red, incredibly smooth, and hard, like the surface of a baked brick. The hills near and far were again flooded about their base with mirage, from which they were reflected as from the waters of a rippled lake. Even the blueness of the distant slopes appeared in the reflection, contrasting with the brown of those nearer at hand. Among my fellow-travellers was a man, typical of many Europeans one meets in South America—a hardened adventurer of twenty to thirty years' experience, who had come out originally on some particular job, full of energy and hope, and meaning only to stay a year or two, but who had remained on, turning his hand to one thing and another. never very successful, often almost ruined, till the hopes of ever seeing home again had faded away with the memory of the friends of his youth and the habits and almost the language of the country of his birth. South America had laid its hand upon him;

all his enthusiasms were gone, and even a temporary success no longer sufficed to overcome the settled sadness of his habit of mind. He had lost energy and initiative, so he told me, and was content, whenever possible (in the manner of the country), to put off till to-morrow anything that he could avoid doing to-day. He had worked in the Argentine, in Chile, in Bolivia, in Peru, and was a mine of reminiscence of strange adventure. Withal, there had developed in him that kindliness of heart and gentleness of demeanor which is one of the charms of South America, expressing itself in ready exchange of cocktails and in other acts of hospitality.

The line crossed the salt, white-banked Rio Grande, which creeps to its death in a saline swamp. Hour after hour the sameness of the scenery continued, yet without monotony to a new-comer. The railroad led on in long stretches, so that, looking forward or back when the air was clear, the traveller saw it disappear in the distance by the mere curvature of the earth. More generally in the hot hours of midday it vanished into mirage. Out of the feigned water there rose the smoke of the freight-train that was following us, like the smoke of a steamer on the horizon. The only thing that altered was the texture of the desert surface, white or gray, rough or smooth, barren or sprinkled with tussocks of grass. Not a bird hovered over it, not a man stumbled along it, never a house came in view, seldom a track, or even a vicuña. At last we entered the volcanic mountain district of the Western Cordillera, and, crossing the Chilean frontier, stopped for lunch at Ollague (12,126 feet).

A volcano, puffing white steam in small jets from its lofty crater, rose above the station, with a small crater at its foot, whereon was fashioned in enormous letters the words " Viva Chile." All the hills and the ground beneath them, utterly bare of vegetation, were red or yellow in color, or of white ashes dotted over with black cinders.

From this point on, for about two hundred kilometres, the journey was most exciting; for the train wandered in and out among volcanoes, streams of lava, and large level sheets of saline deposit like frozen lakes covered with snow. Most of the volcanoes were extinct, but some, notably Carcote, retained the perfection of their form—wide, infinitely graceful pyramids outlined with a pure unbroken curve against the blue sky. The surface of the hills was often colored in the most brilliant fashion imaginable; and the contrast of these rich colors and forms, rising beyond and apparently out of the large, flat, grayish-white surface of the saline deposits, was most beautiful. One of the white lakes was framed in a margin of black volcanic dust and cinders merging upward into gray sand. White dust-whirlpools were dancing on its white floor. A broken hill near by revealed streaks of blood-red, chrome-yellow, and I know not what other colors. Amid such surroundings the engine laboriously dragged us up to the station of Ascotan (13,010 feet), the highest point on the line, whence, running faster down-hill in many a sinuous curve, it brought us round the base of the smoking volcano San Pedro (17,170 feet).

At its foot was a smaller cone, named Poruña, from

Y 337

which there stretched to a distance of two or three miles an astonishing flow of lava, lying on the sandy desert as though newly poured out, and looking for all the world like a big glacier, with steep sides and snout, and the surface much crevassed, all buried in moraine. The railway is carried through this lava-flow in a remarkable cutting. With this strange product of volcanic convulsion for foreground, and volcanoes small and great towering up behind, San Pedro's crest smoking over all, I thought I had never beheld a more weird and inhuman scene. If a man could be suddenly transported to the surface of the moon, near Aristarcus or Gassendi, such, I imagine, would be the landscape that would salute his eyes. Over against these mountains there rose on the other side of the valley a many-colored hill, the Cerro Colorado, covered, they say, with magnetic sand, which leaps into the air and flies about in sheets and masses when a thunder-storm passes over it, to the standing horror of the local Indians. At such a moment, amid the roar of thunder and the electric flashes, surrounded by a desert shaken by earthquakes and dotted over with cinders, with this dancing fiend of a hill close at hand, ignorant people must, indeed, imagine themselves in the midst of a horde of combating fiends.

A little farther on we crossed the red canyon of the Rio Loa, three hundred and sixty feet deep. I stood at the edge of this deep meandering cut, when the low sun struck full on one face of it and a dark shadow fell from the other, and looked across a great flat plain towards countless volcanic hills, many of them perfectly symmetrical in form and shining in the mellow

LAVA STREAM ON THE PAMPA

VOLCANO AND SALT-PLAIN NEAR UYUNI

evening light. The sunset hour is the time to enjoy this clean landscape, as of the moon, enriched by the world's fair atmosphere, when shadows steal across the flat and climb the crimson hills, driving their color up to the soft, still clouds till it fades in the purple pomp of oncoming night.

That evening we put up at the Grand Central Hotel(!) of Calama (7435 feet), kept by a Dalmatian from Lissa, who was full of talk about Tegethof and the great sea-fight. Calama is situated in the midst of a large oasis, artificially irrigated with the waters of the Loa, but it is wretchedly cultivated, and the main crop of many of the fields was weeds. Next day we continued our journey down to the sea. Already at Calama we were conscious of being in a thicker atmosphere, and the sensation of atmospheric weight grew upon us from hour to hour. We traversed alternately through hills and over plains, each flat being at a lower level from the one before—steps of the great staircase that goes down from the high plateau to the sea. But the hills were no longer all volcanic. An hour or two beyond Calama the line was carried through a cutting made in schists. During the morning we crossed the southern tropic and entered the so-called temperate regions; but the change, as far as we were concerned, was only marked by an hourly increment of heat, for our diminution of altitude far more than compensated for our steadily increasing distance from the equator.

Ever since entering Chile, I had been struck by encountering white laborers working on the line. With Bolivia we had left behind the predominance of the

Indian. The visible evidence of the patriotism of Chile, which the inscription, "Viva Chile," on the frontier volcano had first proclaimed, was shown from mile to mile by the numbers of Chilean badges painted or scratched on every prominent rock. The forms of the hills grew less remarkable and more worn down and rounded as we advanced. There were no longer the white saline flats; their place was taken by nitrate fields, being actively worked, especially in the neighborhood of the Salinas Station (4400 feet), which stands by a big nitrate establishment. So easy are the gradients of this line, and so little does the type of scenery change, that it was only by the increasing heat (91° Fahr. at noon in the railway carriage) and the heavier air that we felt we were descending. The hills now became more and more like Dutch dunes. A gale of wind sprang up, carrying the salt dust hither and thither. At last we entered a dry, winding river gorge, the scenery of which was sometimes almost grand. At the ninth kilometre post a little damp oozed through the bed of the valley, giving life to vivid green weeds and moss. A little farther on the ocean burst into view, dazzling bright, and a few moments later we had rounded the corner and were going along the shore of the Pacific, the sand-slopes of the hills merging without change into the sandy beach and sinking beneath the waves, the whole hill-side, as it were, a sandy shore tipped up to the backbone of the continent.

Wonderfully beautiful seemed the Antofagasta Bay, curving round to a fine mountain promontory like a mild Gibraltar, girt with cloud and bathed in bright gray atmosphere. In the midst lay the large town, with a vanguard of ships at anchor. Antofagasta is the prettiest town I had seen since we left Panama : clean, wide-streeted, with houses suggestive of India, and verandas furnished with long-armed chairs. The people, as I saw them, were frank and hospitable. I was carried off to dinner at the club and shown the sights of the place. In the midst of the pretty square is a garden plentifully irrigated by some of the admirable water brought to the town from a distance of three hundred kilometres. Here, as at Uyuni, the church was a small edifice of no architectural pretensions ; it would have looked mean beside the Spanish grandeur of one of the mud-built churches of a mere Bolivian *finca*. I had not been an hour in the place before I heard the clear note of Chilean patriotism, sounding as plainly in the conversation of men of English or Scotch descent as in that of the Spanish Chilean. The whole place had an air of prosperity : good shops and fine houses of business, mostly built of wood and corrugated iron. The town-clock receives the correct hour daily by cable, and the general amenities of modern civilization are provided. The hotel was properly drained and fitted with excellent baths, the rooms were well furnished, and there was real milk wherewith to civilize one's tea, not merely the condensed nastiness which serves the purpose of milk farther north. The steamer from Valparaiso came in during the night. By noon of the following day we had sailed away over a calm sea and beneath a cloudy sky.

Of the remainder of my journey this is not the place

to write. How we landed at Valparaiso and ascended to the summit of Aconcagua, how we navigated Smyth's Sound and the Strait of Magellan, how we climbed in Tierra del Fuego and galloped over the plains of Patagonia—these are other stories which I have related elsewhere. The purpose of this book is to give some description of the mountains and high plateaus of Bolivia, the least known of all South American countries to the remainder of the civilized world. That purpose accomplished, I gladly lay down my pen. At the moment of death it is said that the whole of a man's past life leaps into view in his memory. So now, at the final moment of writing, I seem to behold, in one panorama, those splendid mountains, those wide plains and glorious scenes on which my eye rested as they passed in the long procession of travel; yet my last thought is not so much of them as of the men of many races who gave me their help and friendship by the way. To them, there on the margin of the civilized world, working out their share of the future destinies of mankind, I wave a last adieu!

APPENDIX

A DESCRIPTION OF THE MINERAL SPECIMENS BROUGHT FROM BOLIVIA BY SIR W. MARTIN CONWAY

By L. J. Spencer, M.A., F.G.S.

THE forty-six mineral specimens brought from Bolivia by Sir W. Martin Conway were sent to the British Museum for examination and determination; they are now preserved in the collection of the Mineral Department.

Most of the specimens are from a tin and bismuth mine on the mountain of Huaina Potosi near La Paz, and from the silver and tin mines at Oruro. A few other specimens are from the Pulacayo mine near Huanchaca and from Carangas. In the following description the specimens from each of these localities will be taken in turn.

Of special interest are the complicated twin-crystals of stannite; the occurrence of the rare minerals augelite and wolfsbergite at a new locality; the frequent occurrence of andorite; and the association of fluor-spar with Bolivian tin-stone.

I. Specimens from Huaina Potosi, near La Paz

Native Bismuth and *Bismuthite* (Sulphide of bismuth, Bi_2S_3).

These, showing large, bright cleavage surfaces, occur associated together. On some of the specimens bismuthite is associated with cassiterite and pyrites.

APPENDIX

Cassiterite (Oxide of tin, SnO_2. Tetragonal).

The collection contains several specimens of much the same character: two are labelled Chacaltaya, Huaina Potosi; the others are from the Huaina Potosi mine.

The specimens are compact to fine grained in texture, and light to dark brown in color; they are often iron-stained. Except for the heaviness (specific gravity) of the specimens there would be nothing to suggest on a casual examination that the material was cassiterite. Cavities are lined with minute, very indistinct crystals of cassiterite; these are light to dark brown and translucent to opaque. Quartz, pyrites, and sometimes bismuthite are present in small amounts, mixed with the massive cassiterite. In one specimen the grains of cassiterite are embedded in a dirty green chloritic substance. A thin section of this specimen shows under the microscope an iron-stained aggregate of cassiterite, chlorite, and quartz; the cassiterite grains are frequently twinned.

The most coarsely crystallized specimen is labelled Chacaltaya; it shows in the cavities dark crystals of cassiterite 1 to 2 mm. across. These crystals interpenetrate each other and are difficult to decipher; the faces are very uneven and curved. Sometimes what are apparently hexagonal pyramids can be distinguished. Measurements show that these are really groups of six crystals twinned together in such a manner that the principal crystallographic axes and the twin axes of all the individuals lie in the same plane. The form present is the deeply striated prism m (110), with very narrow planes of the form a (100) on a few of the edges. In Fig. 1, the six individuals are marked m_1 . . . m_6; of these, m_1 is placed in the normal position, with the prism edge and the striations vertical. The second and sixth crystals are twinned on ($\bar{1}01$) and ($10\bar{1}$) respectively of the first crystal; the fifth and sixth are in twin position with respect to the fourth and first respectively, but not with respect to each other. This type of repeated twinning with the twin axes all in the same plane is frequent in rutile, but rare in cassiterite.

APPENDIX

Fluorite (Calcium fluoride, CaF_2. Cubic).

On the most coarsely crystallized specimen of cassiterite, from Chacaltaya, Huaina Potosi, mentioned above, are fairly large crystals of quartz, with limonite, and a group, about 1 cm. across, of corroded crystals of white fluor-spar. The crystals appear to be octahedra, and they have a perfect octahedral cleavage, the cleavage angle being measured as 71° and 109¼°. The specific gravity and hardness are those of fluorite. The material is optically isotropic, and the index of refraction was determined with a cleavage prism to be approximately 1.44. When the material was heated with sulphuric acid, the sides of a glass tube were etched, and crystals of gypsum were observed under the microscope. These details of the determination are given since fluorite is of very rare occurrence in Bolivia, and its association with the tin-stone of this region has been doubted.

II. SPECIMENS FROM ORURO

The matrix of one or two specimens is an altered volcanic rock or ash with kaolinite and blebs of quartz. On another specimen the matrix is slate, and on another blue clay. Most of the specimens are from the San José mine; from the Tetilla and Atocha mines there is one specimen each.

Augelite (Basic phosphate of aluminium, $AlPO_4$, $Al(OH)_3$. Monoclinic).

The massive mineral from Westanå, Sweden, described in 1868 under the name augelite, and found on analysis to have the chemical composition $AlPO_4$, $Al(OH)_3$, was not considered to be a well-established mineral species until crystals from Bolivia were discovered in 1895.* These crystals were from Machacamarca, near Potosi. More re-

* G. T. Prior and L. J. Spencer, "Augelite," *Mineralogical Magazine*, 1895, vol. xi., p. 16.

APPENDIX

cently* crystals of augelite have been found at a second Bolivian locality, namely, in the mines between Tatasi and Potugalete, Department Potosi. The present description of crystals from Oruro adds another to the three localities at which augelite has hitherto been found.

The single specimen from Oruro on which crystals of augelite have been found·has the whole of the free surface, measuring about 28 × 23 cm., covered with crystals of augelite, mispickel, quartz, pyrites, and stannite; there are also some kaolinite and minute yellow globules of cervantite(?) incrusting most of the other minerals. It was not possible to determine with certainty the order of formation of these minerals: the quartz, however, clearly belongs to two generations, there being small crystals on the matrix, and very much smaller crystals incrusting most of the other minerals. The matrix of the specimen consists of massive quartz, pyrites, and tetrahedrite. Cavities at the back of the specimen contain crystals of wolfsbergite, andorite, and stannite.

In themselves the crystals of augelite do not differ from those previously described, but the associated minerals are not the same. The well-developed crystals are 2 to 4 mm. across, and are present in large numbers, so that this is by far the best specimen of augelite that has yet been found. The crystals are colorless and transparent, but usually appear to be yellow and opaque, owing to the surface incrustation of cervantite(?). In habit they are tabular parallel to the basal plane c (001); the forms m (110) and x ($\bar{1}$01) are also largely developed (Fig. 2, p. 351). Five crystals were measured on the goniometer, but the only other forms observed were n (112) and o ($\bar{1}$12), which are rarely present as narrow faces. The cleavages, angular measurements, specific gravity, and optical characters of the crystals are in agreement with previous descriptions, and need not, therefore, be given in detail.

* L. J. Spencer, "Augelite from a New Locality in Bolivia," *Mineralogical Magazine*, 1898, vol. xii., p. 1.

APPENDIX

Stannite (A sulphur compound of copper, iron, and tin, Cu_2FeSnS_4. Tetragonal).

This mineral has long been known from Cornwall, and has been found at a few other localities, but until recently distinct crystals which were certainly stannite have not been described. At various times the crystalline system has been considered to be orthorhombic, cubic, cubic-tetrahedral, and tetragonal. Recently Prof. A. W. Stelzner * has described crystals from Potosi, Bolivia, of which the symmetry is given as cubic-tetrahedral. Blowpipe tests made on these crystals showed them to consist of copper, iron, tin, and sulphur, but a quantitative chemical analysis was only made on the accompanying massive material.

The crystals of stannite from Oruro now to be described do not altogether agree with Stelzner's observations. They are tetragonal, but by twinning they give rise to pseudo-cubic crystals.† An analysis of these crystals has been made by Mr. G. T. Prior; this analysis, which confirms the usually accepted formula for stannite, is the first that has been made on crystallized material. Crystallized stannite from Oruro has been previously mentioned by d'Orbigny,‡ but this has been doubted by Stelzner.§ The numerous crystals which are present on at least four of Sir Martin Conway's specimens would seem to indicate that stannite is by no means a rare mineral at this locality.

A brief description is given below of each of these four

* " Die Silber-Zinnerzlagerstätten Bolivias," *Zeitschr. deutschen geologischen Gesellschaft*, 1897, vol. xlix., pp. 97, 131.

† Since the present account was written, in 1899, the crystals have been further studied and found to possess scalenohedral-tetragonal symmetry, with the angular element $cd = 44° 30'$; twinning on the first law gives rise to pseudo-tetrahedral-cubic symmetry. A detailed account has been prepared for publication in the *Mineralogical Magazine*, 1901, vol. xiii., under the title " Crystallized Stannite from Bolivia."

‡ A. d'Orbigny, " Voyage dans l'Amérique méridionale, 1826–1833," vol. iii., part 3 (Geology), 1842, p. 129.

§ *Loc. cit.*, p. 86.

specimens, since the associated minerals are somewhat different in each case.

1. The best specimen consists of radiated groups of prismatic crystals of mispickel on which are a few crystals of andorite and pyrites. Incrusting all three minerals is the stannite, which occurs abundantly as crystalline crusts and as isolated crystals. It is the crystals from this specimen which were most completely examined and analyzed, and on which the description given below is based.

2. This is the augelite specimen described above. The associated crystallized minerals are augelite, mispickel, quartz, pyrites, andorite, and wolfsbergite, and there are also tetrahedrite, kaolinite, and cervantite(?). The stannite is one of the latest-formed minerals. On the front of the specimen it occurs as black drusy crusts of minute crystals, the form of which cannot be made out even under the microscope. A qualitative chemical examination by Mr. G. T. Prior, however, showed the presence of copper, iron, tin, and sulphur, so that this material is without doubt stannite. On parts of the specimen where the material is more coarsely crystallized, the characteristic twinning described below can sometimes be distinguished. One good twin-crystal of stannite was found on a crystal of andorite in a cavity at the back of the specimen.

3. This is a large piece of massive tetrahedrite, with massive quartz and pyrites. In cavities are crystals of stannite, wolfsbergite, andorite, quartz, and pyrites. One cavity is almost completely lined with bronze-colored crystals of stannite; these are about a millimetre across, and are confusedly grown together, forming a crust. The bronze color is only due to a superficial tarnish, the crystals being black in the interior. The faces are bright, but the crystals are so intergrown that it was not possible to completely determine the crystalline form; several cubic angles were measured, and in general the appearance of the crystals is the same as those on specimen No. 1. A chemical examination by Mr. G. T. Prior showed the presence

of copper, iron, tin, and sulphur. In other cavities are a few of the black crystals of stannite with the pseudo-cubic forms figured below.

4. An aggregate of jamesonite needles, incrusted with small crystals of pyrites and stannite. The stannite crystals are black, and some of the larger ones show the complex twinning.

The following description of the crystallographic, physical, and chemical characters of the crystals of stannite is based on an examination of the first specimen.

The numerous small crystals, averaging about 1 to 1.5 mm. across, are irregularly aggregated and intergrown together, so that only portions of single crystals can be observed. Of the ten crystals measured on the goniometer, only one was apparently a simple crystal (Fig. 3), and even this was afterwards found to show a twin lamella with o (111) as twin-plane; since this crystal was, as is usually the case, partly embedded and intergrown with other crystals, it was probably only a portion of a twin-crystal. The approximate measurements of the angles on this and other crystals agreed closely with those required for a cubic crystal, while the striations and characters of the faces agreed only with *tetragonal* symmetry. The forms noticed on the crystals measured are, in order of predominance:

c (001). Bright and smooth.

m (110). Deeply striated horizontally. The striæ reflect light with the adjacent faces of o (111).

d (101). Often bright and smooth, but also striated horizontally, especially when e (201) is present.

n (112). Bright; faintly striated parallel to its intersection with c (001).

e (201). Deeply striated horizontally. The striæ reflect light in the positions of d (101) and a (100).

o (111). Narrow; bright and smooth.

a (100). Only represented by striæ on e (201).

μ (114). Narrow, deeply striated planes on the edge between n and c.

APPENDIX

p (423). Two minute bright faces in the zone [201, 111, 021]. Measured to *o* 15° 9′ and 15° (calculated for a cubic crystal 15° 13½′).

Of the tetragonal forms given above

    d and *m* correspond to *d* (110) of cubic crystals
    c   "   *a*   "   "   *a* (100)   "   "

and the others have the same indices as the corresponding cubic forms.

The crystals are not suitable for accurate measurement, and the angles obtained varied almost 30′ on either side of cubic angles. For example, for *cd* was measured 44° 34′, 44° 59′, 45° 2′, 45° 9′, etc., and for *co* 54° 16′, 54° 34′; the corresponding cubic angles being 45° and 54° 44′ respectively. On the whole these angles seem to be slightly less than the corresponding cubic angles: the vertical axis *c* would then be, as in copper-pyrites, slightly shorter than the lateral axes *a*.

The most interesting feature of the stannite crystals is the twinning, which takes place according to two laws:

          (i.) Twin plane *d* (101).
          (ii.) Twin plane *o* (111).

The first law is illustrated by Figs. 4–6, p. 351. The simple crystal (Fig. 4), when twinned on (011) or (0Ī1), gives the interpenetrating doublet shown in Fig. 5. When the twinning also takes place on the homologous plane (101) or (Ī01), the three interpenetrating individuals produce a figure (Fig. 6) closely resembling a regular rhombic dodecahedron. In each octant three planes of the tetragonal pyramid *o* (111) become almost co-planar, and correspond to the regular octahedron. These faces bound the edges of deep triangular pits formed by the three faces of the basal plane *c* (001), which in the twinned position are approximately parallel to the three faces of the cube. The prism faces *m* (110) of the simple crystals form the faces of the rhombic dodecahedron in the pseudo-cubic crystal. The edges of this pseudo-dodecahedron are replaced by V-shaped grooves formed by the faces of *d* (101). Each dodecahedral face (*m*) is very nearly

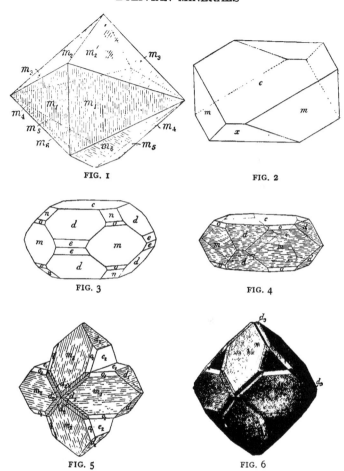

FIG. 1

FIG. 2

FIG. 3

FIG. 4

FIG. 5

FIG. 6

L. J. SPENCER *del.*

EXPLANATION OF PLATE

Fig. 1. Cassiterite from Chacaltaya, Huaina Potosi. Six crystals twinned, together producing a pseudo-hexagonal bipyramid. The only form present is m (110). (Page 344.)

Fig. 2. Augelite from Oruro. Forms: c (001), m (110), x ($\bar{1}$01). (Page 346.)

Fig. 3. Stannite from San José Mine, Oruro. Simple tetragonal crystal with the forms c (001), m (110), d (101), n (112), o (111), e (201). (Page 349.)

Fig. 4. Do. Simple tetragonal crystal with the forms c (001), m (110), d (101), o (111).

Fig. 5. Do. Two interpenetrating crystals, like Fig. 4, twinned on (011).

Fig. 6. Do. Three interpenetrating crystals, like Fig. 4, twinned on (011) and (101), producing a pseudo-cubic crystal. (Pages 350, 352, 353.)

351

parallel to the faces (*d*) in the opposite sides of the four grooves adjacent to it; but the striations on these planes, which are nearly parallel (and sometimes nearly co-planar), are at right angles, as shown in Fig. 6. The fact of these striations being at right angles shows that the crystals are not cubic. Usually, owing to the presence of *e*(201), and its oscillation with *d*(101), the grooves gradually widen out towards the pseudo-tetrad axes.

Doublets as represented in Fig. 5 are rare, but crystals like Fig. 6 are common, especially on specimen No. 1. The actual crystals are often almost as symmetrically and regularly developed as shown in the figure, and in some cases they are developed on nearly all sides; one crystal showed six of the eight possible triangular pits. These twinned crystals bear the closest resemblance to cubic crystals, but the directions of the striations noted above show that they cannot be cubic. This is also supported by the fact that the faces usually give double or multiple images, indicating that the different portions are not quite parallel; the pseudo-octahedral faces, which, as shown in the figure, are represented by three separate areas, sometimes give three very distinct images arranged at the corners of an equilateral triangle.

The crystals are still further complicated by being frequently twinned according to the second law, *viz.*, with *o*(111) as twin-plane. This is often shown by the presence of twin-lamellæ running through the crystals, and by the interpenetration of the pseudo-dodecahedra in the same manner as previously described for stanniferous argyrodite.* This twinning gives rise to two sets of striæ intersecting at an angle of about 70° 32' on the pseudo-dodecahedral faces, while the twinning according to the first law gives rise to two sets intersecting at about 90°. These striæ intersecting at the angles of about 70° 32' and 90° are to be observed on most crystals.

* G. T. Prior and L. J. Spencer, "Stanniferous Argyrodite from Bolivia . . . ," *Mineralogical Magazine*, 1898, vol. xii., p. 7.

APPENDIX

It may be noted that these twin planes, (101) and (111), are the same as those in copper-pyrites, with which stannite appears crystallographically to be somewhat related. The habit of the simple crystals of stannite is, however, more like that of hauchecornite, this being another tetragonal mineral with very nearly cubic angles.

The most striking analogy to these pseudo-cubic crystals (Fig. 6) is given by the twins of phillipsite, the monoclinic crystals of which build up the pseudo-dodecahedra described by Köhler* and others. The optical examination of transparent minerals shows that such composite pseudo-cubic crystals are of frequent occurrence: the rhombic dodecahedra of boracite, garnet, etc., are, for instance, found to be built up of twelve optically biaxial crystals.

Crystals with grooved edges, as in Fig. 6, are illustrated by analcite,† diamond, and haüyne: in the last two cases the grooves are supposed to be due to twinning, while in the first case they are supposed to be due merely to parallel growth.

As regards the physical characters of the crystallized stannite, the following may be noted. The color is iron-black, with a bright metallic to sub-adamantine lustre, somewhat resembling black blende. On one specimen the crystals have a bronze-colored tarnish, which is, however, only superficial. The mineral is opaque. The streak is black and dull. The crystals are not very brittle; the fracture is sub-conchoidal to uneven. $H=3\frac{1}{2}$. Specific gravity$=4.$ $45.‡$

The material collected for analysis consisted mainly of well-developed crystals projecting from the surface of the specimen, but some of the underlying crystalline material was also collected in the belief that it was also

* *Poggendorff's Annalen*, 1836, xxxvii., 561 ; Dana's *System of Mineralogy*, 1892, 6th ed., p. 579, figs. 3 and 4.

† Figures of these are given in Dana's *System of Mineralogy* and *Text-book of Mineralogy*.

‡ Calculated from the specific gravity of the material analyzed (4.52), after deducting 8.58 per cent. of andorite (sp. gr. 5.35).

stannite; the latter, however, contained some andorite, as suggested by the results of the analysis, and as actually seen to be the case upon a further and more careful examination of the specimen. The results of Mr. G. T. Prior's analyses are given below under columns I.–V. Analysis I. was made on 0.3678 gram of material which was decomposed with nitric acid; in II., 0.4215 gram was fused with sodium carbonate and sulphur, and the tin obtained in solution as sodium sulpho-stannate; for the sulphur determination, III., 0.2233 gram was fused with sodium carbonate and potassium nitrate. The mean of these analyses is given under IV. Germanium was tested for, but found to be absent.

	I.	II.	III.	IV. (Mean).	Atomic ratios.
Cu	28.58	28.54		28.56	0.453
Fe	10.95	10.90		10.93	0.197
Sn	25.52	24.90		25.21	0.213
Sb	3.54	3.88		3.71	0.031
Pb	2.02	2.09		2.06	0.010
Ag	0.94	0.82		0.88	0.008
S			27.83	27.83	0.874
				99.18	

The atomic ratios of Sb, Pb, and Ag are approximately those required by the andorite formula $PbAgSb_3S_6$; and the atomic ratios Cu: Fe: Sn: remaining S=.453: .197: .213: .814, which agree approximately with the formula Cu_2FeSnS_4 for stannite; the copper, however, is rather high. Under column V. below is given the percentage composition of the stannite after deducting all the antimony, lead, and silver, and the required amount of sulphur for Sb_2S_3, PbS, Ag_2S. Column VI. gives the calculated percentage composition required by the formula Cu_2FeSnS_4.

	V.	VI. (Cu_2FeSnS_4).
Cu	31.52	29.54
Fe	12.06	13.01
Sn	27.83	27.65
S	28.59	29.80
	100.00	100.00

APPENDIX

This analysis, which is the first that has been made on crystallized stannite, therefore supports the formula usually given for the mineral, namely, $Cu_2FeSnS_4 = CuFeS_2 + CuSnS_2$, or $Fe_2SnS_4 + Cu_4SnS_4$.

Andorite (Sulph-antimonite of lead and silver, $PbAgSb_3S_6$. Orthorhombic).

This mineral has recently been described from Oruro by Profs. Brögger and Stelzner under the names sundtite and webnerite respectively, but these were afterwards shown[*] to be both identical with the Hungarian mineral andorite discovered by Prof. Krenner in 1892. Although andorite is probably not a rare mineral in the Oruro mines, it is as yet represented in only a few collections by one or two small specimens. New material is, therefore, worthy of detailed examination; and in the present case several new crystal forms have been noted.

Crystals were found on four of the new specimens :

1. On the mispickel of the stannite specimen No. 1 from the San José Mine, described above, are a few bright crystals of andorite resembling those described and figured by Prof. Brögger. They are sometimes doubly terminated, and the largest is about 4 mm. long. In habit they are somewhat tabular parallel to the macropinacoid a (100). Pyramids and domes are numerous, but are very irregularly developed, so that the crystals are usually distorted and unsymmetrical in appearance: in Figs. 7 and 8 the crystals are idealized by drawing all the faces of the same form of the same size. A prominent feature of the crystals is the marked striations on all the faces, as illustrated in Fig. 8; in some zones the striations are often so deep and numerous as to render the crystals scarcely suitable for measurement. The pyramids, domes, the brachypinacoid b (010), and the prisms u (130), g (250), and k (120), are all striated horizontally; the macropinacoid a (100) and the remaining prisms are striated vertically, with a few hori-

[*] G. T. Prior and L. J. Spencer, "The Identity of Andorite, Sundtite, and Webnerite," *Mineralogical Magazine*, 1897, vol. xi., pp. 286-301.

zontal striæ, especially on a (100), giving rise to rectangular markings. On the goniometer these striated zones give continuous bands of reflected images, limited, however, between certain points: in the prism zone between a (100) and l (230); in the macrodome zone between a (100) and h (102); in the brachydome zone between b (010) and x (011) or w (035); and in the several pyramid zones [hk0, 00$\bar{1}$] the bands are limited between the zones [001] and [102, 010]. Near the summits of the crystals the faces are less striated and the bands of reflected light much fainter. The pyramid zones showing such bands of light are: [310, 001], [210, 001], [110, 001], [230, 001], [120, 001], and [130, 001]; of these it may be remarked that no pyramidal faces have yet been recorded in the zone [230, 001].

Three crystals were measured on the goniometer, and the following thirty-five forms noted.

Pinacoids: a 100, b 010, c 001.

Prisms: n 210, m 110, l 230, k 120, g 250, u 130.

Macrodomes: h 102, σ 203, f 101, e 302.

Brachydomes: w 035, x 011, γ 021, y 031, η 041.

Pyramids: ξ 312, s 211, A 321, v 112 C 243? ω 132
χ 223 δ 364 β 131
p 111 r 121 E 261
q 221 ϵ 362
ρ 331 D 241
B 441

(Figs. 7 and 8, p. 363.)

The forms present on each crystal were:

No. 1. ab, $nmlkgu$, $x\gamma y$, s, $q\rho$B, ϵD, βE; also deeply striated indefinite macrodomes.

No. 2. abc, $nmlu$, $wx\gamma y\eta$, s, $v\chi p q\rho$B, $\delta\epsilon$; also indefinite macrodomes.

No. 3. abc, $nmlku$, $h\sigma fe$, $x\gamma$, ξ, s, A, $v\chi p q$B, Cr, $\omega\beta$. (Fig. 7.)

The basal plane, c (001), is present on crystal No. 2, as a very small face truncating the brachydomes, and it is faintly curved and striated parallel to the brachy-axis [100]; on crystal No. 3, it truncates the macrodomes and is curved and striated parallel to [010].

APPENDIX

Of the forms given above, u (130) has not been before observed on Bolivian crystals, and the following are new for the mineral:

w (035). Two narrow bright faces, faintly striated horizontally.

η (041). Only as bright striæ; observed twice.

ξ (312). Two small bright faces striated horizontally; in the zones [112, 100], [101, 110], [302, 010], and [310, 001].*

A (321). Two narrow planes on the edges of the horizontal striæ on a (100); in the zones [101, 110], [100, 021], and [320, 001].*

B (441). Small planes, sometimes rather wide; deeply striated horizontally. On all three crystals.

C (243)? Two small planes in the striated zones [120, 001]; the brightest portions of the bands fall just on either side of the zone [203, 010].

D (241). A fairly large plane, deeply striated horizontally; in the zones [120, 001] and [211, 010].

E (261). A small plane deeply striated horizontally and giving no bright image in the reflected band of light; in the zones [130, 001] and [211, 010].

The following are the angular measurements establishing the new forms:

	CALCULATED.		MEASURED.
wb=035 : 010	75°	1½′	74° 22′, 75°
ηb=041 : 010	29°	17′	30°, 29½°
ξe=312 : 302	9°	0½′	9° 7′
ξa=312 : 100	46°	3′	46°
312 : (310)*	44°	39′	44° 42′
Aa=321 : 100	34°	9′	34° 1′
321 : (320)*	24°	46′	24°, 25°
Bm=441 : 110	17°	27′	17° 38′, 17° 18′, 18° 8′, 17° 24′
Dk=241 : 120	24°	17′	24°
241 : (201)*	47°	10′	47° 16′
261 : (201)*	58°	16½′	58° 28′

2. The second specimen is also from the San José Mine

---

*The faces (310), (320), and (201) were not present on the crystals, but their positions were fixed by means of graduations on the crystal adjustment arcs of the goniometer.

APPENDIX

at Oruro. Here several small crystals of andorite incrust the walls of cavities in massive tetrahedrite. It is possible that some of the massive material is andorite, as it closely resembles the crystallized material in appearance; all the fragments tested were, however, found to contain copper, while in the crystals there was no indication of the presence of copper when the material was treated with nitric acid on a microscope slide. The crystals are 1 to 2 mm. in length, and are bright, but deeply striated in the manner described above. On one crystal pyramidal planes were noticed in each of the eight octants. The forms determined by the goniometrical measurement of one crystal were: *abc, nml, hfe,* π(032) γ*y, vpq.*

3. In a cavity at the back of the augelite specimen described above are several crystals of wolfsbergite, but a crystal fragment, closely resembling wolfsbergite in appearance, from one cavity, was found on measurement to be andorite. The forms present are *bmlkyp,* and there are other small pyramids. Resting on the andorite are small twinned crystals of stannite.

4. Small bright crystals in a cavity of the stannite specimen No. 3, described above, were found on measurement to be andorite with the forms *nmlxyyqr,* etc.

Wolfsbergite (= Chalcostibite. Sulph - antimonite of copper, $CuSbS_2$. Orthorhombic).

Two specimens of this rare mineral have recently been described from the Pulacayo Mine, Huanchaca, Bolivia.[*] The present description adds one more to the four localities from which this mineral has hitherto been described.

On two of the specimens from Oruro are bright tabular or blade-shaped crystals of wolfsbergite in cavities in

[*] L. J. Spencer, " On Wolfsbergite from Bolivia, and the Probable Identity of Wolfsbergite and Guejarite," *Mineralogical Magazine,* 1896, vol. xi., p. x. and p. 338.

S. L. Penfield and A. Frenzel, " On the Identity of Chalcostibite (Wolfsbergite) and Guejarite, and on Chalcostibite from Huanchaca, Bolivia," *Amer. Journ. Sci.,* 1897, vol. iv., p. 27, and *Zeitschr. f. Kryst. u. Min.,* 1897, xxviii., p. 598.

APPENDIX

massive tetrahedrite. The crystals are usually small and rarely reach 1 cm. in length and breadth; they are flattened parallel to the basal plane, c (001), and are deeply striated in the direction of the macro-axis. They have a steel-gray color with brilliant metallic lustre; and there is the usual perfect cleavage parallel to the basal plane. A qualitative chemical examination of the crystals showed the presence of copper, antimony, and sulphur, and the absence of silver and lead. Terminal pyramidal planes are not always seen on the crystals; they are usually small and dull and irregularly developed. Three crystals were measured on the goniometer and gave angular values closely agreeing with those obtained by Penfield. The pyramidal planes, though somewhat dull, gave good images, and their indices are high, as is often the case with wolfsbergite. Individual crystals showed the forms:

No. 1. c (001), d (101), g (201), q (863), p (6.12.7).

The planes p are largely developed, and the crystal closely resembles Penfield's Fig. 2 (loc. cit.).

No. 2. c (001), Δ_2 (103), d (101), g (201).

No. 3. c (001), d (101), g (201), t (021), s (065), q (863), τ (261); and other small pyramids not determined, one being in the zone cτ and having the indices (6.18.1) or (7.21.1). Measured to c 86° and 86° 55'. Calculated c: (7.21.1) =86° 23½', c: (6.18.1) = 85° 47½'.

Jamesonite (Sulph-antimonite of lead, $3PbS.2Sb_2S_3$.* Orthorhombic).

1. From the Atocha Mine at Oruro comes a large and very friable mass consisting of numerous delicate acicular crystals loosely aggregated together in radiated or plumose groups, and also confusedly grouped together. The color is iron-black, with a bright metallic lustre. The needles are straight and brittle. They are not in the least flexible, but easily break across, showing a good bright cleavage perpendicular to their length. They are deeply

* Compare *Mineralogical Magazine*, 1899, vol. xii., p. 58.

striated parallel to their length, and are much intergrown with each other in the same direction, so that it is not easy to select simple crystals suitable for measurement. Three fragments were measured on the goniometer, and gave 79° as the approximate value for the prism angle. The basal cleavage forms an angle of about 90° with the faces of the prism.

2. Another small specimen is a firmer aggregate of coarser needles with a bright steel-gray to lead-gray color. The prism angle was measured as about 79°, and there is a good cleavage perpendicular to the length of the needles. Most of the needles are incrusted over with minute crystals, which in places are large enough to be recognized as pyrites and complex twins of stannite. A crystal of quartz is present on the specimen.

3. A specimen from the San José Mine is an incoherent black mass which soils everything that comes in contact with it. Detached pieces are fluffy, and are seen under the lens or microscope to consist of minute black fibres. These are short and straight; they are easily broken, and do not appear to be flexible. The material is therefore more probably jamesonite than plumosite.* Imbedded in the specimen are small octahedra of pyrites.

These three specimens of jamesonite have been examined chemically by Mr. G. T. Prior, and each found to contain lead, antimony, and sulphur.

Tetrahedrite (Sulph-antimonite of copper, silver, etc., $3(Cu,Ag)_2S.Sb_2S_3.$† Cubic-tetrahedral).

Several specimens from the San José Mine consist largely of a massive iron-black mineral with bright metallic lustre and smooth conchoidal or sub-conchoidal fracture. Qualitative analysis of this material from several specimens by Mr. G. T. Prior showed the presence of silver, copper,

---

* Jamesonite and plumosite are to be regarded as distinct mineral species, although since 1860 they have been united in the text-books.

† Compare *Mineralogical Magazine*, 1899, vol. xii., p. 202.

antimony, and sulphur, and an absence of lead. Labels sent with the specimens give the assay value at 10 to 12 per cent. of silver. The material, therefore, appears to be a richly argentiferous tetrahedrite. Cavities in this massive mineral contain crystals of mispickel, wolfsbergite, andorite, stannite, etc., but no distinct crystals of tetrahedrite were found.

Pyrites (Bisulphide of iron, FeS_2. Cubic-dyakisdodecahedral).

Pyrites, either massive or as small crystals, is present on most specimens. Three specimens consist almost entirely of good crystals of pyrites.

1. A fine group of numerous well-developed cubo-octahedra, each about 1 cm. in diameter. Small planes of the form $e = \pi$ (210) are also present (Fig. 9, p. 363). The surfaces of the crystals are coated with a thin drusy layer of pyrites, which easily chips off from the cube and dodecahedral (e) planes, leaving the faces bright and smooth, except for the faint striations parallel to their mutual intersections. In attempting to detach the drusy layer from the octahedral planes, only an irregular fractured surface is obtained. The drusy layer reflects light together with the cube planes of the main crystal. Implanted on these crystals are a few groups of very indistinct crystals of tetrahedrite, and of still later formation are a few small crystals of pyrites, of which the predominating form is the cube.

2. Massive pyrites with the cavities at the back of the specimen lined with small, sharply developed octahedra, with very small a (100) and $e = \pi$ (210). On the front of the specimen are striated cubes with o (111) and $e = \pi$ (210). The octahedral crystals are bright, while the cubes have a reddish tarnish. This specimen is from the San José Mine at Oruro.

3. Massive pyrites with cavities at the back lined with small and bright, sharply developed octahedra; the front of the specimen consists of larger curved octahedra with

an iridescent tarnish. Small planes of the forms a (100) and $e = \pi$ (210) are present.

Mispickel (Sulph-arsenide of iron, FeAsS. Orthorhombic).

Prismatic crystals of mispickel are present on several specimens, and are usually associated with crystals of stannite and massive tetrahedrite. The largest crystals, about 1 cm. long, are those on the best stannite specimen (No. 1) mentioned above. They form more or less radiated groups standing out from the surface. Each crystal is seen to be built up of smaller crystals in not quite parallel position. The prism m (110) is terminated by horizontally striated brachydomes (Fig. 11, p. 363); of these q (011) is small and fairly even; the larger rough area gives a band of reflected images between the positions of t (013) and n (012), with the brightest part near the position of (025). On the augelite specimen the crystals are smaller and more acicular. These crystals (Fig. 10, p. 363) are of much the same habit as those described above, but they have only the forms m (110) and q (011); they are irregularly grouped together on the specimen, and the prisms are often terminated at both ends.

Galena (Sulphide of lead, PbS. Cubic).

One of the specimens is a large mass of galena, showing large cleavage surfaces with a bluish tarnish; associated with it are massive tetrahedrite and small amounts of quartz, chalybite, and copper-pyrites.

Another specimen, from the Tetilla Mine, shows numerous small but well-developed cubo-octahedra of galena; yellow blende is also present.

Blende (Sulphide of zinc, ZnS. Cubic-tetrahedral).

Small indistinct crystals of yellow blende are present on the galena specimen from the Tetilla Mine.

Copper-pyrites (A sulphur salt of copper and iron, $CuFeS_2$. Tetragonal-scalenohedral).

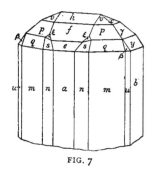

FIG. 7

FIG. 8

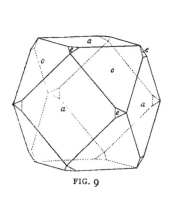

FIG. 9

FIG. 10

FIG. 11

L. J. SPENCER *del.*

APPENDIX

A small amount of massive copper-pyrites is present on one of the galena specimens mentioned above.

Quartz (Oxide of silicon, SiO_2. Rhombohedral-trapezo-hedral).

Quartz is present on several specimens, either occurring massive in the matrix or as small crystals on the surface. Blebs of quartz are present in the altered volcanic rock which carry the metalliferous veins. Larger crystals of quartz, up to 6 cm. in length, are represented by an isolated group of crystals from the San José Mine; they enclose a few black needles with the appearance of jamesonite. Only the usual forms *m r z* were noted.

Cassiterite (Oxide of tin, SnO_2. Tetragonal).

The compact tin-stone from Oruro is of much the same character as that from Huaina Potosi. The heavy, pale-brown, compact masses contain numerous cavities which are lined with minute crystals of cassiterite. In the cavities of one specimen are pentagonal dodecahedra $e = \pi$ (210) of pyrites, and in another the cavities are lined with small quartz crystals. Massive pyrites and a black mineral with metallic lustre occur in small quantities, intermixed with the massive cassiterite. A thin section of a specimen from the San José Mine shows under the microscope a porous aggregate of small, interlocking, pale-yellow crystals of cassiterite. The index of refraction and the double refraction are high. Twinning is frequent, and sometimes often repeated; the line of junction between the individuals of a twin is always sharp and straight.

Chalybite (Carbonate of iron, $FeCO_3$. Rhombohedral).

Small indistinct crystals of chalybite are present on the large galena specimen mentioned above. The cleavage angle was measured on the goniometer as $73°$ $0'$.

Kaolinite (Hydrated silicate of aluminium, $Al_2O_3.2SiO_2.2H_2O$. Monoclinic).

APPENDIX

White powdery kaolinite is sometimes present, filling cavities and dusted over the free surfaces of the specimens. It has no doubt been derived by the alteration of the felspar in the volcanic rocks which carry the mineral veins.

Alunite (Hydrated sulphate of aluminium and potassium, $3Al_2O_3.K_2O.4SO_3.6H_2O$. Rhombohedral).

The occurrence of alunite at Oruro has recently been noticed in the *Mineralogical Magazine* (1897, vol. xi., p. 298). It is present on one of Sir Martin Conway's specimens as white patches in massive tetrahedrite. It is usually incoherent, but in places is more compact. Under the microscope it is seen to consist wholly of minute rhombohedral crystals, having the appearance, but not the optical characters, of regular cubes.

III. SPECIMENS FROM THE PULACAYO MINE, HUANCHACA

From this locality are four small specimens on which are pyrites, copper-pyrites, galena, blende, quartz, and stibnite, both massive and in crystals. The crystals of copper-pyrites, though small, are fairly good. On one of the specimens are minute black crystals with a brilliant metallic lustre, from which several good measurements were obtained, but not sufficient for identifying the crystals: they appear to be orthorhombic, but the measurements do not agree with wolfsbergite, bournonite, andorite, or stephanite.

IV. SPECIMENS FROM CARANGAS

Barytes (Barium sulphate, $BaSO_4$. Orthorhombic).

The specimens consist of an irregular cellular aggregate of large, thin-tabular crystals of barytes up to 10 cm. in length. Small crystals, grown in nearly parallel position on a main crystal, and small fragments are colorless and transparent; the mass of crystals as a whole is white. As determined by goniometric measurements, the forms present are c (001), m (110), l (104), d (102), u (101) and o (011). Small crystals of pyrites are enclosed in, and in-crust the surface of, the barytes. Galena, kaolinite, and quartz are also deposited on the barytes.

NOTES ON ROCKS COLLECTED BY SIR W. M. CONWAY DURING HIS EXPEDITIONS IN THE ANDES

By Professor T. G. BONNEY, D.Sc., LL.D., F.R.S.

THE rock specimens collected by Sir Martin Conway dur-ing his travels in the Bolivian Andes have been intrusted to me for examination. The ends which he had especially in view made it difficult to secure a large number of speci-mens, but some of them possess an exceptional interest as representing localities previously untrodden, so far as we know, by the foot of man. These enable us to deter-mine the nature of the rocks which constitute two of the highest summits in the eastern and more elevated Cor-dillera of the Bolivian Andes, and to infer that its crest in other parts is not volcanic. This fact, and the results afforded by some other specimens, are valuable additions to the mass of information on the geology of the Bolivian Andes embodied by the late David Forbes in his classic paper,* and of the predecessors to whom he refers. That excellent petrologist, while showing that Palæozoic and later sedimentaries, together with igneous works of con-siderable antiquity, entered very largely into the com-position of these mountains, pointed out that volcanic rocks of the ordinary Andean type also occurred, calling especial attention to their similarity in Bolivia, Peru, and Chile. Specimens brought by Sir Martin Conway from three localities fully bear out his predecessor's observa-tion, though none of them happen to contain the crystal-

* *Quart. Jour. Geol. Soc.*, xvii. (1861), pp. 7–62.

lized quartz which he mentions, or, on the other hand, to range themselves with the basaltic group. The rocks also of Ecuador, as we learned from Mr. Whymper's valuable collection, belong in the main to the same great group, the andesites, though several of them contain amblystegite, a variety of rhombic pyroxene, which I have not noted in the specimens which I have examined from Bolivia or Chile. That difference, however, is hardly of secondary importance. The specimens collected by Sir Martin Conway during his ascent of Aconcagua confirm the inferences to which I was led by examining those obtained by Messrs. FitzGerald and Vines, while the few from Mount Sarmiento in Tierra del Fuego show that mountain to be composed, not of volcanic material, but of crystalline rock, greatly modified by subsequent pressure.

(1) ILLIMANI

From the upper part of this mountain Sir Martin Conway brought back eleven specimens, some of them representing the ridge of the Pic de Paris, from the last rocks which he traversed. Grouping them for description according to localities, we find: (1), "from the first camp on Illimani," resembles a hard dark mudstone, possibly with a rude cleavage; (7) and (8) are from the "rock wall below the fourth camp." The former is a dark, minutely granular rock, the nature of which is doubtful; the latter is stained a rusty brown outside, and is very decomposed. It is apparently a holocrystalline rock, possibly once a felspathic granite, but is not likely to repay microscopic examination; (9), "behind camp four," is another puzzling, dark, minutely granular rock, resembling (2) and (7). "From the top of the shoulder of the Pico del Indio" comes a crystalline and subporphyritic rock (10). Of the specimens from the ridge of the Pic de Paris, (2) is another of these minutely granular dark rocks, with a little cupriferous pyrites on a joint surface, and (3), a similar rock, also with the same mineral, but more distinctly sedimentary in aspect. The beds are said to strike southwest and northeast, and to be nearly vertical; (4) is permeated with pyrite, and is possibly a fine-grained mudstone, gritty or even pebbly in places, but is so affected by mineralization that its origin is not easily determined; (5) is deeply stained with limonite, and may only be a vein product; (6), which shows slickensides, is another of these puzzling dark rocks, but (11) appears to be crystalline, though fine grained, as if possibly a darkish banded gneiss. Taking first the most difficult group, from which I selected (2,) (6), (7), and (11) for slicing, a glance at the preparations through the microscope explained the uncertainty whether they were igneous or sedimentary. They were rather minutely crystalline; nevertheless they belonged to the latter group; in other words, they have been affected by contact metamorphism, which, however, owing no doubt to the original constitution of the material, has not developed some minerals which usually are conspicuous. They have much in common, though exhibiting certain varietal differences. The groundmass chiefly consists of the following minerals: brown mica, a white mica, in extremely minute flakes, aggregated in little patches, opacite, granules of quartz, and perhaps of felspar. These constituents are unequally distributed, the first and third showing a tendency to cluster. As to the varietal differences, (2) exhibits a number of irregularly outlined dusky spots which, with crossed nicols, look like cloudspots on a brighter field; (6) affords rather similar but less dusky spots, which, however, often are darker at the centre, while the brown mica tends to gather round these in an irregular ring. In (7) the spots are yet darker than in (2), and the dominant mineral in them acts rather feebly on polarized light. There is not sufficient evidence in any one of these specimens to show what this mineral may be, but the rocks themselves may be reckoned among the "spotted schists," the fruits of contact metamorphism. In (11) the process has gone further, and the rock is practically crystalline, the cloudy spots have disappeared; the constituents are quartz (possibly some felspar), brown mica, some iron oxides, and brownish-yellow grains resembling idocrase. The specimen shows a banded structure, parts being more micaceous than others.

The igneous rock (10) is shown on microscopic examination to have a microgranular groundmass composed mainly of grains or imperfectly formed crystals of felspar, in which are imbedded the following more conspicuous crystals: (a) felspar, fairly idiomorphic, varying in amount of decomposition: perhaps more than one species, but only plagioclase recognized; (b) quartz, occasionally retaining traces of crystalline outlines, but not seldom corroded by groundmass; (c) biotite, more or less altered, and a little chlorite; (d) zircon; (e) iron oxide—very little; (f) a mineral occurring in grains, in one or two cases showing crystalline form, but more commonly irregular in outline, and once in aggregated granules: rather strongly pleochroic, varying from a greenish gray to a rather tawny red: polarization tints generally rather low, extinction oblique but not at high angles. The mineral has some resemblance to piedmontite, and I think it probably a manganese silicate, though it does not 'actually correspond with any known to me. The crystalline condition of this rock is not such as to suggest that it alone has been the agent of metamorphism in the sedimentaries on the upper part of Illimani, but (8) indicates more coarsely crystalline masses to be also present. Thus the peak of Illimani is not volcanic, as has been sometimes asserted; neither is it wholly granitic, as affirmed by D'Orbigny, nor sedimentary Silurian, as by D. Forbes,* each of them having seen only one side of the shield.

(2) SORATA

FIRST EXPEDITION

The specimens numbered from (17) to (28) were collected by Sir Martin Conway during his first expedition to Illampu or Sorata, when he attained an elevation of 20,000 feet.

* *Ut supra*, p. 53.

APPENDIX

(17). One and a half hours northwest of Huarina; "this rock crosses the road and forms a mass of low hills to east, the beds striking northwest and being nearly vertical." It is a small piece of a hard brown mudstone, defined mostly by bedding and joint faces, the former showing slight variations in the texture of the material; also, small flakes of fragmental white mica are more thickly scattered on some of them than on others. The rock has a Palæozoic aspect.

(18). "A bed of this, horizontally stratified, just north of where (17) crosses the road." A pale buff, compact rock, crumbling and very decomposed, much resembling a domite; possibly an indurated volcanic dust, but more probably a rotten, compact andesite.

(19). "Near Achacache. This rock goes striking away parallel to the Cordillera to south, forming skeleton of low line of hills." It is a piece of hard, fine-grained sandstone or quartzite, containing some minute flakes of white mica, and defined top and bottom by bedding planes. It shows sharp, irregular jointing and external zones of a ferruginous infiltration—probably it is a Palæozoic rock.

(22). "Specimens from the ridge of Hiska Haukaña glacier, by which we ascended to Rocktooth Camp, Ancohuma." (See Mr. Spencer's report, page 343.)

(23). Specimens from the Rocktooth Camp, Ancohuma. (See Mr. Spencer's report, page 343.)

The next group of specimens come from localities high up on Sorata, slightly to the east of a line drawn south from the summit.

(20), (21) are labelled "just above north side of Hiska Haukaña lake-basin, Ancohuma. The red rock forms bulk of hills on both sides of the basin and spreads away to southeast; strikes north, dip 30° to west." The two specimens appear to be identical: a hard, compact, gray mudstone, probably with signs of a cleavage. As their aspect under a lens was slightly abnormal, I had a slice cut from (20). The larger portion is composed of a clear, minute, micaceous mineral, exhibiting a somewhat foliated

370

structure, in which occur small grains of a water-clear mineral, probably quartz, and granules or clustered grains, generally rather tabular in form, of iron oxide (hematite?) also fairly abundant films of brown mica, rather irregular both in dispersion and size. In this groundmass are fairly numerous patches, about .01 inch diameter, some approximately circular, others prismatic, but rounded at the corners. These enclose much of the matrix, but when seen with a low power appear as brownish spots. On crossing the nicols they are found to act feebly on polarized light, those of the former shape remaining almost dark as the stage is rotated, those of the latter apparently extinguishing parallel to their axes. The data are insufficient for an accurate determination, but I suspect them to be a mineral allied to dipyre. The rock shows the effect of pressure and of moderate contact action, the second, I suspect, being the later in date.

(24). "From Hiska Haukaña." Two vein-specimens: one consisting of quartz, cupriferous pyrite, and a metallic mineral, with a hardness less than 3, a brown streak and a distinct cleavage ; the other composed of granular pyrite.

(25). "Common among débris all over west slopes of foot of Ancohuma." A compact, hard, black rock, sharply jointed, apparently a variety of siliceous argillite.

(26), (27). "Form the rock over which lay all our descent to Sorata town—strike parallel with the Cordillera, dipping at very varied angles." The former is a small piece of well-banded, rather gritty felspathic mudstone, containing some fragmental mica. The latter is a more compact but banded mudstone, with some mica on the bedding plane. These perhaps belong to the same series as (17), (19), (20), and (21).

(28). "Picked out of adobe wall of Tambo de Patamanta." A hard, brown, compact material, probably siliceous, showing on its surface impressions of cubes (probably of pyrite) which have disappeared. No doubt a vein specimen.

APPENDIX

From the last rocks on Sorata, which, however, were nearly 3000 feet below its snowy summit, Sir Martin Conway brought a considerable number of specimens. But as the majority are vein products, they are only indirectly illustrative of the rocks which form this portion of the *massif*. Of them a brief notice will suffice, and as any interest which they possess is mineralogical, rather than geological, I have not had any of them sliced for microscopic examination; (a) may be taken as a type of a group. It consists of felspar, mottled with a rather minute, dark green mineral, probably a chlorite. The crystalline grains of the former are fairly coarse, cream white in color, more or less decomposed, but retaining in places indications of oscillatory twinning. With this specimen we may place (b), (f), (j), (l), (o), (v), (w), and perhaps (x). In (e), some small quartz crystals occur in cavities; to (l) a bit of rock, somewhat similar to, but coarser than, (k) is attached; in (w), the green mineral occurs in larger crystals, and resembles a hydrous biotite rather than a true chlorite. Among the remaining specimens, (p) consists of quartz and black tourmaline, the latter occurring in bunches of acicular crystals; (q) is the same, but in one part is a fair amount of felspar; (c), a lump about 5 inches long, consists almost entirely of radiating groups of acicular black tourmaline, with some interstitial quartz, felspar, and, occasionally, a little ferruginous dust. Tourmaline is present in (r), (s), (t), (z), but these are a little more varied in composition; they also contain a mineral, which, though bearing some resemblance to tourmaline (giving straight extinction, and not to be scratched with the knife), is of a rather unusual color (brown, inclining to olive in small fragments), with weak pleochroism, and fairly well-marked transverse cleavage.

We infer from these specimens that the rocks of the *massif* are crystalline, and have undergone some subsequent changes. The next group shows the former supposition to be correct. Of them, one, (*g*), is so much decomposed that I have not thought it worth slicing. It is, however, a moderately coarse holocrystalline rock, consisting of a decomposed white felspar, a greenish pyroxenic mineral, probably hornblende, and some rather irregularly distributed quartz. Hence it is a quartziferous syenite or diorite, probably the latter. The remaining specimens have been examined under the microscope; (*d*) is a moderately coarse holocrystalline rock, consisting of quartz and felspar, the latter decomposed and largely replaced by minute flakes or fibres of a micaceous mineral, but in places showing plagioclastic twinning, with a little altered biotite, one or two zircons, and a fair number of small grains of a translucent, rich sienna-brown mineral. The last show a slight tendency to a prismatic habit, and appear once or twice to assume a dull olive or bluish tint, or be connected with a mineral of that color. As a rule, they resemble pseudobrookite more than any other mineral known to me. Here and there are small irregular veins of a mosaic of granules, apparently quartz, probably indicative of some ancient mechanical disturbance. The rock may be named a granite, but it belongs to the miarolite type; (*m*) is also a similar holocrystalline rock, consisting of quartz, somewhat decomposed felspar, much of it certainly plagioclase, a fair amount of biotite, and a little iron oxide and zircon. The constituent crystalline grains vary a little in size, and we find, as in the last, some indications, but less marked, of mechanical disturbance. This rock also is a granite (miarolite); (*n*) is generally similar to the last-named rock, but with more signs of alteration, especially in the case of the biotite. The quartz also more frequently shows a mosaic structure; (*n*) is a fine-grained granite or aplite, with only a little mica (both brown and white). Except for the absence of the supposed pseudobrookite we might suppose it a comparatively compact variety of (*d*); (*k*) represents a biotite granite (containing two or three zircons), bearing a general resemblance to (*m*). This is cut by a microgranite, which here and there exhibits an approach to a graphic structure. It includes a few grains of iron oxide and flakes of altered biotite, together with a few larger grains of felspar and quartz, which may have been derived from the other rock.

These specimens, taken as a whole, show that Sorata in its highest visible part is composed of holocrystalline rocks,* and is not one of the volcanic peaks.

(3) VARIOUS LOCALITIES IN BOLIVIA

(12). "Buttress at angle going to Cohoni." Crystals of white felspar (up to about .2 inch diameter), of biotite, and a little pyroxene about half that size, are imbedded in a rather speckled gray groundmass. The microscope shows that the first mineral is plagioclastic; the second is much affected by corrosion, and is sometimes reduced to a mere framework of granular iron oxide, and the third is a much-altered, light-colored augite (?). These minerals are imbedded in a pale greenish or brownish glass, studded with minute felspar microliths. The rock accordingly is a mica-andesite, and no doubt belongs to the volcanic group of the South American chain.

(13), (14). "Near Cohoni." Two specimens of very minutely granular decomposed red rocks. Without microscopic examination (and they do not seem worth it) I cannot determine whether they are compact andesites or indurated volcanic dust. But they probably represent the same group as the last-named specimen.

(15). "Southeast angle, Esquina de Pongo." Two specimens of a rough gray mudstone (no effervescence with hydrochloric acid), containing some minute parallel-lying flakes of white mica.

(16). "Just north of Mellocato, on west side of La Paz Valley (striking parallel with the Cordillera)." A very

---

* D. Forbes (*ut supra*, p. 53) says that Sorata is composed of Silurian strata, " fossiliferous, as I have proved . . . up to its very summit." Obviously this phrase must be employed with great laxity.

APPENDIX

fine-grained, reddish, felspathic grit, bearing some resemblance to (13) and (14), but a little coarser.

(29)–(31). "Common in débris above Huarisata on pass to Sorata (large mass of red rock seen at foot of Ancohuna)"; (29) is a red-colored grit, moderately coarse. A little felspar may be present, but the grains are chiefly quartz, some being well rounded, others showing crystal faces due to secondary deposition; (30) is a buff-colored quartzo-felspathic grit, and (31) is a holocrystalline rock, very much decomposed, but felspar with some biotite and a little interstitial quartz may be recognized in one or two places. The rock probably was a mica-syenite or diorite.

(32). "Not far from Huarina (see my note book, Oct. 17th)." A very decomposed, compact, buff-colored rock, containing a few scattered crystals; the light-colored probably decomposed felspar; the dark biotite. The rock is probably a domite or very decomposed andesite.

(33)–(36). "From Cusanaco placer mine, below Palea." Of these (33) is a small piece of a very ferruginous (partly limonite) rock, probably sedimentary in origin. A little streak of gold may be detected in one place, but some one may have used the specimen as a test-stone; (34) is a very fine-grained felspathic grit, stained with hematite; and (36), a speckled, grayish-colored rock, is extremely decomposed, but is probably an andesite.

(40)–(46). "From Vilahaque Hill." Of these (40), said to be the "main material of the hill," is composed of more or less subangular fragments, ranging up to over an inch in diameter, apparently a compact quartzite, which are cemented by a dark ferruginous matrix; (41) is a rather fine-grained, soft, crumbling, red, felspathic sandstone,* and (42) is similar, but browner in color; (43) is more variable in structure, containing a few small pebbles, and is intermediate in color. In all, some of the quartz

* The occurrence of red sandstones in Bolivia is noted by D. Forbes (*Quart. Jour. Geol. Soc.*, 1861, p. 38), who assigns them to the Permian Period.

grains are fairly rounded; (44), "from loose stones on the hill-side," is a finely speckled, rather dark, reddish rock, probably igneous, but belonging, I think, to an older group than the ordinary volcanics of the Andes; (45) is reddish in color, iron stained, and probably a very fine-grained quartz-grit, while (46) is a vein specimen, chiefly consisting of quartz.

(47). "A heap of this in Santa Ana Hacienda for building." It is a dark, rather peaty-looking mud, in which are traces of plants.

(48). "This and a conglomerate like (40) dip to the western plain at 60° from Peñas Hill." It is a fine-grained, red, felspathic grit, like (41) and its associates.

(49). "Conformably underlies (48)." The rock appears to be a dark, gritty mudstone, in which is some minute mica. Microscopic examination shows it to be a fine-grained grit, rather iron-stained, in which quartz, felspar, and white mica can be recognized, with a few granules of zircon, one or two possibly of tourmaline, and of pseudo-brookite (?).

(50)--(54). "On slope of hill approaching Milluni"; (50) is gray, felspathic argillite, possibly affected by cleavage; (51) is a gritty, gray-colored mudstone, in which are thin micaceous layers. The specimen is traversed by cracks which are filled with quartz, etc.; (52) is a dark mudstone, rather heavy, jointed, and possibly cleaved; (53) is less easily determined. It is gray in color and veined. Under the microscope it is seen to consist of grains of quartz, with some felspar and flakelets of brown mica, a little of the translucent brown mineral (pseudobrookite?), and a few small zircons, the interstices being filled by aggregated minute granules which afford bright tints with crossed nicols. The rock is sedimentary in origin, but apparently is slightly altered, possibly by contact metamorphism.

(54)--(59). From Milluni mine; (54) is attached to three specimens, from veins, apparently in a mudstone. They consist of quartz, pyrite, ordinary and cupriferous, etc.; (55) is part of an impure quartz vein, crystals of that mineral covering one surface; (56) is a dark mudstone, containing minute flakes of white mica, and affording a rough fracture. It exhibits markings, probably vegetable, one of them resembling the impression of a stem of a plant; (58), probably, is a fine-grained, felspathic grit; a vein in one face contains many small crystals of quartz, colored by hematite; (59) is a hard, gray rock, with an irregular fracture, probably a fine-grained, rather felspathic grit, but (57) presents some resemblance to a pale-colored andesite. The structure, on microscopic examination, is seen to be rather minute, but appears on the whole to be related to (53). Hence I am disposed to look upon it as sedimentary, though possibly slightly affected by contact metamorphism.

(60), (61). "*In situ* on ascent of a spur of Cacaaca, crossing from Milluni." The first is a darkish gray, gritty mudstone, felspathic and micaceous, with distinct indications of bedding and jointing; the second, a gritty rock containing fossils.

(71). "Rock in which the lode is found, Huaina Potosi." A fine-grained, dull-colored rock, containing several cubic crystals of pyrite and traces of stibnite (?). The microscope proves it to be a grit, composed of quartz, felspar, more or less decomposed, some biotite, chlorite, and white mica, a few small zircons, and iron oxide, in which occur larger crystals of pyrite. It has the aspect of a Palæozoic rock.

(80), (81). "Pampa crust at Uyuni." In the former, grains of quartz, mostly subangular to subrotund, with some rounded and larger (not exceeding a hemp seed in size, and generally less than a mustard seed), are scattered throughout a mass of rather compact tufa. The specimen is nearly an inch thick, and its surface is irregular and lumpy; (81) is more cavernous, gives a brisker effervescence, and contains less grit. Some lichen is growing on the surface.

(82), (83). Lava from Ascotan. The former exhibits felspar crystals up to about one-fifth of an inch in diameter, in a rather dark, compact matrix, which becomes redder on weathering. Microscopic examination shows the more conspicuous crystals to be plagioclastic felspar, biotite, and hornblende (the two being often blackened by iron oxide), with a little paler-colored augite. These are imbedded in a dirty brown glass, studded with microliths of plagioclastic felspar. The rock, accordingly, is a biotite-hornblende-andesite. The second specimen is generally similar, but its reddish matrix is more distinctly mottled with darker tints. The more conspicuous minerals are as before; the biotite and hornblende are more easily recognized. The microscope shows no material difference to exist, though the biotite and hornblende are less affected, and the base affords slight indications of a fluxional structure; (83), also from Ascotan, is a pale, cream-colored granular rock, either a decomposed trachyte or fine trachytic ash, in which a large quantity (perhaps nearly half the mass) of lemon-yellow sulphur is interspersed. The exact nature of the matrix cannot be determined microscopically, and the specimen is hardly worth microscopic examination, which, indeed, might give no result.

(85)–(89). Don Pedro Volcano; (85) is dull-red scoriaceous rock, with a fair number of small spots; some black, about as large as pinheads, indicating a pyroxene; others light colored, probably felspar; (86), a compact, pale-pinkish matrix, is studded with small crystals of a glassy felspar and of biotite (often idiomorphic), in both cases not exceeding 1 inch in diameter. The rock under the microscope has a general resemblance to the last described, but contains augites slightly larger in size, and has a rather clearer base; (87) is a purplish black, minutely vesicular rock, containing some minute crystals of felspar. On microscopic examination it is found to be studded with plagioclastic felspar, ranging from microliths to about .03 inch in longest diameter, with grains and granules of iron oxide, and the same (not very regular in outline) of augite. There is a little residual glass, but it is difficult to detect among the crowd of small minerals.

(90), (91). "Railway cutting west of Sal Gema." A piece of rather hard, compact, gray shale, slightly irregular in shape, with joint surfaces, brown stains, and dendritic markings; (91) is generally similar in shape, browner, and very rotten. The outside is shale, but a layer, about half an inch thick, is probably a rotten felspathic grit. The specimen is hardly worth cutting to determine the nature of the latter.

(92). Near Salinas railway station. This specimen has a tufaceous aspect, and is harder than the finger-nail, but, as it does not effervesce with acids, cannot be a carbonate; possibly it is anhydrite.

(4) From the Western Face of the Peak of Aconcagua

These specimens were collected, not from rocks *in situ*, but from the great slopes of débris which cover so much of the mountain, and are traversed during the upper part of the ascent. On this account, and as their general character was readily ascertained by study with a lens, I have contented myself with an occasional examination of the powder. While the varietal differences are numerous, as might be anticipated in samples from a number of successive lava flows, they all represent one group, the andesites, and it is interesting to observe the general absence of scoriæ and even of vesicles. I was struck with this fact in examining the specimens brought from Aconcagua by Messrs. FitzGerald and Vines, and called attention to it in the note contributed to their volume,* because I had reason to think that their collection, though a small one, was likely to be representative. The specimens also fully bear out an interesting observation made by Sir Martin Conway, that the fragments in this débris were often more or less subangular. This, no doubt, is due to their rubbing, one against another, in sliding

* *The Highest Andes*, p. 331.

down the mountain-side. On a lofty peak, such as Aconcagua, subject to great variations of temperature, the movement of loose débris probably is much increased by the action of snow, in the same way as was suggested by Professors A. C. Ramsay and J. Geikie in the case of certain breccias on the Rock of Gibraltar.*

The following is a list of the specimens:

(1). Andesite, containing a little brown hornblende. On one face (doubtless a joint) small crystals of idocrase are rather numerous, some a yellow-brown in color, others more yellow.

(2). A subangular piece of gypsum with some superficial red stains (hematite).

(3). Small and rather flat fragments, cream white in color, apparently representing a compact trachyte (probably andesite), in a very decomposed state.

(4), (5). Small and irregular-shaped fragments, of a greenish color, probably due to malachite; one being compact, the other porphyritic. Two of the latter contain crystals (up to about ⅛ inch diameter) of a blackish mineral, which proves to be a very dark hornblende with a rather small extinction angle; the same mineral, but of a smaller size, occurs in others. They are varieties, rather decomposed, of andesites, mostly hornblendic.

(6). Part of a rather smoothed subangular fragment of a compact olive-green rock, in which are some very small dark prisms. Probably a hornblende-andesite, slightly stained with malachite.

(7). An elongated triangular fragment, defined by joint faces, showing some very small crystals of felspar in a compact matrix. An andesite.

(8), (9). Small fragments of a rather dark, finely speckled andesite, "powdered" in places with a minute, yellow-green mineral (epidote?).

(10). A small flat chip of a dark andesite, partly coated with a greenish mineral. Probably epidote.

* *Quart. Jour. Geol. Soc.*, **vol. xxiv.** (1878), p. 515, etc.

(11), (12). Compact dark-gray andesites.

(13), (14). Dark but finely speckled augite-andesites, as proved by examining the powder from one under the microscope.

(15), (16). Minutely speckled andesites, very decomposed, with external stains of limonite.

(17). The groundmass is compact, and a rather dark gray color. It contains crystals of a dead-white felspar, probably plagioclase, up to ⅛ inch diameter, with a few, smaller in size, of a dark pyroxene, probably hornblende. A variety of andesite.

(18). A very similar rock, but with a dull reddish groundmass. The spots of the dark pyroxene are fewer and smaller. Andesite.

(19). Similar to (17) and (18); but with a greenish-gray groundmass, little of the pyroxenic constituent, and some specks of pyrite. The felspar as before, but it contains some granules of epidote (?). Andesite.

(20). The groundmass is a dull purplish color, the minerals in visible crystals are smaller, the felspars whitish, being generally rather more elongated; the dark constituent, smaller in size but more abundant, proves to be a rich brown-colored hornblende. A hornblende-andesite.

(21). A gray groundmass, in which small crystals are fairly abundant, representing the following minerals: (a) white felspar; (b) a blackish pyroxenic mineral, often columnar in form, not seldom nearly ¼ inch in length, and in one case rather more; mostly, if not wholly, hornblende. A hornblende-andesite.

(22). A similar groundmass, but the felspars are slightly fewer and smaller. The hornblende, however, is quite as abundant, is more frequently columnar, and shows traces of a parallel ordering. Hornblende-andesite.

(23). Resembles the last two, but the felspars are larger, nearly attaining to ¼ inch, the hornblende as in (22), but without the fluxional structure. Hornblende-andesite.

(24), (25). Probably from one mass; presenting a general

resemblance to the last three; perhaps most closely allied to (23), but considerably more decomposed.

All these rocks, (17) to (25), are closely related varieties of andesites, but I should expect them to represent at least three distinct masses of lava.

(26). A pale, slightly purplish, gray-colored, compact groundmass, including many small crystalline grains of white felspar and a few of pyroxene. The rock is an andesite, obviously decomposed, and speckled with minute pyrite.

(27)--(31). Pieces of compact dull purplish-red lava, one or two showing a few very small cavities; another contains two or three stout crystals of hornblende, almost $\frac{1}{4}$ inch long, and yet another many minute crystals of felspar. Varieties of andesite.

(32). A block rather irregular in form, about 4 inches in the longest diameter, brick-red in color, with indications of minute felspar and of some hornblende. A rather decomposed andesite. There are some small external patches of a soft black mineral with metallic lustre—stibnite (?).

(33). A fragment, considerably less than a cubic inch, of a reddish-brown color resembling a chert or possibly a pitchstone. This I have examined under the microscope. The slice includes on one side a small piece of andesite, with little crystals of plagioclase, in a groundmass of microliths of the same and ferruginous specks, together with a limited amount of glassy base showing traces of devitrification. The remainder of the slice consists of an irregular, sometimes labyrinthic, sponge-like structure of a reddish to very dark-brown material, associated generally with a thin outer band of light-yellow or occasionally reddish-brown color (the latter, when both are present, being the exterior one). The interspaces are filled with a clear mineral. Between crossed nicols this proves to be chalcedonic quartz, with a slightly radial arrangement, and the yellowish or reddish bands to be also chalcedony, but iron-stained. I think this specimen to be a piece of rather basic scoria, which has included a fragment of andesite, and in which chalcedony has been afterwards deposited, probably as a result of solfataric action; or, in other words, it is a specimen of silicified scoria.

The general absence of scoria, as already mentioned, is noteworthy, especially in a mountain of such great elevation. No doubt Aconcagua has suffered much from denudation, and the lighter materials, which hardly can fail to have entered into the composition of its crater ring, have been swept away. But even if we allow for this, lava flows must be much in excess of ash, at any rate in the part which has been examined by Messrs. FitzGerald, Vines, and Conway. In these, hornblende-andesite seems to be the dominant variety.

(5) Mount Sarmiento, Tierra del Fuego.

(1). A rather thin slab, measuring approximately 3 inches by 2 inches, the broader surfaces indicating a cleavage-foliation, and of a grayish-green or olive color; apparently a gneiss or a rather micaceous schist, which has undergone great pressure. This inference is confirmed by microscopic examination: the rock has been much crushed and has afterwards been recemented. It was originally crystalline, banded, and probably traversed by small quartz-veins. More felspathic or micaceous layers once alternated with more quartzose, the latter now forming more or less irregular, often crumpled, streaks. The former consist of a fine-grained mixture of a micaceous mineral with granules, mostly earthy, but in part water-clear. The flakes vary from a rather pale dull green to almost colorless, the one being very feebly pleochroic, and giving dull tints with crossed nicols, while the other produce more brilliant tints and resemble an ordinary white mica. Probably they are all varieties of a hydrous mica, but perhaps in some cases a chlorite may be present. Similar flakes also occur in the more quartzose streaks. In these the water-clear mineral, commonly, when quartz (though a secondary felspar may also be present), is rather polygonal in outline and exhibits a distinct grouping; the grains, like the flakes, varying in diameter from about .003 to .001 inch; occasionally, though rarely, being as much as .005 inch. These show a distinct grouping by size; the larger, which are more free from mica, probably representing original veins; the smaller, in which it is more abundant, the more quartzose layers of the original rock. The earthy granules, on examination with a high power, appear to be decomposition products from felspar, with some epidote, which mineral occasionally occurs in rather more distinct grains. A somewhat rounded zircon is also to be seen. On the whole, a pressure-modified mica-schist seems the best name for this specimen.

(2). A fine-grained rock, speckled greenish white and dull green, with faint indications of foliation, resembling a diabase or diorite, somewhat pressure - modified. The microscope shows that it consists of a pale - green horn-blende, in not very well-formed crystals, which vary considerably in size (the larger being rather rich in small enclosures), together with epidote, white mica, perhaps some chlorite, and possibly a few grains of secondary felspar. The rock is slightly foliated, has probably been somewhat affected by pressure, and is an altered diorite, which may once have been a dolerite.

(3). A rather pyramidal specimen, probably bounded by irregular joint surfaces, deeply stained with limonite. On chipping away a corner, the rock is found to be holocrystalline, moderately coarse, consisting mainly of decomposed felspar and a somewhat altered biotite. It is hardly sufficiently well preserved to be worth slicing, but it appears to be either a mica-syenite or a mica-diorite.

(4). A holocrystalline rock, having a rather dark but speckled matrix, in which are scattered (with a slight fluxional ordering) whitish crystals, apparently of felspar, with a rather irregular outline; the former seemingly consisting of this mineral and a dark-green hornblende, with some specks of pyrite. On microscopic examination, it becomes evident that the rock has undergone considerable secondary change, initiated possibly by pressure; for the outlines of all the principal constituents are more or less irregular. In the matrix, the felspars have undergone much molecular rearrangement; small granules, probably in part epidote, in part kaolinitic, having formed, with occasionally a water-clear mineral resembling quartz, which, however, may in some cases be a secondary felspar. The hornblende is of a pale-green color, not unfrequently speckled with granules, apparently of epidote, having also flakelets of brown mica, and rather larger flakes of the latter developed around the edges, as if formed at the expense of the hornblende and the felspar. The larger crystals, which to the unaided eye appear to be the latter mineral, are found to be mainly composed of microliths. The majority are rudely prismatic in form, inclining sometimes to flaky. At first sight two minerals apparently are present: one, a fairly normal epidote; the other, rather less regular in form, giving low blue polarization tints, but, as the one sometimes seems to pass into the other in the same crystallite, I doubt whether the difference indicates more than some slight variety in composition. With them a little white mica and residual felspar (?) is associated. Pyrite happens not to be present, but there is a decomposed iron oxide, which, as it is associated with brown granules resembling sphene, probably represents ilmenite. Thus the rock is a modified diorite.

Examination with the microscope confirms the impression which was formed from the hand specimens; namely, that this is a group of rocks of considerable antiquity, long anterior to the date of the ordinary lavas and scoriæ of the Andean chain. They have been affected by the great earth movements which have given it birth, and belong to the folded mass of older crystalline and sedimentary rocks, which serve as a foundation to the newer volcanic summits. Mount Sarmiento not improbably belongs to the same part of the great mountain system of South America as the eastern range of the Bolivian Andes (explored by Sir

William Martin Conway), and we must remember that Mr. Whymper found Sara-urcu (15,502 feet), in the easternmost range of the Ecuadorian Andes, to consist wholly of metamorphic rocks.*

ON SOME PALÆOZOIC FOSSILS FROM BOLIVIA OBTAINED BY SIR WILLIAM MARTIN CONWAY

By R. BULLEN NEWTON, F.G.S., British Museum

Among the geological specimens collected by Sir William Martin Conway in Bolivia are two rocks exhibiting certain organisms which have been submitted to the writer for determination. The largest of these is a tabular mass of micaceous, gray sandstone, measuring 5 by 6 inches in extent, and having a thickness of $1\frac{1}{4}$ inches. Its structure is impregnated with minute speckles of what appears to be limonite, and a similar material fills up the numerous fine veins which intersect the slab in all directions. On the upper surface occur the fossils; these consisting of Brachiopod-shell impressions, together with some other remains which, on account of their fragmentary nature and bad preservation, are a good deal problematical, although they apparently belong to a crustacean or a fish. It is through the Brachiopods, however, that the age of the sandstone can be furnished, since one of the examples is identifiable as *Anoplotheca flabellites*, a characteristic species of Lower Devonian rocks of both North and South America, the Falkland Islands, and South Africa. A further Brachiopod valve is also observable, which appears to belong to the genus *Atrypa* (?); but this as well as the other specimens will be subsequently referred to under more detailed observations. The locality of the sandstone, as given by Sir William Martin Conway, is as follows: "*In*

---

*See *Proc. Roy. Soc.*, No. 234 (1884), for descriptions of the specimens and references to similar occurrences in the Andes.

APPENDIX

situ, on ascent of spur of Cacaaca, in crossing from Milluni to Huaina Potosi mine"; at a height of 16,500 feet above the level of the sea. The other rock specimen is a thin fragment of dark slaty-shale, tinged superficially with a reddish brown color. One of its surfaces is covered with the valves of a small Brachiopod, all in an extremely compressed state, and presenting resemblances to the genus *Orthotetes*. It was obtained at "Cerro Antajahua, Mina Milluni, La Paz," and is probably of Devonian age.

One of the most valuable contributions on the Palæozoic fossils of Bolivia was furnished by Dr. A. Ulrich in 1892, from some rich material supplied him by Dr. G. Steinmann. Ulrich demonstrated that the clay-slates and sandstones, so widely distributed over Bolivia and Brazil, could be synchronized with the Oriskany sandstone, the Upper Helderberg and the Hamilton groups of North America, on account of the occurrence of such typical Brachiopods as *Anoplotheca flabellites* and *Vitulina pustulosa*. From similar data he also traced an analogy between these Bolivian deposits and those of Brazil, the Falkland Islands, and South Africa.

Several other authors have written on the palæontology of Bolivia, but without reviewing their works it may be of interest to append the following list of memoirs on this subject:

DERBY, O. A. — "Notice of the Palæozoic Fossils (from Lake Titicaca); with notes by Alexander Agassiz." *Bull. Mus. Comp. Zoology, Harvard College*, 1876. Vol. iii., No. 12, pp. 279–286.

FORBES, DAVID— " On the Geology of Bolivia and Southern Peru." *Quart. Journ. Geol. Soc.*, 1861. Vol. xvii., p. 762 (with geological map).

GABB, W. M.—" Description of a Collection of Fossils, made by Dr. Antonio Raimondi, in Peru." *Journ. Acad. Nat. Sci.*, Philadelphia, 1877, new series. Vol. viii., part iii., p. 302.

KAYSER, E.—"Beiträge zur Kenntniss einiger paläozoischer Faunien von Süd-Amerika." (*a*) Devonische Versteinerungen vom Titicacasee." *Zeitschr. Deutsch. Geol. Ges.*, 1897. Vol. xlix., pl. 12, p. 303.

ORBIGNY, ALCIDE D'.—" Voyage dans l'Amérique Méridionale (La République de Bolivia, etc.)" *Paléontologie et Géologie*, 1842. Vol. iii., parts iii. and iv.

APPENDIX

SALTER, J. W.—" On the Fossils from the High Andes (Bolivia) collected by David Forbes." *Quart. Journ. Geol. Soc.*, 1861. Vol. xvii., pp. 62-73, pls. 4 and 5 (Palæozoic Fossils).

STEINMANN, G.—" Zur Kenntniss der Jura- und Kreideformation von Caracoles (Bolivia)." *Neues Jahrbuch*, 1881, Beilage Band 1, pp. 239-301, pls. 9-14.

STEINMANN, G. —"A Sketch of the Geology of South America." *American Naturalist*, 1891, p. 585.

ULRICH, A.—" Paläozoische Versteinerungen aus Bolivien," in " Beiträge zur Geologie und Paläontologie von Südamerika " (edited by G. Steinmann). *Neues Jahrbuch*, 1892, Beilage Band 8, p. 116, pls. 1-5.

DESCRIPTIONS OF THE SANDSTONE FOSSILS

BRACHIOPODA

Anoplotheca flabellites.—Conrad. (See fig. 1, page 389.)

ATRYPA FLABELLITES. Conrad. *Fifth Ann. Rep., New York Geological Survey*, 1841, p. 55. (Not figured.) (North America.)

(?) TEREBRATULA PERUVIANA. D'Orbigny. *Voy. Amérique Mérid.*, 1842. Vol. iii., part iv., p. 36; vol. viii., pl. 2, figs. 22-25 (=Bolivia).

ATRYPA PALMATA. Morris and Sharpe. *Quart. Journ. Geol. Soc.*, 1846. Vol. ii., pl. 10, fig. 3, p. 276. (Falkland Islands.)

ORTHIS PALMATA. Sharpe. *Trans. Geol. Soc.*, London, 1856. Ser. ii., vol. vii., pl. 26, figs. 7-10, p. 207. (South Africa.)

LEPTOCŒLIA FLABELLITES. Hall. *Pal. New York*, 1859. Vol. iii., pl. 103*b*, fig. 1, pl. 106, fig. 1, p. 449. (North America.)

ORTHIS AYMARA. Salter. *Quart. Journ. Geol. Soc.*, 1861. Vol. xvii., pl. 4, fig. 14, p. 68. (Bolivia.)

LEPTOCŒLIA ACUTIPLICATA. Hall. *Pal. New York*, 1867. Vol. iv., pl. 57, figs. 30-39, p. 367.

LEPTOCŒLIA FLABELLITES. Ulrich. *Beitr. Geol. Pal. Südamerika—Paläozoische Versteinerungen von Bolivien*, 1892. Pl. 4, figs. 9-13, p. 60. (Bolivia.)

LEPTOCŒLIA FLABELLITES. Hall and Clarke. *Pal. New York*, 1893. Vol. viii., part ii., pl. 53, figs. 40-46, 53, p. 137.

ANOPLOTHECA FLABELLITES. Schuchert. *Bull. U. S. Geol. Survey*, No. 87, 1897, p. 144.

This form, as represented by Sir William Martin Conway's specimen, appears to be an external view of the dorsal or smaller valve, exhibiting an orbicular contour, and ornamented with twelve rather rounded ribs, of which the two or three central ones thicken out in the anterior

FIG. 1

ANOPLOTHECA FLABELLITES
Conrad sp.

FIG. 2

ATRYPA ? sp.

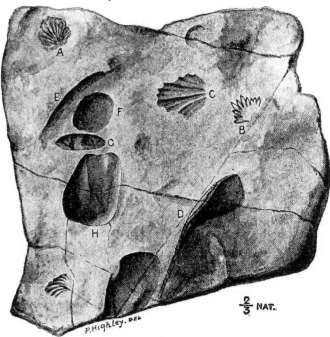

FIG. 3

SANDSTONE SLAB EXHIBITING FOSSIL REMAINS ON ITS SURFACE

A = ANOPLOTHECA FLABELLITES (exterior of dorsal valve).
B =   Ditto   (an impression of the anterior half of a smaller valve).
C = ATRYPA ? sp.
D = Fragmentary head of shield of probably a Trilobite or Cephalaspidian fish with a pos-
      tero-lateral cornu.
E = Marginal rim of a head-shield belonging to a similar organism and showing obscure
F   )   linear striations.
G   }   Evenly margined, oval, and oblong excavations of doubtful origin.
H   )

FIG. 4

FIG. 5

ORTHOTETES SP.

direction. Under a favorable light, obscure indications seem to be present of concentric striations decorating the ribs. The flabellate character of the species is well expressed in the specimen.

Dimensions—Length = 12 } millimetres.
　　　　　Width = 12 }

Conrad originally recorded this species from the Oriskany sandstone of North America, but through the researches of Ulrich and other writers it is now recognized from the Devonian beds of South American countries, the Falkland Islands, and South Africa, although not known as a European form. The genus suggested for the species on this occasion is that adopted by Dr. Schuchert, one of the latest authorities on systematic Brachiopoda.

Atrypa (?) (See fig. 2, page 389.)

Under this genus a rather doubtful impression is included. The specimen is elongate, slightly convex, and with moderately oblique sides; its ornamentation consists of three or four prominently raised ribs, which appear to trifurcate, these main ribs being separated by fairly wide grooves. There are no indications of transverse sculpturing, and in the absence of such a character it is possible, as my colleague, Dr. F. A. Bather, points out, that this valve may belong to the genus *Spirifer*, and not to *Atrypa*, although in some of its characters there is a resemblance to such forms of this genus as *Atrypa marginalis* (Dalman). The specimen has the beak curved inward, and it probably represents the pedicle (or ventral) valve.

Dimensions—Length = 20 } millimetres.
　　　　　Width = 18 }

PROBLEMATICAL ORGANISMS

The problematical remains, previously mentioned, now require to be considered. They resemble portions of head-shields which may have belonged to either a crustacean or a fish. One is furnished with a long, lateral, tapering spine, forming the produced extremity of what

APPENDIX

appears to be the cheek-surface of a trilobite or a ceph-alaspidian fish ; the other represents a rim or margin of a possible head-shield of a similar organism, showing obscure-linear striations. Adjacent to this last-mentioned fragment are some curiously excavated spaces, which seem to be connected with it, from the fact that they exhibit perfectly even margins. Those lying close to the rim are of oval design, whereas another is of oblong shape, with the lateral margins narrowing slightly towards the rounder excavations. Neither Dr. Traquair nor Dr. A. S. Woodward are able to acknowledge definitely that these remains belong to the fish-group of animals, although the latter thinks there is a resemblance in that direction. It is, of course, more probable that they should be crustacean, since trilobites have been described from Bolivia, and no vertebrates, so far as can be ascertained, have yet been recorded from the Devonian rocks of that country.

Therefore, as these curious bodies offer no structure of sufficient importance to connect them decidedly with any known fossil, we must await further collections from this sandstone formation before a more accurate statement can be made regarding them.

It may be interesting to mention, however, that a similarly spined fossil of doubtful affinity from the Palæozoic rocks of Bolivia was described by Salter* in 1861 as *Boliviana bipennis*; although it need not be mistaken for the present specimen, as it differs in possessing surface ridgings and furrows, besides in other details appearing to be an entirely separate organism. (See fig. 3, page 389.)

DESCRIPTION OF FOSSILS ON THE SPECIMEN OF SLATY SHALE

BRACHIOPODA

Orthotetes sp. (See figs. 4 and 5, page 389.)

The dark slaty-shale rock exhibits several compressed casts of Brachiopod-valves which probably belong to a

* *Quart. Journ. Geol. Soc.*, 1861, vol. xvii., pl. 5, fig. 11, p. 72.

species of *Orthotetes*. Unfortunately, the reddish-brown surface of the matrix serves to obscure the specimens, and it is only by the aid of a lens and a good bright light that they can be traced out. In shape they are transversely oblong, and their sculpturing consists of numerous fine, closely set ribs which bifurcate a little below the centre of the valve. There are indications also that the ribbing is crossed by delicate concentric striations, which would suggest relationship to such a form as *Orthotetes umbraculum* (Schlotheim). The hinge is long and straight, but whether the cardinal angles are rounded or not is somewhat difficult to discern, either on account of imperfect margins or because the impressions are rather crowded and frequently overlap each other. A general resemblance may also be noticed to *Orthotetes sp. A.* of Ulrich,* a form from the same horizon and country, although not showing the striated character of the ribs.

Dimensions—Length = 13 }
$\qquad$ Width = 9 } millimetres.

LIST OF PLANTS COLLECTED BY SIR WILLIAM MARTIN CONWAY IN THE BOLIVIAN ANDES—1898–99.

RANUNCULACEÆ.

Anemone integrifolia, H. B. K.
37. Near the top of Huallata Pass, 14,110 ft.
65. The Puna—"Common fuel-moss."

CRUCIFERÆ.

Draba affinis, Hook f.(?)
This very meagre specimen was mixed with *Werneria pygmaea*, Gill.(?), and *Saxifraga Cordillerarum*, Presl, from the neighborhood of Rocktooth Camp, Mount Sorata, at about 18,000 ft.

* "Beitr. Geol. Pal. Süd-Amerika," *Paläozoische Versteinerungen von Bolivien*, 1892, pl. 4, fig. 30, p. 76.

APPENDIX

VIOLACEÆ.

Viola pygmaea, Juss.

38. Near the top of Huallata Pass, 14,110 ft.

CARYOPHYLLACEÆ.

Cerastium mucronatum, Wedd.

6. Illimani, camp 3, 16,500 ft.

HYPERICACEÆ.

Hypericum thesiifolium, H. B. K.

48. High up on the south side of Huallata Pass, at about 14,000 ft.

MALVACEÆ.

Malvastrum flabellatum, Wedd.

35. On ascent from Hiska Haukaña to Rocktooth Camp, at about 18,700 ft.

GERANIACEÆ.

Erodium cicutarium, L'Hérit.

63. La Paz race-course; 18, Umapusa, 14,270 ft.

Oxalis lotoides, H. B. K.

46. High up on south side of Huallata Pass.

LEGUMINOSÆ.

Adesmia spinosissima, Meyen.

54. Hiska Haukaña and neighborhood.

Astragalus uniflorus, DC.

39. Near the top of Huallata Pass, 14,110 ft.

Medicago denticulata, Willd.

64. La Paz; on the race-course (introduced).

Lupinus sp.

9. Illimani, near first camp, 14,000 ft.

SAXIFRAGACEÆ.

Saxifraga Cordillerarum, Presl, var. *trigyna*, Engler.

Near Rocktooth Camp, about 18,000 ft.

LOASACEÆ.

Blumenbachia chuquitensis, Hook. f.

23. Frasciya, 15,000 ft.

CACTACEÆ.

Echinocactus sp.

16. Umapusa, 14,270 ft.

393

APPENDIX

UMBELLIFERÆ.

Azorella diapensioides, A. Gray.

 65. Vilahaque Hill, about 14,500 ft.

VALERIANACEÆ.

Valeriana nivalis, Wedd.

 34. On the ascent from Hiska Haukaña to Rocktooth Camp, about 18,000 ft.; common; 52, Puna.

COMPOSITÆ.

Aster limnophilus, Hemsl. and H. H. W. Pearson.

 28. Hiska Haukaña, at about 16,500 ft.

Baccharis genistelloides, Pers.

 8. Illimani, near first camp, at 14,000 ft.

Baccharis subpenninervis, Sch.-Bip.

 10. Illimani, near first camp, at 14,000 ft.

Baccharis alpina, Wedd. (?)

 24. Frasciya, about 15,000 ft.

Baccharis microphylla, H. B. K.

 11. Illimani, near first camp, at 14,000 ft.

Erigeron Brittonianum, Rusby.

 36. Hiska Haukaña; 44, High up on the south side of Huallata Pass.

Senecio adenophylloides, Sch.-Bip.

 4. Illimani, on moraine, at about 16,000 ft.

Senecio linearifolius, Poepp. (?)

 25. Frasciya, at about 15,000 ft.

Senecio sp.

 13. Illimani, near first camp, at 14,000 ft.   ·

Werneria dactylophylla, Sch.-Bip.

 32. On ascent from Hiska Haukaña to Rocktooth Camp, at about 18,000 ft.

Werneria Mandoniana, Wedd.

 29, 30, and 31. On ascent from Hiska Haukaña to Rocktooth Camp, at about 18,000 ft.

Werneria pygmaea, Gill.

 21. Umapusa, 14,270 ft., and without number, near Rocktooth Camp, about 18,000 ft.

Werneria heteroloba, Wedd.

 51. Puna.

APPENDIX

Barnadesia polyacantha, Wedd.

40. On the way down towards Sorata.

Perezia caerulescens, Wedd.

2. Illimani, near first camp, at 14,000 ft.; 56, Hiska Haukaña and neighborhood, at about 16,000 ft.

Hypochaeris sessiliflora, H. B. K.

55. Hiska Haukaña and neighborhood; 61, South slope of Huallata Pass.

CAMPANULACÆ.

Lobelia nana, H. B. K.

45. High up on south side of Huallata Pass; 59, Hiska Haukaña and neighborhood; 60, Theodolite station 6, Puna, near Achacache.

Centropogon, sp. nova.?

42. On the way down towards Sorata.

VACCINIACEÆ.

Vaccinium penaeoides, H. B. K.

7. Illimani, Camp 3, at 16,720 ft.

PLUMBAGINACEÆ.

Plumbago scandens, Linn.

43, 44. On the way down towards Sorata.

GENTIANACEÆ.

Gentiana sedifólia, H. B. K.

1. Illimani, near first camp, at about 14,000 ft.; 20, 22, Umapusa, at about 14,500 ft.; 50, Puna.

BORAGINACEÆ.

Eritrichium, species indeterminata.

62. South slope of Huallata Pass.

SOLANACEÆ.

Solanum pallidum, Rusby.

43. On the way down towards Sorata.

SCROPHULARIACEÆ.

Fagelia deflexa, O. Kuntze.

41. On the way down towards Sorata.

Mimulus, species indeterminata.

57. Hiska Haukaña and neighborhood, at about 16,000 ft.

Ourisia muscosa, Benth.

26. Hiska Haukaña, at about 16,500 ft.

APPENDIX

LABIATÆ.

Bystropogon canus, Benth.

    12. Illimani, near first camp, at 14,000 ft.

Micromeria boliviana, Benth.

    3. Illimani, near first camp, at 14,000 ft.

AMARYLLIDACEÆ.

Bomarea glaucescens, Baker.

    5. Illimani, Camp 3, at about 16,700 ft.

Bomarea glaucescens, Baker, var. *puberula*, Baker.

    14. Illimani, at about 11,500 ft., just below Atahuaillani.

GRAMINEÆ.

Deyeuxia glacialis, Wedd.

    33. On the ascent from Hiska Haukaña to Rocktooth Camp, at about 18,000 ft.

OTHER COLLECTIONS

Owing to absence from England I have been unable to obtain detailed lists of these in time for publication. All are deposited in the British Museum (Natural History). The undescribed collections included:

A number of birds.

Two human skulls, man and woman, both artificially distorted.

Two lizards, *Liolamus cyanogaster* and *Lilamus multiformis*, from high above Umapusa.

Four batrachians, *Paludicola bibronii* and *Bufo spirulorus*.

One fish, *Oustias owenii*, from the slopes of Mount Sorata, about 15,000 ft.

Nineteen Arachnida and about fifty insects. "Among the beetles collected by yourself in Bolivia," writes Mr. Charles O. Waterhouse, of the British Museum, "there are two specimens of a species which is quite new, and which I have described under the name of *Plastica polita*."

APPENDIX

Two land shells were identified by Mr. E. A. Smith: *Epiphragmophora estella* (d'Orbigny) [=*Helix estella*, d'Orbigny], habitat, Illimani; *Bulimulus culmineus* (d'Orbigny) [=*Bulimus culmineus*, d'Orbigny], habitat, Illimani and Umapusa.

BIBLIOGRAPHY

THE following are the works to which I have referred or attempted to refer. Some of them were inaccessible to me. This list, of course, makes no claim to be a complete bibliography of Bolivia.

AHUMADA MORENO, P.—*Guerra del Pacifico*. 6 vols. Valparaiso, 1884–9. Fol.

√ ALCEDO, ANT. DE—*Geographical and Historical Dictionary of America* (G. A. Thompson's edition). 5 vols. London, 1812–15. 4to.
——Atlas. London, 1816. Fol.

Annals of the Astronomical Observatory of Harvard College. Peruvian Meteorology (S. I. Bailey and E. C. Pickering). Chapter on the Configuration and Heights of the Andes, with Bibliography. Cambridge (Mass.), 1899. 4to.

ARAMAYO, AVELINO—*Proyecto de una nueva via de comunicacion entre Bolivia y el oceano Pacifico*. London, 1863.
——*Bolivia*. London, 1874.

ARARA(?)—*Voyage dans l'Amérique méridionale*. Paris, 1809. (Not in Brit. Mus.)

ARCHIVO BOLIVIANO—*Coleccion de Documentos relativos a la Historia de Bolivia, durante la época colonial, con un catalogo de obras impresas y de manuscritos que tratan de esa parte de la America Meridional, publicados por V. de Ballivian y Roxas*. Paris, 1872, etc. 8vo. In progress.

BALLIVIÁN, M. V., and E. IDIAQUEZ—*Diccionario Geografico de la Republica de Bolivia*. La Paz, 1890.

BELLESSORT, ANDRÉ—*La jeune Amérique. Chili et Bolivie*. Paris, 1897. 8vo.

BILLINGHURST, GUILLERMO E.—*Reconocimiento Militar del Rio Desaguadero y de la Altaplanicie Andina*. Lima, 1880. Fol. (*vide* Proc. R. G. S. 1882, p. 647.)

BOLIVIA, FOREIGN OFFICE REPORTS ON—Annual Series, Nos. 1053, 1499 (C. Akers), and 1841 (A. St. John).

BOLIVIA, HANDBOOK OF—Bulletin No. 55 of the Bureau of the American Republics. Washington, 1892. 8vo.

BRAVO, C.—*La Patria Boliviana: Estado geografico*, being vol. v. of the *Biblioteca Boliviana de Geografia e Historia*. La Paz, 1894. 8vo.

BIBLIOGRAPHY

BRESSON, ANDRÉ—*Bolivia. Sept années d'explorations, de voyages, et de séjours dans l'Amérique australe.* Paris, 1886. 4to.

CASTELNAU, FRANÇOIS DE—*Expédition dans les parties centrales de l'Amérique du sud.* 7 pts. Paris, 1850–59. 8vo, 4to, and fol.

CHARLEVOIX, PIERRE F. X. DE—*Histoire du Paraguay.* Paris, 1756. 4to. English translation, 2 vols. London, 1769. 8vo.

CISNEROS, C. B., and R. E. GARCIA—*Geografia comercial de la America del sur. Tercera Entrega. Rep. de Bolivia.* Lima, 1897, etc. 8vo. In progress.

CORTÉS, MANOEL JOSÉ—*Ensayo sobre la Historia de Bolivia.* Sucre, 1861.

——*Bolivia.* Paris, 1875.

DALENA, JOSÉ MARIA—*Bosquejo estadistico de Bolivia.* Sucre, 1851 and 1878 (?).

DE BONELLI, L. HUGH—*Travels in Bolivia.* 2 vols. London, 1854. 8vo.

DESJARDINS (?)—*Le Pérou avant la Conquête espagnole.* (Not in Brit. Mus.) l. and d.? This is stated to contain representations of pre-Inca Bolivian ruins as observed and drawn in 1847 by M. Angrand.

✓ FORBES, DAVID—*The Aymara Indians.* Journal of the Ethnological Society, new series, vol. ii., p. 193 et seq. London, 1870, 8vo.

——*Geology of Bolivia and S. Peru.* Quarterly Journal of the Geological Society, vol. xvii., pp. 7–62, with map and sections. London, 1861. 8vo.

✓ FORD, ISAAC N.—*Tropical America.* London, 1893. 8vo.

GRANDIDIER, ERNEST—*Voyage dans l'Amérique du sud. Pérou et Bolivie.* Paris, 1861. 8vo.

HUMBOLDT, ALEX. VON—*Aspects of Nature.* Translation by Mrs. Sabine. 2 vols. London, 1849. 8vo.

MATHEWS, E. D.—*Up the Amazon and Madeira Rivers, through Bolivia and Peru.* London, 1879. 8vo.

MILLER, GENERAL—*Memoirs, in the Service of the Republic of Peru.* 2 vols. London, 1829.

MINCHIN, J. B.—*Bolivia.* Proceedings R. Geographical Soc., p. 671. London, 1882. 8vo.

MORENO, J. L.—*Nociones de geografia de Bolivia.* Sucre, 1889.

MUSTERS, G. C.—*Notes on Bolivia.* Journal of the R. Geographical Soc., vol. xlvii., p. 201. London, 1877. 8vo.

ORBIGNY, A. DESSALINES D'—*Descripcion geografica, historica, y estadistica de Bolivia.* Paris, 1845. 8vo.

——*Voyage dans l'Amérique méridionale de 1826 à 1833.* 9 vols. and atlas. Paris, 1835–47. 4to.

PAZ SOLDAN, M. F.—*Guerra de Chile contra Peru y Bolivia.* La Paz, 1884.

PENTLAND, J. B.—*Memoir on the Andes and on the Great Plateau.* Journal of the R. Geographical Soc. London, 1835 and 1849. 8vo. See also *Annales de Chimie et de Physique,* Paris, 1829.

BIBLIOGRAPHY

✓ PRESCOTT, W. H.—*History of the Conquest of Peru*, edited by J. F. Kirk. 2 vols. London, 1884. 8vo.

QUERBEUF, ABBÉ DE — *Lettres edifiantes et curieuses écrites des missions Etrangères.* 26 vols. Paris, 1780–83. 12mo.

RECK, HUGO—*Geographie und Statistik der Republik Bolivia.* With map. *Petermann's Mittheilungen.* Gotha, 1865, 1866, and 1867. 4to.

RENÉ-MORENO, GABRIEL—*Biblioteca Boliviana.* A bibliography of Bolivia. Santiago de Chile, 1879. 4to.

＼ REISS, W., and A. STÜBEL—*Reisen in Süd.-Amerika.* Berlin, 1886, etc. 4to.

✓ ———— and R. KOPPEL—*Kultur und Industrie südamerikanischer Völker.* 2 vols. Berlin, 1889. Fol.

✓ RÜCK, E. O.—*Guia General de Bolivia.* Sucre, 1865.

✓ SQUIER, E. G.—*Peru: Incidents of Travel, etc.* London, 1877. 8vo.

TEMPLE, EDMOND—*Travels in Various Parts of Peru, including a ✓ Year's Residence in Potosi.* 2 vols. London, 1830. 8vo.

TSCHUDI, J. J. VON—*Reisen durch Südamerika.* 5 vols. Leipzig, 1866–69. 8vo.

✓ ———*Travels in Peru during the years* 1838–42. London, 1847. 8vo.

URSEL, COMTE C. D'—*Sud Amérique: Séjours et voyages . . . en Bolivie, etc.* Paris, 1879. 12mo.

VALDÈS, J. C.—*La Paz de Ayacucho.* La Paz, 1890. 8vo.

WEDDELL, H. A. — *Voyage dans le ord de la Bolivie.* Paris, ✓ 1853. 8vo.

✓ WIENER, CHARLES—*Pérou et Bolivie.* Paris, 1880. 8vo.

INDEX

INDEX

INDEX

THE END

Printed in Great Britain
by Amazon

THE
HOUSE
WITH THE
GOLDEN
DOOR

THE WOLF DEN TRILOGY

The Wolf Den
The House with the Golden Door